"Most Thai restaurants are terrific, but some are more terrific than others, and Kamolmal qualifies for the latter category. . . . *Wow* is the word for the food!"

—*Los Angeles* Magazine

Thai cooking is an excitingly different and distinctive Asian cuisine. Influenced by both Indian and Chinese cooking, its exotic taste is unique and utterly delicious. Now Western cooks can learn to prepare a fascinating range of authentic dishes from Thailand as perfected by master chef Kamolmal Pootaraksa and recreated with integrity by William Crawford. These simply wonderful and naturally healthful dishes offer the best in this exquisite, subtle cuisine . . . a new world of tastes, blends, and glorious dining.

THAI HOME-COOKING FROM KAMOLMAL'S KITCHEN

"A clearly written, step-by-step sort of book, offering recipes for Thai dishes both familiar and obscure . . ."

—*Los Angeles Times*

"Explains this appealing cuisine admirably well."

—*Library Journal*

WILLIAM CRAWFORD is an accomplished Thai cook. A former student of Kamolmal, he spent over a year helping her compose and adapt her recipes for the North American market. Dr. Crawford, a psychologist, is on the faculty of UCLA and maintains a private practice in Los Angeles.

KAMOLMAL POOTARAKSA was born in Bangkok, Thailand, where her parents owned and operated a large restaurant. She is owner-chef of Kamolmal, an authentic Thai restaurant in Tarzana, California, which earned a high rating from *Los Angeles* Magazine for its outstanding cuisine. She has taught Thai cooking through the UCLA Extension Division and currently teaches Thai cooking at Los Angeles City College.

THAI HOME-COOKING

FROM KAMOLMAL'S KITCHEN

❋•❋•❋•❋•❋

William Crawford
and Kamolmal Pootaraksa

A PLUME BOOK

This book is dedicated to
CHOOMPOL and GARY,
who know who they are
and need no introduction.
∗•∗•∗•∗•∗

PLUME
Published by the Penguin Group
Penguin Books USA Inc., 375 Hudson Street, New York, New York 10014,
U.S.A.
Penguin Books Ltd, 27 Wrights Lane, London W8 5TZ, England
Penguin Books Australia Ltd, Ringwood, Victoria, Australia
Penguin Books Canada Ltd, 2801 John Street, Markham, Ontario,
Canada L3R 1B4
Penguin Books (N.Z.) Ltd, 182-190 Wairau Road, Auckland 10, New Zealand

Penguin Books Ltd, Registered Offices: Harmondsworth, Middlesex, England

Published by Plume, an imprint of New American Library, a division of Penguin
Books USA Inc.

BOOKS ARE AVAILABLE AT QUANTITY DISCOUNTS WHEN USED TO PROMOTE PRODUCTS OR
SERVICES. FOR INFORMATION PLEASE WRITE TO PREMIUM MARKETING DIVISION, PENGUIN
BOOKS USA INC., 375 HUDSON STREET, NEW YORK, NEW YORK 10014.

 REGISTERED TRADEMARK—MARCA REGISTRADA

Designed by Barbara Huntley

Library of Congress Cataloging in Publication Data

Crawford, William R., 1936–
  Thai home-cooking from Kamolmal's kitchen.

  Includes index.
  I. Cookery, Thai. I. Pootaraksa, Kamolmal. II. Title.
TX24.5.T5C73   1985   641.59593   85-352
ISBN 0-453-00494-6
ISBN 0-452-26133-3

First Plume Printing, August, 1986
  7 8 9 10 11 12 13 14

PRINTED IN THE UNITED STATES OF AMERICA

Acknowledgments

COOKBOOK AUTHORS can never acknowledge all the people who contributed to their work; the influences are so widespread that they become untraceable. Nonetheless, we want to recognize those people who stand out in the contributions they made to this book. However well one understands cooking, it is another matter to put instructions on paper in a meaningful way, particularly when writing about procedures and ingredients that may not be familiar to the cooks who will be using the book. That takes trial and error and relies on feedback from test-kitchen "guinea pigs."

The most significant assistant in the development of this book was our good friend Allen Chivens, who encouraged us from the beginning, cooked, cooked, and cooked to test recipes, and provided us with countless suggestions and unfailing encouragement. This book is almost as much his as ours, and we are grateful to him beyond measure.

In addition to the many students who sliced, chopped, cooked, tasted, and tested draft versions of the recipes, the following people provided significant assistance and encouragement:

Alan Malyon, Charles Elliott, Joseph Gaudioso, Dorothy Small-berg, Bronwyn Anthony, Jane Hoose, and Rheba and Rudy deTornyay. A special note of thanks to Gary Simmons, who cooked, ate, and helped describe more Thai food than he probably would have thought possible. To each of these we are indebted for his/her unique contribution.

Molly Allen, our editor, was patient, encouraging, and totally supportive throughout the long, tedious process of shepherding the manuscript through the many stages of publication. We couldn't have done without her. We are also very grateful for the efforts of our agent, Evan Marshall, who was enthusiastic from the very beginning.

Last, but certainly not least, are Kamolmal's parents and grandparents, who began teaching her how to cook at an early age. They laid the groundwork for an abiding love and respect for good food, and are the original architects for this book.

Contents

1
Introduction

THE CUISINE OF THAILAND, although distinct from that of any other nation, is a combination of many cuisines, most notably those of China and India. The earliest influences came from China, from whence the ancestors of the modern Thai people migrated. That influence is seen today in the Thai inclination to blend contrasting tastes (sweet, sour, hot, bitter, and salty) and textures. The influence of India can be seen in the use of curry pastes and stewed dishes. A notable example is Beef Musman, which was developed directly by Indian merchants residing in Thailand. Other neighboring countries probably had similar, though lesser, influences on Thai cuisine. In spite of these outside influences, Thai food has a character distinct from that of the other countries in Southeast Asia. This is due in part to the rugged independence of the Thai people, but perhaps more to the fact that Thailand is the only country in Southeast Asia that was never colonized by a Western power. In addition, it stands at the crossroads of Southeast Asia. A glance at a map shows clearly that it would be difficult to cross Southeast Asia without passing through Thailand.

Through the centuries, Thai cooks have followed specific

techniques for combining ingredients, techniques that are as valid today as they were when they were first developed. For example, grinding in a mortar and pestle is a centuries' old technique for pounding ingredients to a smooth paste and grinding seeds and grains to a fine powder. Today's blenders and food processors may be more efficient in terms of human labor, yet they do not produce a final product of as fine a quality as does the time-honored mortar and pestle.

Similarly, time has shown the wok to be an exceptionally versatile and efficient cooking utensil. It can be used to stir-fry, steam, and deep-fry and uses relatively little fuel in the process.

As is true in other Asian cuisines, rice is the mainstay of the Thai diet. It is consumed in large quantities at every meal as well as with between-meal snacks and is so central that most dishes (with the exception of dessert and beverages) serve as accompaniments to rice, adding flavor and additional nutrients. In almost every recipe we have indicated that the dish should be served with rice. Most Thai preparations, particularly the curried dishes, have enough sauce to flavor the rice. Those that do not produce sauce of their own are usually accompanied by an auxiliary sauce which serves the same purpose.

The Thai people love snacks and eat often throughout the day, stopping at restaurants or, more frequently, purchasing snacks from vendors who push carts through the streets or maneuver boats through the crowded canals, advertising their wares in loud, lyrical voices. For that reason, there is a large repertoire of snack foods. In the chapter on Appetizers and Snacks we describe several of the most popular snack foods. Any of them may also be served as part of the main meal, as is sometimes done in Thai homes.

Pork and fresh fish are the main animal products in the Thai diet. Chicken, traditionally used less extensively than either pork or fish, has become more popular in recent years. Items like sweetbreads, liver, heart, kidneys, stomachs, and intestines are widely used in Thailand and are considered a delicacy by some people. We have therefore included some recipes using "innards," and we urge you to try some of them; we hope you will be pleasantly surprised at the result.

Although the number of strict vegetarians in Thailand is relatively small when compared to some other countries, the Buddhist religion does require abstinence from meat for several days each month, and most of the Thai people follow that mandate. For that reason, as well as for reasons of economy, excellent dishes have been developed using tofu (beancurd) as the main source of protein. We have included some of these because they are excellent and provide a nutritious, low-calorie change of pace as well as being very economical.

In general, Thai food is highly spiced and very hot because of the extensive use of spices, herbs, and chilies. Initially, black or white pepper provided the hot peppery taste, but in the sixteenth century international traders introduced chilies to Thailand and the Thai people quickly incorporated them into their cuisine. Today both pepper and chilies are used extensively and each makes its own unique contribution. The extent to which chilies and pepper are used varies with each cook and from household to household according to individual taste. Some dishes are mild, and others so hot that they are considered inedible by most Westerners. In preparing this book, we have used ingredients and proportions that are in the middle of this range, recognizing that the dishes may be too hot for some and too mild for others. Thus, you should feel free to modify the amount of chilies or pepper to suit your own taste. In any event, the spiciness is under the control of the diner to some extent, because he or she may reduce or intensify the "bite" of the food by eating more or less rice with it. Whether you are dining at home or in a restaurant it is important to understand the moderating effect that rice has on spiciness. A good, authentic Thai restaurant will serve ample rice and willingly supply more on request, sometimes at no extra cost. Increasing the amount of rice consumed reduces the "bite" without sacrificing the accompanying flavor. Reducing the amount of chilies or other flavorings would not accomplish that nearly as effectively, because the chilies add a rich flavor as well as "heat."

For the convenience of the user, this book is organized into chapters that conform to traditional Western ideas about food, i.e., appetizers, soups, salads, various meats, etc. In Thailand the organization would probably be handled quite differently because the Thai people are much more likely to consider the cooking process and the curries or sauces as the major factors in organization rather than the main ingredients or the serving sequence. On the one hand, our organization makes it easier to decide which meats or vegetables you wish to prepare and then find the recipes. On the other, it produces some artificial designations that could result in overlooking a particular recipe because it appears in a different chapter. For example, Saté (page 153) is described in the chapter on Appetizers and Snacks, but it could be served as a main course. Stir-Fried Cabbage with Shrimp is listed under Vegetables but could be served as a main dish if you increase the number of shrimp or decrease the amount of cabbage. We suggest that you look through the entire book making note of the recipes that interest you since these recipes can be used as flexibly as you wish in a menu.

In Thailand there is no set course sequence since most dishes are served at the same time or at least in close succession as they are prepared. Most or all of the dishes are placed on the table at once and each diner selects what he or she wishes, alternating between different foods. This is very practical, because it allows the diner to first eat a very spicy food, then a refreshing, cooling soup, salad, or relatively bland main dish, then the spicy dish again, and so forth. We suggest you try this approach and suspect that once you become accustomed to it you will appreciate its appeal.

Similarly, servings and portions are viewed differently in Thailand than they are in Western countries. When guests are expected in Thailand, it is as common to prepare additional dishes as it is to increase the amount of any one dish. This adds variety and interest to the meal and, since most Thai food is quickly and easily prepared, means little additional effort for the cook. A dish that would serve only two or three if served alone with minimal rice might serve four, six, or even eight if served in combination with other dishes and with ample rice. This method posed a major problem for us in listing the number of servings for each recipe. In some instances, Sarong, for example, we have listed the number of pieces of food produced, so you may decide how much you want to make. For the most part, however, we have based the number of servings on the assumption that two or three main dishes will be served with rice, an appetizer or snack, a soup, and perhaps a salad. If you plan to serve in the Thai manner and present a number of dishes at the same time, you may need to reduce the quantity of each. In most cases that can easily be accomplished by reducing all ingredients proportionately. You could also choose to prepare the *full* amount and eat the leftovers the next day, which is done a great deal in Thailand. In fact, some dishes, such as Beef Musman, actually improve in flavor if prepared in advance. This is not recommended, however, for deep-fried foods, which should be hot and crisp when served. In many recipes we have provided ahead-of-time notes suggesting how far in advance various dishes may be prepared and held for use later.

We have provided both the English and Thai names for all recipes (and some ingredients), the former so that you may remember them more easily and the latter so that you may recognize them in markets and restaurants. However, there is no standard way to translate Thai words into English, and even language scholars engage in lengthy debates on the correct transliteration. This is because Thai is a very lyrical, tonal language, and the same word may have several meanings depending on the inflection. You will probably see variant spellings for many of the words we have used, and about the only solution we can offer is to suggest you try to pronounce the words yourself and compare the sounds to see which are similar. For example, the letters "K" and "G" could be used interchangeably in most words because the actual sound lies somewhere in between. With our friend Allen Chivens, the authors spent many hours checking references and listening to one another pronounce the words in Thai and English before we derived the spellings used in this book. We offer no apologies for our spellings and only hope that it will not be too confusing if you see other versions.

HOW TO USE THIS BOOK

We have presented precise and detailed steps in preparing the recipes and instructions in this book, and in most instances we have tried to describe the final product. For some readers the instructions may be too explicit, but we hope they are not too general for anyone. In some instances, the instructions may seem long, but we wanted them to be complete. The number of steps in a recipe does not necessarily mean it is more difficult, just that we wanted to let you know how to approach each task. Although sometimes we have given approximate times, timing is often difficult to define exactly, because we have no way of knowing the conditions under which you will be cooking. A cook who is experienced in any cuisine knows that the best way to determine when a dish is prepared properly is by smell, appearance, taste, and touch. Unfortunately, those qualities can be difficult to describe.

With respect to ingredients, we have been very precise in the amounts listed. However, you should feel free to modify them according to taste, and in some recipes we have suggested that. Chilies provide a good example. Our recipes for dishes using chilies produce what we consider to be moderate "heat." However, these may prove too mild for some people and too hot for others. They are, in any case, very mild compared to what you would find in Thailand. A taste for hot chilies is usually acquired, and if you eat a lot of Thai food (for some reason it becomes addictive) you will probably find that you will want to increase the number of chilies by quite a bit.

Please follow the sequence of preparation exactly, at least the first few times you use a recipe. It has been developed for ease and efficiency of preparation and following it will lead to authentic results. For example, if a recipe instructs you to add coconut milk in small increments, please do not dump it all in at once. The dish probably won't be ruined, but it will lack the subtle blending of flavors that results if the recipe is followed carefully. Read the instructions for each recipe several times before beginning, so that you have the sequence firmly in mind. Above all, have all your ingredients prepared and measured before you begin cooking. This is particularly important in stir-fried dishes, where everything goes at a very fast pace once you begin to cook. The instructions and procedures in our recipes are presented in the sequence that Thai tradition and our kitchen tests have shown produce good results.

After you select the recipes you wish to prepare, read about the ingredients before going shopping so that you can be sure to get the right ones, or, if they are not available, that you use the recommended substitutions. It is always best to use the freshest possible ingredients. If there are Thai markets in your community, be sure to visit them. Stepping into a Thai market can be a bewildering experience at first because the shelves are lined with strange-looking (and strange-smelling) ingredients in bottles, cans, and cellophane packages. Some of them will be labeled only with Thai letters or, at best, the Anglicized version of the Thai word. Don't hesitate to ask questions; most proprietors of Thai markets will be happy to help you. The recipes in this book use only a small sample of the host of available products.

Preceding most recipes we give a general description of what to expect and, when appropriate, how substitutions can be made. Following some recipes are variations that we hope you find useful and that may stimulate you to introduce variations of your own in other recipes. Although Thai cooking does follow certain set guidelines and procedures for preparation, there is great flexibility in the proportions of ingredients. We have also indicated those instances in which substitutions of ingredients or changes in procedure should not be made.

Once you have learned the basic techniques and have acquired an idea of how flavors and textures are combined in Thai food, you can be innovative and develop your own dishes. As with any other cuisine, there are as many ways to prepare a dish as there are cooks to prepare it. Please remember that we have presented Thai home cooking, not haute cuisine. In a Thai home, meals are usually prepared with what is available and in season (although, because of the tropical climate, few staples in Thailand are ever out of season), and the cook needs to be creative and bold.

2
Cooking and Serving

A TRADITIONAL Thai kitchen is simple and straightforward, and the preparation of food is accomplished very efficiently. Foods are served attractively, but that is accomplished by garnishing and decorating rather than through the use of complex tableware or serving pieces. A completely equipped Thai kitchen is a masterpiece of simplicity and could contain nothing more than a wok, a saucepan, steaming pans, a knife or cleaver, a chopping block, a simple stove, a mortar and pestle, and stirring and straining devices. Virtually every kitchen in America contains several times as much equipment and many more resources than are required for basic Thai cooking.

In this chapter we provide descriptions of basic equipment and procedures used in preparing and serving Thai food, including suggested menus as well as suggestions for planning your own. It is not necessary to have all the equipment for either cooking or serving, nor is it necessary to follow our suggested menus slavishly. However, the cooking procedures we describe are essential for proper results, regardless of the equipment you use.

You may decide for yourself which cooking and serving equipment you wish to have and what substitutions you wish to make. To illustrate that it is not essential to buy a great deal of new equipment, we have included some standard items, which you probably already have in your kitchen and which are readily available if you don't.

The equipment we describe is available in some parts of the country and not in others, so you may need to improvise. For example, a brass Foy Tong maker may be difficult to find, but the same result can be achieved with a piece of wax paper and some tape, as we describe following the recipe for Foy Tong.

Because so much of the food preparation is done before any actual cooking begins, Thai food takes less time to cook than many other cuisines. Advance preparation includes slicing, chopping, grinding, and grating, none of which is complicated and most of which goes pretty quickly. The methods of cooking are stir-frying, deep-frying, or steaming, each of which goes quickly, which is why it is important to have all ingredients ready to use. It is a mystery to us why people who complain that "It takes so much chopping and slicing" will spend even more time and effort to produce a Western dish. Cooking times will vary depending on whether you use electricity or gas and on the specific characteristics of your stove or range. For that reason we have chosen, in most cases, to describe the effect to be achieved rather than give precise cooking times, although we sometimes mention approximate times to give you an idea. Ovens are a relatively new introduction to Thailand and still are not as widely used as in the United States, so there are few baked preparations, and those are confined to desserts. Almost everything is cooked in a wok or other stove-top vessel.

COOKING EQUIPMENT
Barbecue Grill

A barbecue grill or hibachi can help add flavor to certain dishes like Barbecued Chicken. It is not essential, however; a similar effect may be obtained by using the broiler of a stove. A barbecue grill or hibachi should always be used outdoors because the amount of carbon monoxide it produces can be lethal without adequate ventilation.

Blender

A blender may be substituted for the mortar and pestle (described on page 12) for grinding ingredients and preparing curries. However, because the quantities to be ground in some recipes are small, you may find that the ingredients fly around in the container and do not grind. In that event you will need to add liquid to aid in grinding. We have suggested this in certain recipes. The necessity for this procedure depends on the size and shape of the blender-container as well as on the amount of food you are preparing. If your blender is equipped with a 1–cup minicontainer, it is excellent for making curry pastes.

Cleaver

In Asian and Oriental cooking almost all chopping and slicing is done with a cleaver. Cleavers are about 7 inches long by 3 inches wide and are generally heavy. The weight is part of the usefulness because it does much of the work for you; most of your task is simply guiding the blade. As with knives, carbon-steel cleavers are easier to sharpen at home than are stainless-steel ones. Although you may find a cleaver unwieldly to use at first, once you become accustomed to it you will probably swear by it. However, useful as it is, for chopping and slicing, a cleaver is not essential. (See entry on knives.)

Coconut Grater

The traditional Thai coconut grater is a low rectangular stool with a small, round piece of metal attached to one end. The metal has sharp pointed edges that are used to gouge and grate the coconut directly from the shell. The operator sits on the stool and pulls the coconut toward him or her with a twisting motion. It is still used in many traditional Thai kitchens, but we find the method for cracking and grinding coconuts described in Chapter 3 more efficient, and do not recommend this traditional technique unless you want to do it for fun.

Coffee Grinder

An electric coffee grinder is effective for grinding small quantities of roasted seeds, dried chilies, or roasted rice. If you already own one for coffee, it can be used providing you clean it thoroughly before and after grinding non-coffee ingredients. To clean it, place some cornmeal or uncooked rice in the grinding container and grind thoroughly. Repeat until the rice or cornmeal comes out clean—usually two grindings is enough. Use a toothpick or small brush to remove any particles which cling to the sides or crevices.

Food Processor

A food processor is convenient for grinding and chopping ingredients, but even more than the blender it may cause small amounts of ingredients to spin around rather than grind. Its principal use for this book would be in chopping coconut, grinding meat, or making large quantities of curry pastes based on multiples of the recipes. Because the size of food processor containers varies, we are not able to provide precise instructions on amounts, and you will need to use your own judgment and experience.

Grater

A grater is useful for producing small shreds of vegetables for garnishing, and it may also be used to grate coconut to make coconut milk. If you have a food processor with slicing and grating disks, a hand grater may not be necessary.

Knives

One or more sharp, heavy knives are essential for any kitchen, especially a Thai kitchen, where so much depends on proper slicing and chopping. There should be at least one large, very sharp knife for slicing and chopping and a small, very sharp one for peeling and boning. We suggest knives with smooth blades rather than those with serrated or scalloped blades because smooth-bladed ones are much easier to keep sharp. We do not recommend stainless-steel knives because in general they are much more difficult to sharpen at home. (See cleavers.)

Microwave Oven

A microwave oven is useful, but not essential; we use one to precook some items like Stuffed Chicken Wings, but excellent results may be obtained without it. It is also useful for reheating cooked rice and leftovers but represents a sizable investment if used solely for that purpose.

Mortar and Pestle

A mortar and pestle is an indispensable tool in a traditional Thai kitchen and is used for pounding ingredients to a paste or powder. The major advantages over a food processor or blender are that the mortar and pestle can handle small quantities easily and the ingredients are mashed rather than chopped, which releases the oils and flavors more effectively. We suggest a mortar about 6 to 8 inches in inside diameter and about 2 to 4 inches deep. It should have sloping sides, a relatively smooth interior, and be made of heavy stone that will not chip or crack. The heavier the pestle the more efficient it will be, because it will do some of the work for you. We strongly recommend that you include a mortar and pestle in your kitchen equipment. It is useful for grinding and mashing many ingredients and its use is not limited to preparing Thai food.

Ranges and Stoves

Traditionally, woks are placed on top of a small stone brazier that is filled with red-hot coals, so that cooking proceeds very quickly. This technique is still used by street and boat vendors as well as in some homes. It can be simulated by placing a wok on a bed of hot coals in a barbecue for easy outdoor cooking in the summer.

Otherwise, the best heat source for cooking Thai food is a gas stove capable of producing a high, hot flame. Commercial gas stoves are best, and are available in restaurant supply stores, often at no more cost than standard home models, particularly if you can find a good used one. If you are stuck with an electric range, the easiest way to cook Thai food is to turn a burner on high and move the wok on and off the burner to regulate the heat. It can be done effectively with just a little bit of practice. If you do not have gas and you really want a good heat source, try one of the small tabletop units that use bottled gas. They are available in restaurant supply stores with from one to four burners and work very well. Also available in some restaurant supply stores are one- or two-burner tabletop units specifically designed to hold a wok.

Rice Cooker: Electric

An automatic electric rice cooker is useful if you prepare large quantities of rice frequently, but is unnecessary in the average kitchen. We find that it is no more trouble to cook rice in a saucepan following the procedure described in the chapter on rice (page 95).

Rice Cooker for Glutinous Rice

For the best results, glutinous (sweet) rice must be steamed in a container that holds the rice above a large quantity of boiling water. Although a special piece of equipment has been developed for that purpose, any kind of steamer can be used. If the steamer you use has holes large enough to allow the rice grains to slip through, line it with a piece of damp cheesecloth. The traditional glutinous rice cooker consists of an urn-shaped pot with a flared top. This is filled about one third full of water. Soaked rice is placed in a cone-shaped basket, which is inserted into the opening of the metal container, pointed end down, and a lid is put over that. The water is then brought to a boil and the rice is steamed in the basket. (See page 96 for instructions on cooking glutinous rice.)

Scales

A kitchen scale graduated in markings of one ounce or fractions of an ounce is very handy until you become accustomed to estimating the amounts of ingredients. It is not essential to have one, however, and we have indicated volume as well as weight measures. We find that a small "dietary" scale is most useful, because it is easier to measure small amounts accurately. A postage scale can be equally effective, and for some strange reason is often less expensive than scales designed for kitchen use. Whatever you use, we suggest getting into the habit of weighing ingredients rather than measuring volume. It is more accurate and no more difficult.

Steamers

Traditional Thai steaming equipment consists of round, stackable, perforated metal pans that fit over a container in which water is placed. Three or four perforated pans can be placed on top of each other and the steam rises through all of them. As with other Thai cooking equipment, it is efficient and effective. Any type of steamer can be used that permits food to be placed far enough apart to allow steam to circulate freely, and in which enough water can be placed to generate sufficient steam to last through the cooking process. Some woks come with a steaming rack made of concentric rings instead of a perforated pan. In that case you need to put the food on a heatproof plate and set the plate on the rings. Bamboo steamers are also available and work well, but they are difficult to keep clean.

Strainer

The traditional strainer used for deep-frying has a long wooden handle and a slightly concave, loosely woven brass basket. It is effective but, alas, should not be washed in a dishwasher. An effective and equally useful adaptation is a long-handled metal strainer with a round, almost flat, perforated metal scoop. It is widely available in houseware departments.

Tea or Coffee Strainer

A Thai tea or coffee strainer is a cloth bag about 1 foot long, which tapers from an opening about 5 inches in diameter. The open end consists of a metal ring to which the bag is attached and a protruding metal handle. Tea is placed in the bag and water is poured through it into a medium-size bowl or saucepan. Then the bag is placed in another bowl or pan, the brew is poured through it again into the second container, and the procedure is repeated until the desired strength is obtained. The strainer may also be used for draining pureed rice when preparing dishes like

Sweet Rice Tarts. The bag will be darkly stained after using it for tea or coffee, but if it is washed well the stain will not affect the rice puree. Any bag made of fine cloth can be used. (See instructions for preparing tea, page 279).

Vegetable Peeler

This is not an essential item but it is useful for producing paper-thin slices of daikon (white radish), carrot, and other vegetables to be used for garnishing. It is the easiest way to punch out the soft "eye" of a coconut to drain the liquid before cracking the coconut.

Wok

The wok is probably the most versatile and efficient cooking utensil in existence. It can be used to stir-fry, deep-fry, roast, or steam. In Western cultures, Dutch ovens or deep skillets are the closest equivalent and can be substituted, but they are less desirable because they are less fuel-efficient; the straight sides make stirring and food removal more difficult; and they require more oil when deep-frying. The sloping sides and narrow bottom of the wok are what make this pan so efficient and easy to use. Woks come in a variety of sizes and are usually made of spun carbon steel, stainless steel, or aluminum. Fancy copper-plated ones are also available; we see no reason for having one. They are usually heavy, difficult to keep clean, and virtually impossible to season. We recommend a spun carbon steel wok because it is a good heat conductor and can be seasoned to help prevent sticking. Aluminum is a reasonable second choice, but because it does not season as well, you may need to use more oil when stir-frying foods that tend to stick, such as rice or noodles. Stainless steel neither seasons well nor conducts heat well and should be avoided. For some reason, woks with "no-stick" surfaces such as Teflon or SilverStone tend to cause foods to stew in their own juices rather than produce the fine, almost-dry texture that bare metals produce. They are adequate for deep-frying, but not stir-frying. We do not recommend electric woks because they do not heat as quickly and are not as responsive to heat changes as free-standing models.

There are basically two types of handles on woks: square loops and straight. Either type can be made of metal or wood. The square-loop type has the advantage that it takes up less space, but the disadvantage that it is more difficult to use with one hand. The straight handle, which looks much like a standard saucepan handle, is easier to maneuver with one hand, but takes up more space. Best of all for most stir-frying is the type that has a straight wooden handle on one side and a wooden square loop on the other side. This allows the most flexibility in handling, and the wood negates the need for potholders because it stays cool.

The woks usually available for home use are 14 inches in diameter and 4 inches deep, although the sloping sides make them seem deeper. This size fits well on most home stoves, has enough room for vigorous stir-frying or deep-frying of several large pieces at a time, and is the size most often available in housewares departments and Thai and Oriental markets. Smaller woks, designed primarily for cooking omelets, are available, and we find them quite useful for that. Larger woks are also available, but are not recommended for home use unless you have a commercial gas stove in your kitchen, because most home ranges cannot provide enough heat for them.

If you have a gas stove, a round-bottomed wok is best, because the round bottom permits smoother movements of the scoop and food than does a flat one. If you have an electric range, a flat-bottomed wok will be more efficient, easier to keep in place, and safer, because it is less likely to tip over. A flat-bottomed wok, however, interferes with the smoothness of movements in stir-frying. A flat-bottomed wok may be used on a gas stove, but a round-bottomed one should not be used on an electric range because the heat transfer is less efficient.

With time and frequent use, a well-seasoned wok takes on a nice dark appearance inside and out. Do not try to keep it shiny bright, because the dark coating signifies proper use and, most important, aids in preventing food from sticking. Once seasoned, a wok should not be scrubbed with steel wool or cleansing powder unless it becomes rusty through neglect or improper use. Treat it much as you would a non-stick pan. A plastic scrubber and mild soap with water may be used for the occasional pieces of stuck food, as may happen with noodles. Ordinarily, all you need do is add hot water while the wok is still hot, swirl it around, and brush with a stiff fiber brush, such as a vegetable brush. Dry the cleaned wok with a paper towel or cloth, then heat it for about 30 seconds over high heat to make sure it is completely dry.

Seasoning a Wok

A new spun-carbon-steel wok should be cleaned thoroughly and seasoned prior to its first use. When purchased, it will be coated with an oily substance that reduces the risk of rust during shipment and storage. The following procedure will result in a nicely seasoned wok:

1. Remove the oily coating by scrubbing the wok thoroughly with soap and water, scouring powder, and, if necessary, steel wool. It will probably be necessary to repeat the scrubbing and rinsing several times to remove all the coating. This is the only time that steel wool or scouring powder should be used on a wok, unless the wok gets rusty from lack of use. Dry the wok thoroughly.

2. Place the wok over low heat until it is hot all the way up the sides. This may take no more than 1 minute over a strong gas flame, 2 or 3 minutes over a weak gas flame or on an electric range. Remove the wok from the heat.

3. While the wok is still hot, pour in 1 or 2 tablespoons of vegetable oil and spread it evenly over the surface of the wok, inside and out. Let the wok cool to room temperature, then wipe off any excess oil that has not been absorbed by the metal.

4. Heat the wok again, as you did before, and repeat the oil treatment. At this point, part of the bottom of the wok will have begun to turn dark and perhaps glossy. The size and intensity of the dark area will depend primarily on the intensity of heat generated by your stove.

5. Repeat the procedure two more times. After the fourth treatment, store the wok in a dry place.

6. Each time you use the wok it will become more seasoned, and the dark area will grow, eventually covering the entire wok inside and out.

Wok Cover

A wok cover is used for steaming, or when preparing foods that need to simmer, like Beef Musman. Wok covers are high round or flattened domes with a handle on top. The best are those with heat-resistant handles so you don't need a potholder to remove them. In any case, the cover should fit smoothly around the inside edge of the wok to prevent excess steam from escaping. If a wok is to be used for steaming, the cover should fit about ½ to 1 inch below the top of the wok. This allows you to add more water by pouring it around the edge of the cover without lifting the cover and letting steam escape.

Wok Ladle

A wok ladle is about 16 to 18 inches long and has a bowl about 4 inches in diameter. It is used with the wok scoop to lift prepared dishes out of the wok and put them into serving bowls. Any sturdy ladle with a relatively large bowl can be used. The particular advantage of the wok ladle is that the angle at which the bowl is attached to the handle matches the angle of the scoop part of the wok scoop, making it easier to use them together.

Wok Scoop

This is a metal scoop about 3 inches wide at the working end, with a wooden or metal handle 12 to 19 inches long. It is used for stir-frying and folding. If you dislike the sound of metal scraping against metal when you are stir-frying you may use a stiff wooden or plastic spatula of about the same dimensions. Be sure that whatever you use is very stiff and has a handle long enough to allow maximum control over the movement of ingredients and to allow you to stand far enough from the wok to avoid being burned by spattering oil or other ingredients.

SERVING EQUIPMENT
Rice Server

Although any covered bowl can be used, the traditional rice server is a deep, covered container that comes in several sizes, ranging from one large enough to serve a dinner for eight to small individual ones. It is usually made of stamped aluminum covered with intricate Thai designs, and comes with an aluminum spoon similarly decorated. It lends an authentic touch, is very decorative, keeps the rice warm, and holds in special aromas, such as that from jasmine rice. To help keep the rice warm, the container should be filled with hot water, then emptied and dried just before the rice is added.

Serving Dishes

Each food prepared should be placed on the table in a separate dish, which can be passed or reached by each diner, since in Thai dining each person chooses from among the dishes, shifting back and forth at will. Small casseroles about 8 to 10 inches long are useful, as are platters and soup bowls.

Soup Server

A doughnut-shaped, chimney-equipped server is generally used to keep soup steaming hot. Inexpensive aluminum ones are available in Thai and Oriental markets. You may also find more expensive servers made of tin-lined copper or brass. These containers are usually larger, and are sometimes referred to as Mongolian Hot Pots. If you choose a brass or copper utensil, be sure it has a non-corrodible lining such as tin. To use the server, place 1 to 2 teaspoons of jellied fuel (Sterno) on the metal grate and ignite it *through the bottom opening* after filling the container with soup. Each diner scoops out the amount of soup he or she desires. If you are serving more than four persons it may be more convenient to have two small servers rather than one large one. Never attempt to pass the container at the table when it is full of hot liquid.

Tableware

Contrary to popular belief, the Thai make relatively little use of chopsticks. Spoons and forks are more commonly used. Spoons are particularly useful for eating rice and sauces. Forks are useful when eating noodles, although fingers or chopsticks may be used if you prefer. Actually, almost everything except soup may be eaten quite effectively and properly with the fingers, a messy procedure but one that can be fun.

COOKING TECHNIQUES

The techniques used in Thai cooking are straightforward and easy to master. There are no complex procedures to be learned, nor are there elaborate preparations of basic ingredients. Because most of the preparation is done before the actual cooking begins, cooking proceeds quickly even if you are preparing several dishes. This is particularly true if the instructions for advance preparation given in Chapter 3 are followed. The cooking techniques used in this book are described in the following sections.

Stir-Frying

Stir-frying is the basic technique in Thai cooking, and it is used more often than any other. The food is stirred and lifted rapidly and almost constantly in very hot oil or lard to increase the amount of contact each particle of food has with the hot surface of the wok. This reduces the cooking time significantly and increases fuel efficiency. A wok is extremely well suited to this purpose because the sloping sides and wide top allow for more vigorous stirring and mixing of the food than would be possible in a flat-bottomed, straight-sided container. You may demonstrate this for yourself by cooking the same stir-fried dish in a wok and then in a Dutch oven or deep skillet. Traditionally, a lot of lard or oil is used, but we have reduced the amount in our recipes.

To stir-fry, you should always heat the wok well before adding the oil; pour the oil around the middle of the sides first, allowing it to run down, then swirl the oil over the surface of the wok. This coats the cooking surface evenly and permits better transfer of heat from the pan to the oil, allowing the oil to heat instantly. Heating the wok before adding the oil also helps keep the ingredients from sticking during cooking.

Traditionally, the wok is placed over a very hot fire or on coals. Gas resembles this most closely and provides continuous, quick heat that can be controlled easily. Electric heat may be used, but the heat recovery time is usually slower after ingredients are added, and the cooking time may be longer. With an electric range it is more effective to adjust the heat level by removing the wok from the burner than to try and regulate it by turning the heat control knobs. Another electric-range method is to keep one burner on "high" and an adjacent one on "low," transferring the wok back and forth. Either procedure takes practice.

Some foods, like chopped garlic, coriander root, and ginger, need to be stirred constantly and rapidly to keep them from sticking, burning, and becoming bitter. Others, like sliced meat or vegetables, may be stirred more slowly and even allowed to stand without stirring for a few seconds. The object is to cook everything evenly in the least amount of time.

Add the ingredients as directed in the recipes and stir-fry until the desired effect is obtained. Because the sequence of adding ingredients is important, the recipes should be followed carefully the first time or two until you get the basic ideas in mind. In some cases the sequence is important for the sake of flavor. For example, garlic, coriander root, and ginger are usually cooked first to allow the oil or lard to absorb their flavor and transmit it to the other ingredients as they are cooked. In other instances; the sequence is based on the cooking times of the ingredients: those ingredients that take longer to cook are added first and those requiring less cooking time are added later. We cannot overemphasize the importance of having all ingredients ready to use, premeasured in containers near the cooking area. Once cooking has begun it must proceed quickly and smoothly; stopping to chop, slice, or measure ingredients can be an incredible nuisance as well as possibly contributing to a different effect in the finished dish. If you have an opportunity to watch an experienced Thai cook at work, please do so. At the risk of sounding overly romantic, we can describe it only as poetry in motion.

Deep-Frying

Deep-frying is second only to stir-frying in Thai cooking, and a wok is marvelously adapted to this technique. Its sloping sides provide a larger oiled surface on which to cook the food, resulting in less oil (and less fuel to heat the oil). To deep-fry, add the oil to the wok before heating the wok; then bring the oil to the appropriate temperature. Although an instant-reading cooking thermometer may be used to determine the temperature, it is not essential. You can determine the correct temperature for deep-frying without a thermometer by adding a small piece of scallion, garlic, or ginger, or a few drops of batter to the oil. If it rises to the surface quickly and begins to turn light brown without burning, the oil is the correct temperature. If it drops to the bottom of the oil and just sits there, the oil is too cold. If it gets crisp or burns immediately upon contact, the oil is too hot.

Steaming

Steaming is used less often in Thai cooking than in some other cuisines of Asia, but it is essential for some preparations. Traditional steaming equipment consists of perforated metal pans that can be stacked on top of an accompanying solid-bottomed pan in which a little water has been placed. Up to four perforated pans can be stacked on top of one another, so that a number of foods can be steamed at once. However, any type of steamer you have, or can improvise, will work perfectly well provided that it keeps the steam contained and you are easily able to add more hot water as needed. Exercise some caution when adding water or unloading the steamer to avoid burns.

Traditionally, steamers in Thailand are lined with banana leaves, and the foods to be steamed, particularly desserts, are also wrapped in banana leaves. Banana leaves are generally unavailable in the United States, but if you can get them, please try this technique. Otherwise, waxed paper, parchment paper, cheesecloth, or aluminum foil may be substituted. If food is to be placed directly on metal steaming pans, the pans should be oiled lightly to prevent sticking. If bamboo steamers are used, put the food on a heat-resistant plate to help keep the bamboo racks clean.

POUNDING AND GRINDING TECHNIQUES

A mortar and pestle is by far the best tool for pounding ingredients to a paste and for pulverizing herbs and spices. A little salt added to moist ingredients acts as an abrasive and aids in pulverizing them. The pounding action helps release oils and flavors better than the grinding action of a food processor or blender, but these appliances may be substituted if a mortar and pestle is not available. A blender is more effective than a food processor for grinding curries and preparing coconut milk, because the ingredients are less likely to whirl around without being processed. For small amounts of dry ingredients, such as seeds, a coffee grinder or spice grinder is useful but not essential.

PORTIONS, MENUS, AND SERVING

By Western standards, the portions of each dish in Thailand are often relatively small both because the Thai eat frequently in small amounts and because several dishes are likely to be served at the same meal for variety and contrast. That allows each diner to select those items of most interest and to switch back and forth between them as taste dictates. The portions provided for each recipe in this book are based in part on that custom. We have provided a range of servings for the recipes: the smaller value should be used if you plan to serve fewer dishes, and the larger one if you plan to serve several dishes at the same meal. As in all cooking, your own judgment and experience must be the final criterion, and our suggested portions should be viewed merely as guidelines.

Planning a traditional Thai meal is a straightforward procedure. One need remember only two things: (1) serve three to five dishes that compliment each other in taste, color, and texture, and (2) always include rice. Rice is the hub around which the entire meal revolves, but it is not counted as one of the dishes; it is simply expected. Beyond those simple "rules," your own imagination and taste prevail. Main dishes are often selected to include hot and mild dishes, sweet and savory dishes, meat or poultry and fish dishes, a soup, and a vegetable or salad or both. Here again we find a difference between Western and Thai serving practices. Thai salads and vegetable dishes frequently contain meat or seafood and are served with what we would consider main dishes. Sweets are not considered part of a routine meal in a Thai home, but rather are used as between-meal snacks during the day or, more rarely, later in the evening after dinner. In Thailand there is no demand to serve food steaming hot, except for soup and steamed rice, as there is in most Western cuisines. Many dishes are served at room temperature and most others can be served lukewarm. Soup and steamed rice, however, should be served steaming hot.

Many people in Thailand eat their main meal at midday, with a lighter meal in the evening and snacks in between. Like so many aspects of Thai cuisine, this has a practical value. The Thai believe that one can sleep better if a light meal is eaten in the evening. (Certainly it helps in weight control, because it is well known that going to sleep soon after a big meal contributes to weight gain.) The Thai are pragmatic about eating, and subscribe to the idea of eating when they are hungry, as is evidenced by the many street vendors from whom one can purchase all kinds of food from early in the morning until well into the evening.

The appetizers and snacks in this book are only a sample of the snacks available in Thailand. These may, of course, be used as main courses at a sit-down meal, but traditionally they are eaten between meals and, more often than not, purchased from the carts of street vendors or the boats of vendors plying the waterways of the *klongs* (canals). To provide hot foods, some street vendors carry cooking equipment, a supply of hot coals, and the necessary ingredients on a long pole balanced over their shoulders. Others carry all ingredients and cooking utensils in a small pushcart. In either case, food can be cooked anywhere at a moment's notice.

Some of the dishes in this book are particularly easy to prepare and require few, if any, ingredients that are not widely available. They can serve as a very good introduction to Thai cuisine and hopefully will encourage you to venture further and make any efforts required to obtain special ingredients for other recipes and to learn some of the more detailed techniques. A partial list of these dishes includes: Deep-Fried Bread and Pork, Stir-Fried Pork with Seasonings, Thai Dried Beef, Salty Dried Beef, Garlic Pork, Chicken Cashews, Chicken or Fish Balls, Barbecued Chicken 1 and 2, Stir-Fried Cucumber and Egg, Deep-Fried Tofu, Deep-Fried Vegetables, and Stir-Fried Broccoli. If you have never attempted cooking Thai food before and wish to get an easy introduction, try some of these dishes first.

To help you in planning menus we have provided sample menus, each with a different focus. They should be viewed only as guidelines to show typical combinations that balance flavor and texture: they are not intended to be followed slavishly.

A Mild Menu for 6 to 8

Won Ton Soup
Stuffed Chicken Wings
Sweet and Sour Pork
Beef with Oyster Sauce
Chicken with Cashews
Deep-Fried Vegetables
Green Salad
Rice

A Mild and Hot Menu for 6 to 8

Fish Maw Soup
Noodles with Coconut Milk, Pineapple, and Ginger
Beef Panang
Garlic Pork
Hungry Shrimp
Stir-Fried Broccoli
Thai Salad
Rice

A Hot and Spicy Menu for 6 to 8

Hot and Spicy Shrimp Soup
Stir-Fried Beef with Mint
Chicken with Green Curry
Pork with Green Beans
Fish Cakes
Hot and Spicy Mushrooms
Pickled Vegetables
Rice

A Light Meal for 4 to 6

Thai Dried Beef
Barbecued Chicken 1 or 2
Green Papaya Salad
Rice with Coconut Milk or Steamed Rice

The buffet as we know it in the United States is not used in Thailand, but Thai foods can be used effectively to create a tasty and colorful buffet. In fact, it could be argued that every Thai meal is a buffet, because, in general, several dishes are served at one time. In selecting foods for a buffet, keep in mind the following suggestions for the most effective presentation: (1) select mostly dishes that can be made ahead and served at room temperature; (2) include a variety of colors, textures, tastes, and levels of spiciness; (3) for contrast and interest, include a few hot dishes that hold well and that can be kept warm in chafing dishes; (4) avoid hot shellfish dishes, which must be kept warm, since the shellfish will continue to cook and may get tough; (5) avoid hot noodle dishes, which may get gummy and sticky while standing; (6) avoid deep-fried foods, which are likely to get soggy after standing; (7) and last, but certainly not least, decorate the table and garnish the food as attractively as you can. Carved fruits and vegetables are traditional, but flowers may be used if their fragrance does not overwhelm or conflict with the fragrance of the food.

A Sample Buffet for 16 to 20

Beef Musman
Ground Pork Wrapped in Noodles
Galloping Horses
Beef Salad
Egg Crepes
Fried Chicken Curry Won Tons
Steamed Won Tons
Grilled Beef with Thai Seasoning
Pickled Vegetables
Chicken in Roasted Curry Sauce
Chicken Fried Rice
Steamed Rice

As a further aid in planning menus, we have classified the recipes in this book as "mild" and "hot," in which "hot" refers to the intensity of the flavors of chilies and pepper. The hot dishes are marked with the symbol ✳✳✳ near the English name. Those with no ✳✳✳ are considered mild. Within each range, some dishes are hotter or milder than others, so the classifications should be viewed as only a general guideline, one that is largely subjective. You may wish to indicate levels of heat to your diners by garnishing the dishes. You could use chilies to garnish the hot ones and omit the chili garnish from mild ones. If you prepare some dishes hotter than others you could use red chilies to garnish the hottest ones and green chilies for the milder ones. You may wish to reclassify some items based on your own taste and the taste of your family or friends. Also remember that some of the mild dishes are accompanied by hot sauces or dips, which each diner may add according to taste, so that a "mild" selection need not be too mild even for an asbestos-mouthed diner. Furthermore, you may modify the heat by adding or deleting chilies or pepper to taste. We have provided recipes that are only moderately hot by Thai standards.

As we have indicated, there is generally no provision for serving dishes in courses in a Thai meal, as there is in most Western countries. Remember, the Thai approach food from the point of view of "eat what you want to eat when you are hungry." Most foods are served at the same time, or in the sequence in which they are prepared, and diners choose what they want. The usual procedure is to put a large portion of rice in the center of your plate or bowl and place two or more foods at the edge of the rice. An effective way to keep the sauce and flavors separate is to form pockets around the edge of the rice and spoon a different food into each. Bowls are particularly useful because they retain the various sauces, which can then be absorbed by the rice.

Place settings may consist of either a standard plate and a soup bowl for each diner, or two soup bowls, one for soup and the other for solid foods. If a plate and soup bowl are used, the soup bowl should be placed beside the plate, not on it, so both may be used at the same time. All the dishes should be placed within easy reach of each diner. If you are serving more than four people, it may be better to serve each dish in two separate bowls on different parts of the table so that nothing has to be passed.

Each diner should be provided with a large spoon and a fork. Knives are not necessary because the food will have been chopped or sliced beforehand. Chopsticks are used relatively little by the Thai people. A spoon is the principal eating utensil, and the fork is used mainly as a food pusher and guider. Unless you are left-handed, the spoon is held in the right hand and the fork in the left. The back (convex) side of the fork is held facing the spoon and food is pushed into the bowl of the spoon with it. The fork may be used to eat noodles and some solid pieces, like chicken wings or won tons, but fingers are just as appropriate for those foods. In fact, it is perfectly all right to use your fingers for almost anything except soup. Even sauces may be eaten with the fingers by forming a small ball of rice and using it to sop up the sauce from your plate. It may be less elegant, but it certainly is enjoyable. Most Thai restaurateurs in the United States keep a supply of chopsticks on hand for people who ask for them, and it is not unusual to see people struggling with chopsticks in the mistaken belief they should, while at an adjacent table a Thai family may be eating comfortably with fork and spoon.

Fish sauce, vinegar sauce, and ground roasted chilies are almost always on the table in the same way that salt and pepper would be in Western countries. There is a major difference, however, between Thai and Western attitudes toward the use of table condiments. Whereas in Western cultures it might be considered an offense to the cook to use additional condiments at the table, the Thai people expect it. They recognize that individuals do have different tastes and reactions to food, and believe that each diner should feel free to modify the taste, particularly when it comes to spiciness.

GARNISHES

Garnishes add the extra touch that makes the presentation of Thai food even more appealing. They can be as simple as lettuce leaves and sliced chilies or vegetables, or as elaborate as vegetables intricately carved to resemble animals, objects, or flowers. The variety of garnishes is limited only by your imagination, although space permits us to describe only a few of them in this section. Once you get the idea, you may wish to develop garnishes of your own. You can also refer to one of several books that provide detailed instructions on food carving, or, better yet, take a course in decorative food carving.

Special tools are available for carving vegetables into intricate shapes, and some of the procedures are very complicated.

The procedures we describe here, however, require nothing more than a sharp paring knife, some cold water, and a little patience.

BROCCOLI—Broccoli florets provide a natural garnish, and the stems can be formed into decorative shapes.

1. Remove the florets. Peel the tough skin from the stems. Trim the stems and slice them crosswise or lengthwise into pieces of uniform size and shape (determined by the shape the final decoration will be). (Pieces should be about ⅛ to ¼ inch thick.)

2. Carve the edges of the slices to form silhouettes of animals, flowers, leaves, or geometrical designs.

CHILIES—Select green or red chilies, depending on the color contrast you desire. Fresh chilies make the best decorations, but dried ones may be used if they are soaked in warm water for 20 or 30 minutes until they are partially reconstituted.

Chili Flowers

1. Using scissors or a sharp knife, cut the chilies lengthwise in 5 to 8 places, leaving the strips attached to the base and stem.

2. Remove the center rib and seeds if you wish.

3. Place the chilies in a bowl of cold water until the strips fold back, forming "petals."

CUCUMBERS—Cucumbers (or zucchini) provide several easy carving possibilities.

Cucumber Slices

1. Cut V-shaped wedges lengthwise down the cucumber at ¼-inch intervals. The most attractive results come when you cut carefully with a sharp knife. If you are in a hurry, pull the tip of a vegetable peeler down the length of the cucumber.

2. Slice the cucumber crosswise into circles about ¼ inch thick.

Boat with Riders

1. Slice a cucumber in half lengthwise. Slice off just enough of the "peel" side opposite the cut to allow the cucumber to stand securely with the cut side up.

2. With a spoon, remove the seeds and part of the flesh to make a hollow "boat."

3. Insert a toothpick lengthwise through a ripe olive so that about ⅛ inch extends from one end. Break the other end of the toothpick so that it extends about ¼ inch. Insert the longer end of the toothpick into the bottom of the inside of the "boat." Repeat with other olives, placing them about 1 inch apart.

4. Place a thin, round slice of carrot on top of each olive and secure it by pushing down on the toothpick.

EGGS—We are all familiar with slices of hard-cooked eggs used as garnishes, and one of our examples includes just that. The other may surprise you.

Egg Wedges

1. Hard-cook several eggs in simmering water. Peel them when they are cool enough to handle.

2. Slice each egg lengthwise, and slice each of those halves lengthwise into 2 or 3 wedges. Move the knife back and forth as you cut, so that a slight ripple effect is produced.

Egg Nets

1. Put 5 or 6 eggs in a mixing bowl with ⅛ teaspoon of salt. Beat lightly until they are smooth, but not frothy. Strain them through a fine sieve.

2. Heat 1 inch of oil to 350° in a wok. Dribble the beaten, sieved eggs over the surface of the hot oil in the wok to form narrow strands. Hold the bowl of eggs in one hand and dip the other hand into the eggs. Hold your hand about 12 to 18 inches over the oil and let the egg run in a thin, steady stream from your fingertips while moving your hand in a circular motion so the surface of the oil is covered with a thin net of egg. Or, dribble the egg from the tines of a fork.

3. You will need to repeat this procedure about four times. The intent is to form a thin net of egg strands which will cook quickly, without massing together. When the strands are set completely and light golden on the bottom, flip them over carefully and brown the other side.

4. Remove them from the oil, drain them on paper towels, and repeat with the remaining eggs.

GREEN ONIONS—Green onion "brushes" are easy to prepare and can help turn even the most mundane-appearing dish into something special.

Onion Brushes

1. Remove the root of a green onion neatly. Cut off enough of the green part to leave the rest about 6 to 8 inches long.

2. With a very sharp knife, slice the onion lengthwise, beginning 1 or 2 inches from the root end. Rotate the onion 90° and repeat. Rotate and slice 3 or 4 more times. Or, cut from both ends, leaving an uncut center portion about 1 inch long.

3. Place the onion in cold water until the strips turn outward and form a brush.

LETTUCE—Most dishes can be made more attractive simply by placing them on a single layer of 1 or 2 whole lettuce leaves. In some recipes we have suggested specific types of lettuce because we have found they are attractive and effective. For example, red lettuce, with its contrasting red and green leaves, is very pretty when topped with stir-fried shrimp dishes. If the type of lettuce we recommend is not available, substitute other types (preferably not iceberg). Lettuce is the most basic garnish of Thai cuisine and has the advantage that the leaves may be eaten. It is surprising how many people in the United States leave the lettuce on the serving plates in Thai restaurants, mistakenly thinking that the leaves are for decoration only. Not only are they missing the pleasure of the crisp, contrasting texture, but they are also discarding the sauce trapped in the leaves or underneath them.

TOMATOES—Tomatoes provide a versatile vehicle for carving various shapes. Three of the easy-to-carve designs are:

The Tulip

This method produces four "petals," but more petals look even nicer and can be produced easily by making more cuts.

1. Slice a very thin piece of tomato from the stem end to form a flat base for the tomato to stand on.

2. Starting about one third of the way from the base of the tomato and going over the top, make a shallow incision through the skin from the point where you began to a similar point on the opposite side of the tomato. Repeat with another incision over the top at right angles to the first one. The skin will be cut into 4 triangular pieces whose tips are at the top of the tomato. Cut as shallowly as you can—the goal is to cut the skin but not deep into the flesh.

3. Use the point of a small knife to cut shallowly under each triangular flap; and peel the flap down carefully almost to the base of the incision. Repeat with the other flaps.

The Basket

1. Slice a very thin piece of tomato from the stem end to form a flat base for the tomato to stand on.

2. Visualize a ½-inch strip going across the top center of the blossom end of the tomato and about halfway down each side. This will be the handle of the basket. Starting about ¼ inch from the center of the tomato, cut through the skin and flesh to a point halfway to the stem end. Repeat on the other side of the visualized handle to outline the handle. At the base of each of these cuts, cut horizontally through the tomato to the vertical cut, and remove the wedge-shaped piece that results. (Use this wedge as additional garnish or in dishes that call for tomato wedges as an ingredient.)

3. Remove the seeds and flesh from the handle part of the basket. Remove the seeds and flesh from the bowl part of the basket.

4. Cut out a series of small V-shaped wedges around the edge of the bowl of the basket to form a ridged rim.

The Rose

1. Slice a paper-thin circle of tomato skin, about ½ inch in diameter, from the blossom end of the tomato, but do not remove it. It will form the base of the rose.

2. Leaving the circle attached, slice a paper-thin strip about ½ to ¾ inch wide around the tomato. Continue all the way to the stem end, being careful not to break the strip. As you slice, move the knife up and down slightly to produce a ripple effect in the edges of the peel.

3. Starting with the circle from Step 1, form a loose spiral with the strip of skin, allowing it to flare outward a little at the top.

4. Place the spiral circle side down on a plate. It will resemble a rose. Mint, coriander, or basil leaves may be placed at its base to simulate leaves.

3
Ingredients and Advance Preparations

FROM THE BEGINNING we thought it important to prepare this book using authentic Thai ingredients and techniques. The special ingredients needed include lemon grass, coriander, coriander root, *kah*, fish sauce, and chilies. These ingredients can usually be found in most markets selling products of Southeast Asia or the Orient. Except for coriander root, which is unique to Thai cuisine, they are used throughout Southeast Asia. Because some ingredients may not be available, we have included substitutions when that is possible without sacrificing the nature of the preparation. In a few instances we have indicated that no substitutions are available. We are aware that in those few cases some readers may have to omit a limited number of dishes from their Thai repertoire until the ingredients become available. It would have been easy to introduce many substitutions that only approximate Thai flavors and textures, but we felt it would be a disservice to the cuisine and to serious cooks to do that. Some fruits and vegetables are almost impossible to find in the United States, even in locales in which there is a large Thai community. In that case we have either completely omitted dishes using those items or made very close substitutions with ingredients that are available.

It is well worth the trouble of getting authentic ingredients whenever possible. Some things are available by mail order and, alas, some others are not because they must be fresh. An example is fresh rice noodles (see recipe, page 101). We have found no totally satisfactory substitute that captures the flavor and texture of fresh rice noodles, just as there is no fully adequate substitute in Italian cooking for fresh homemade pasta. That should not deter you from preparing the various dishes using the recommended substitutes, which provide similar textures and tastes.

Because Thai ingredients are often new to Americans we have described them in this chapter. We hope this will help avoid the feeling of confusion you may experience upon first stepping into a Thai market and being confronted with shelves of strange-looking ingredients. When we thought it would be useful, and when our test kitchen "guinea pigs" suggested it, we have included comments on ingredients that are familiar to American cooks.

We strongly recommend using absolutely fresh ingredients whenever possible. The quality of some preparations is dependent to a very large extent on the freshness of ingredients, especially vegetables and meats. We recognize that in some areas of the country certain fresh foods may not be available all year. In that case you may wish to substitute frozen foods, but please understand that the resulting dish may suffer somewhat.

MSG (monosodium glutamate) is not used at all in the recipes in this book. It is a white crystalline powder that is claimed to enhance the flavor of food. We believe that it only helps mask the flavor of inferior ingredients and we recommend against using it at any time. In spite of claims to the contrary in commercials and advertisements, it seems to us that it adds a taste of its own. Further, some people are very sensitive to it and develop what has come to be known as the "Chinese restaurant syndrome," often experienced as sneezing, a feeling of tightness around the temples, or fullness or pain over the cheekbones. When quality ingredients are used, and proper cooking procedures followed, there is no reason to resort to MSG or similar preparations.

INGREDIENTS

AGAR—is derived from seaweed that is harvested commercially in large quantities, and it has a wide variety of uses. It is also known as Chinese or Japanese gelatin and comes in several varieties and in shades of white and light brown. The dessert recipes in this book call for the white variety. Its principal characteristic is that it acts as a superb jelling agent and as such it is used in pharmaceuticals, cosmetics, commercial food products such as ice cream, and many other preparations. It may be familiar to you from your days in biology class, where it was used as the medium on which various kinds of microorganisms were grown for study under the microscope. It is available in Thai and Oriental markets and in health food stores, and comes in dried strips about 15 inches long or in powdered form. Our recipes use both forms, and unless powder is specified, strips should be used.

BAMBOO SHOOTS—are generally available only in cans in this country, so our recipes are based entirely on the canned variety. You may find them in chunks, sliced, julienned, or whole. They are always available in Thai and Oriental markets and usually can be found in the canned vegetable or specialty foods sections of larger supermarkets. They should be crisp, tender, and have a mild taste. If the ones you buy are soft or have a "tinny" taste that remains even after you rinse them, try another brand if possible. Some merchants buy bamboo shoots in large cans and remove the shoots to smaller containers so you need buy only as much as you need. However, the shoots have still been canned.

BANANA LEAVES—are used extensively in Thailand to line steamers and to wrap food, especially desserts, for steaming. When steamed, the leaves impart a faint banana flavor to some foods. They are sometimes available in Puerto Rican or Mexican markets and may be frozen if wrapped tightly in aluminum foil. They are not essential; aluminum foil, waxed paper, parchment paper, or cheesecloth may be substituted.

BANANA SQUASH—See Squash.

BASIL—is known as HORAPA in Thailand. It is widely available and relatively inexpensive there. It is used in Thai dishes as an ingredient as well as a garnish and adds a flavor that is slightly peppery and cooling at the same time. In the United States it is less widely available and is usually quite expensive, even in season. Fortunately it is easy to grow, and in mild climates it can be grown well into the winter. Unfortunately, it loses texture and color when frozen, and therefore loses much of its value in Thai cooking. Fresh basil can be used in many places where we call for mint, and conversely, fresh mint, if available, is an excellent substitute for basil even though their flavors differ.

BEAN PASTE (BROWN)—is made from fermented soybeans and may be found in bottles or cans in Thai and Oriental markets and some supermarkets. There is no true substitute. Because part of the desired effect is the salty flavor of the beans, soy sauce may be added as a substitute; it will not provide the "beany" flavor or texture, however.

BEAN PASTE (WHITE)—is also known as fermented white beans. The Thai name is TAO JIEW KAOW or TAO JIEW LEUNG. It is made from fermented soybeans and is found in bottles and cans in Thai and Oriental markets and some supermarkets. Sometimes it is labeled "Yellow Bean Sauce" or "White Bean Sauce." Even though the label often says "sauce" the beans are still whole. They may be white or slightly yellow, depending on the brand. Some brands are more salty than others; we suggest you taste them before using, and rinse them in cool water if they taste too salty for you.

BEAN SPROUTS—which add a delicate, crisp texture without contributing much flavor of their own, can be found in most major supermarkets and are always available in Thai, Oriental, and health food stores. The bean sprouts to which we refer are sprouted from mung beans, but soybean sprouts may be substituted. However, other types of sprouts, e.g., alfalfa, wheat, rye, etc., should not be used. If bean sprouts are not generally available they can easily be grown in your own kitchen; they require neither light nor soil to sprout. (For instructions, turn to the section on preparing ingredients.) To obtain the maximum crispiness they should be soaked in cold water for about 15 minutes or more just prior to use. Occasionally bean sprouts can be found canned, but they should *never* be used because processing completely destroys their texture and flavor. Rather than use these soggy messes it is much better to omit bean sprouts from the dish. There is no substitute for fresh.

BEAN THREAD—See Noodles, Transparent.

BEEF—of any kind may be used, but we suggest the less tender cuts because they are less likely to fall apart during stir-frying or stewing. Flank steak is particularly good because it can be cut across the grain easily, and it produces attractive, ragged-edged slices.

BOK CHOY—is also known as Chinese or Oriental cabbage in some areas and markets. It has large, dark-green leaves and white stems that are about twice the size of celery stalks.

CABBAGE (CHINESE)—is a term loosely applied to several vegetables, including bok choy and Napa cabbage. To avoid confusion, we have specified the type to use in each recipe. (See Bok Choy and Napa Cabbage.)

CABBAGE (NAPA)—is is about a foot long and several inches in diameter at the widest part. It has soft leaves that are pale green and white. It is sometimes known as celery cabbage, Chinese lettuce, or Chinese cabbage. The flavor is delicate, and the texture crisp.

CARDAMOM—is a member of the ginger family. It grows in Ceylon and southern India and is one of the most expensive spices. Ground cardamom is much more widely available than dried seeds, but ground cardamom loses its flavor much more quickly than the seeds. When purchased whole, the seeds are often encased in beige pods, which should be removed before the seeds are used. The Thai name for cardamom is KRAVAN.

CATSUP—is a surprising ingredient for Thai food until you realize that it was originally developed in India, even though most people associate it with American food.

CHILIES (FRESH)—exist in hundreds of recognized and classified varieties and probably many more that have never been classified. A complete description of all the kinds you are likely to find commercially available or listed in seed catalogues is far beyond the scope and purpose of this section. We have provided brief descriptions of some of the most common varieties below, but the list is *far* from complete. The general Thai name for chilies is PRIG. In traditional Thai cooking they are used with what might seem to be reckless abandon, but our recipes use them in moderation. Feel free to increase or decrease the amounts in the recipes according to your taste, provided that you do not omit them altogether. In addition to "heat," chilies add a rich flavor which can be obtained no other way. Traditionally, the seeds are left in fresh chilies and removed from dried ones. The seeds produce much of the heat, so removing them will reduce that, but still leave the rich flavor.

For fresh chilies we have used Serrano chilies, because they are widely available and produce a very good effect. You may substitute Jalapeño or any other hot chilies, but the proportions needed will vary with the type used, and the flavor will be somewhat different with each. If available, the tiny, fiery-hot Thai chilies known as "bird peppers" have a particularly good flavor, but the amount used should be about one fourth that of Serranos if measured in weight, unless you like fiery hot food. Preserved chilies in bottles may be used in salads or as garnishes, but they are too sour to be used in main dishes.

Fortunately, chilies are very easy to grow from seeds or small plants; they thrive in a sunny, dry location and make very decorative garden plants. If you grow your own you will find that the intensity of heat and flavor will vary from chili to chili from the same bush, and there is no sure-fire way to determine which will be hotter without tasting. If you grow your own you may wish to freeze them for use in the winter, following the instructions we provide in the section on preparing ingredients (page 59). Dried chilies (page 40) are used in some of the curry pastes and for preparing ground roasted chilies.

Cayenne Chilies—are about 3 inches long by ¼ inch wide. They are allowed to mature and turn red before being harvested.

Jalapeño Chilies—are green, gently tapered, and about 2½ inches long and ¾ inch wide at the stem end. They are widely available in fresh or pickled form, but the pickled variety should be used only in salads, never in curries.

Serrano Chilies—are widely available and easy to grow and freeze for later use. They are usually green but sometimes may be found red, and are about 1½ inches long and ½ inch wide. They have a very strong, hot, rich flavor.

Thai Chilies—are more widely available frozen than fresh and are usually found only in Thai markets. They are about 1 inch long, ⅛ inch wide, and may be green or red. In Thailand they are known as "bird peppers," partly because mynah birds love to eat them—and when they do, the birds seem to talk more. (Another reason is that small objects, and these chilies are very small, are referred to as being "bird-sized.") These chilies are fiery hot and have a fuller, richer flavor than either Serranos or Jalapeños. They may be substituted for Serranos or Jalapeños by using about one fourth as much Thai chilies as you would the others, when measured by weight.

Yellow Chilies—are small and very hot. They are slightly larger than Jalapeños, bright yellow with a hint of green, and are sometimes called "small yellow wax" chilies.

CHILIES (DRIED)—are usually packed in cellophane packages, although they are often available woven or sewn into long, decorative garlands, particularly in Mexican markets. The general Thai name is PRIG HANG. Dried New Mexico or California chilies are much milder than the small red Japanese dried chilies, which in turn are milder than the tiny dried Thai chilies. Any of these may be used interchangeably, depending on availability and your own taste. A general rule of thumb is that the smaller the chili the hotter it is likely to be, but, like any rule of thumb, there are exceptions. If you aren't sure, it is better to ask than to expect "fire" and not get it or, worse, not expect it and have to throw the food away because it is too hot.

California Dried Chilies—are dark red, about 5 inches long, and 1½ inches wide at the stem end. They have a relatively mild, rich flavor and should be roasted before use to allow the flavor to develop fully.

New Mexico Dried Chilies—are similar in appearance to California chilies and the flavor is only slightly hotter.

Small Dried Red Chilies—may be known as Thai chilies or Japanese chilies. The very smallest ones are extremely hot. The ones we suggest are about 2 to 3 inches long and about ¼ inch wide, and could be described as very hot. In Mexican markets they may be labeled "Chilies arbol."

CHILI PASTE (GROUND)—is usually labeled with its Indonesian name as SAMBAL OELECK, and that is the name you are likely to find on the bottle. The Thai name is PRIG BOD. It comes in several varieties, some of which contain garlic, onions, and other herbs and spices. Our recipes are based on plain chili paste. The quantities we suggest may be varied according to your taste. It should be stored in the refrigerator after opening. Like other Thai ingredients, chili paste should not be omitted altogether, because even in small quantities it adds necessary tang. In large quantities it is downright fiery. You can make your own version by coarsely grinding fresh red chilies (include the seeds but not the stems), and adding vinegar and salt to make a coarse, thin paste. However, since homemade chili paste is really no better than the commercial variety and has a shorter shelf life, commercially prepared ground chili paste is recommended. Different brands vary in hotness and you may need to try several before you find the one you like. There is no substitute.

CHIVES—are an herb with a flavor somewhere between that of garlic and onion. Only the green shoots, which look like miniature green onion stalks, are used. Fresh chives should be used whenever possible, but you may substitute frozen ones. Do not substitute the "freeze-dried" chives commonly found in the spice section of many supermarkets. Fortunately, chives are extremely easy to grow in a sunny location in the garden or in a very sunny window. Either Chinese or American chives may be used, with the knowledge that Chinese chives have a sharper flavor.

CLOUD EARS—are known in Thailand as HET HOONOO, which translates literally to "rat's ear," which is what they look like. They have virtually no taste and are used primarily for their texture. They are available in Thai and Oriental markets and are also known as "tree fungus" or "dried tree ears." They should not be confused with Oriental dried mushrooms, which they do not resemble in either taste or texture. Cloud ears are a fungus that grows on trees in Asia and are available only in the dried form in the United States. Because they add no flavor of their own they can be omitted if not available or if you do not like the crunchy, gelatinous texture they provide. There is no substitute.

CLOVES—are know as GAHN PLU in Thailand and are widely available in American supermarkets. They are very aromatic and strongly flavored, so use them in moderation.

COCONUT MILK—is prepared by grinding coconut meat with water and pressing out the liquid. It is not the thin, watery liquid found inside the coconut. Thick coconut milk is produced the first time liquid is pressed from the ground mixture and thin coconut milk is produced the second time. The procedure is described in detail on pages 62–63. Coconut milk is available canned and frozen. We recommend that you use homemade or frozen coconut milk if possible, because it will have a fresher flavor than canned. This is particularly true for dishes in which coconut milk is a predominant ingredient, e.g., Coconut Chicken Soup. If you use the canned variety, you may need to try several brands to find the one that is the freshest-tasting and most flavorful. We have found "Chef's Choice" to be quite good. We have seen references in some sources which suggest simulating coconut milk by adding coconut flavoring to dairy milk, but we find the flavor of this preparation totally unappealing. Furthermore, fresh dairy products are used rarely in traditional Thai cooking, so introducing dairy milk as a substitute for coconut milk seems wrong on two counts. There is no substitute.

COCONUTS—See Preparing Ingredients, page 60.

COFFEE—from Thailand is finely ground and contains additives such as corn, rice, sesame seeds, and sugar. Each of these adds its own flavor, making Thai coffee unique. Standard American coffee should not be substituted in Thai coffee preparations.

CORIANDER—is also known as cilantro or Chinese parsley. In Thailand it is known as PAK CHEE. It has a unique, pungent, earthy flavor and can be found in Thai, Oriental, Mexican, and Near Eastern markets as well as most large supermarkets.

Fresh coriander can be kept in the refrigerator for one week by placing it upright in a small container with barely enough water to cover the roots and covering the tops with plastic wrap or a small plastic bag. The wrap or bag should be put on loosely to allow air to circulate. There is no substitute, and the dried leaves found in the spice section of supermarkets should never be used. Please also read the entry on Coriander Root.

CORIANDER ROOT—is used extensively in Thai cooking, and is one of the "secret ingredients" that provide much of the unique flavor of Thai food. Coriander plants have fairly extensive root systems composed of many hairlike strands, but these are lost in the process of commercial harvesting and shipping. You may be able only to find coriander with small stubby roots ¼ to ½ inch long and about 1/16 to 1/8 inch in diameter. You may find that every trace of root has been removed from the coriander in your market or that the vestiges that do remain are almost invisible. There are three solutions: (1) ask your produce manager for coriander with roots—sometimes they are cut off for aesthetic reasons and the unmolested variety is still in the storage area; (2) grow your own—it's really quite easy if you have a yard or a sunny window; (3) use the bottom 1 inch of the stems as a substitute. If you do grow your own, harvest the plants when they are about 6 to 8 inches high. If coriander with roots is rare in your area and you suddenly find some, get as much as you can, remove the roots, chop them, and freeze them.

CORIANDER SEEDS—are readily available in Thai, Oriental, and Near Eastern markets and usually can be found in the spice section of supermarkets. They have a slightly sweet flavor. In a Thai market they go by the name MELLET PAK CHEE. If all else fails, try looking in the seed section of your local nursery or plant store. They will be more expensive there, but at least they will be available. If you grow your own coriander, let several plants go to seed and you'll have an ample seed supply for cooking as well as for starting a new coriander patch. There is no substitute.

CUMIN—is known as YIRA in Thailand. The seeds are readily available in the spice section of most supermarkets or in Thai, Mexican, Oriental, or Indian markets. They have a pungent aroma and slightly sharp taste and should be used in moderation. Fennel seed may be substituted if you prefer a mild licorice-like flavor.

CURRY OR CURRY PASTE—refers to a group of preparations made by pounding or grinding several spices, herbs, and other ingredients to a smooth paste. The term "curry" is sometimes confusing, because many people think of the powder found on supermarket shelves. Actually, the term is a generic one and refers to any herbs and spices that are ground and cooked together. Curry in Thai cooking is in no way synonymous with the "curry powder" found in supermarkets, and the commercial powder should be used only when specifically mentioned in a recipe. There are probably as many subtleties in preparing curry as there are cooks, and you may wish to modify the proportions in our recipes to your taste. The procedures, however, should be followed carefully. Curry pastes are available commercially, and some of the moist ones are quite good, but they vary in flavor and hotness so you may need to try several before finding one that you like. Commercially prepared curry pastes are also very expensive and, in the interest of economy, flexibility, and freshness of taste, we suggest you make your own. Most curries can be prepared in larger quantities than needed at the moment and stored in the refrigerator for several weeks or frozen for a longer period. Preparing larger quantities also makes grinding in a blender or food processor much easier and it results in a smoother paste.

CURRY POWDER—is universally available in markets that have spice sections. It is a blend of several spices and the specific ingredients may vary from manufacturer to manufacturer. It is not used widely in Thai cooking, and dishes in which it is included are probably Indian in origin.

EGGPLANT—in Thailand is quite different than that found in the United States. There are several varieties of Thai eggplant, ranging from small ones that look like large green peas to elongated green ones about the size of a banana. They are usually not available except in areas where there is a large Thai community, and even then they are generally quite expensive. In recipes calling for eggplant we have suggested the type to use. Fortunately, American or Japanese eggplant can be substituted in many dishes. In Thailand, eggplant is sometimes eaten raw as a snack with sauces or dips. Try it; we think you will be surprised at how good it tastes, once you get over the idea that it can only be eaten cooked.

EGG ROLL WRAPPERS—are made from wheat flour, eggs, and water. They tend to puff up when fried and are used less extensively in Thai cooking than spring roll wrappers. (See the entry on spring roll wrappers, page 55.)

FENNEL SEEDS—are widely available in the spice section of most supermarkets. They add a faint taste of licorice. Cumin seeds may be substituted, but the flavor will be different.

FISH OR SHRIMP BALLS—may be purchased fresh or frozen in Thai markets, but it is easy to make your own if they are unavailable commercially. We provide instructions on making them in the chapter on fish and seafood (page 236).

FISH MAW—is dried swim bladders or stomachs and intestines that have been deep-fried. It comes in cellophane bags and looks very much like large fried pork skins. It must be soaked before use and will expand up to four times the dried size. It adds little flavor of its own and is used primarily for texture. It is rarely found outside Thai and Oriental markets, and it is not unusual to find it in several price ranges in the same market. We generally buy the less expensive brands and find them totally acceptable. There is no substitute, but it can be omitted.

FISH SAUCE—is known in Thailand as NAM PLA. It is a liquid that looks like soy sauce and smells like fermented anchovies, which is exactly what it is. When you first smell it you may be tempted to omit it from the recipe, but do not give in to that temptation because it is an essential contributor to the elusive flavor that is typical of Thai cuisine. It is cooked in most of our recipes, but in Thailand it is usually found on the table to be added as an extra flavoring, in much the same way that soy sauce is served with Chinese food. Many brands are available, but some are too salty, particularly those made in Vietnam. Because fish sauce is inexpensive to begin with, we suggest that you do not try to be over-frugal and buy the cheap brands. There is no substitute.

FIVE-SPICE POWDER—is usually made of ground

star anise, cinnamon, cloves, fennel, and peppercorns, but some manufacturers make minor changes in the ingredients. It is not used widely in Thai cooking, but does add a unique flavor when it is used. It is always available in Thai and Oriental markets and can often be found in the spice section of larger supermarkets.

GARLIC—is used extensively and in large quantities in Thai cooking. Fortunately, there is no major difference in taste between Thai and American garlic, but Thai garlic has a very thin skin that is not removed before the cloves are used. The tough, papery skin on American garlic, however, must be removed, and the weights and measures in our recipes are for garlic that has been peeled. Use the recommended amount—it won't be too strong unless you abhor garlic in any amount. In that case, Thai food is probably not for you anyway. Garlic, like onions, fish sauce, and shrimp paste, is usually cooked thoroughly to reduce the strong bite of the raw form. (For tips on peeling, chopping, and storing, see page 64.) Garlic powder or garlic salt should not be substituted, but you may use commercially pureed or chopped garlic.

GINGER—provides a sharp, pungent flavor and pleasing aroma. Fresh ginger is available in the produce section of most large supermarkets and in Thai and Oriental markets. Most ginger available in the United States is "old ginger" and has a medium-brown skin, which must be removed. "Young ginger" has a soft, translucent skin edged with shades of pink and purple, and does not need to be peeled. They are interchangeable in our recipes. We recommend using only fresh ginger, because the prepared or processed forms never have the same quality or intensity of flavor. There is no substitute.

GROUND FISH—fresh or frozen, is sometimes available in Thai and Oriental markets. You may make your own very easily by grinding fresh fish fillets to a puree in a food processor or meat grinder fitted with the finest blade. A firm-fleshed fish such as red snapper or catfish works best.

KAFFIR LIME LEAVES—the leaves from the Kaffir lime tree, add a unique, not-quite-bitter, lemon-lime flavor. In Thailand they are known as MAKRUT. They are available either dried or preserved, and these two forms are interchangeable.

Powdered leaves, known as BAI MAKRUT, are also available. One whole leaf is equivalent to ¼ teaspoon powder. The preserved type does not need to be soaked before use, but the briny preserving liquid should be rinsed off completely. Whole dried leaves must be soaked for some recipes and not for others. All of our recipes assume dried leaves, because they are more widely available and are less expensive. If you use bottled leaves omit the soaking instructions. There is no substitute.

KAFFIR LIME RIND—the rind of the fruit of the Kaffir lime tree is available in both dried and preserved form. The dried form must be soaked before use in most recipes, and the preserved kind must be rinsed thoroughly to remove the briny preservative. Our recipes assume the dried type because it is more widely available and is less expensive. If you are using preserved rind, omit the soaking instructions. There is no substitute.

KAH—is also known as GALANGAL or LAOS and is a form of ginger. It is found most frequently in dried slices about ⅛ inch thick, and is usually packed in small cellophane packets. Dried KAH will keep indefinitely in a closed container, unrefrigerated. A powdered form is also available, and a ⅛-inch thick slice of dried KAH is approximately equal to ½ teaspoon powdered. Slices of dried KAH are not uniform in size. An average one would be about ¾ inch on each side, and about ⅛ inch thick. Some Thai markets carry frozen KAH. It does not need to be peeled, and should be sliced crosswise into pieces about ⅛ inch thick at the time it is to be used. There is no substitute.

LARD—is traditional for stir-frying and deep-frying in Thailand, but it is gradually being replaced by vegetable oils. Its principal advantage is that it makes foods crisper and more flavorful, but the disadvantages are that it congeals and becomes unpalatable when it cools.

LEMON GRASS—looks something like large, fibrous, pale green onions, and it has the aroma and flavor of lemons. When young and fresh it is tender, and when older it is more fibrous. Our recipes use only the bottom 6 inches of the stem. It is very easy to grow in mild climates and produces new plants quickly as the adult ones are used. It is also available in dried or powdered form. The dried version is acceptable if soaked in hot water for about 1 hour before use, but the powdered form should not be used. There is no substitute.

LETTUCE—comes in a variety of textures and colors in some parts of the United States. In some instances we have indicated a particular type of lettuce to add color or for a specific texture. If the type of lettuce we recommend is not available, substitute any other kind.

LIMES—are used more often than lemons in Thai cuisine. In developing the recipes in this book we have used small, green "bartender's limes" because they are more widely available commercially than any other kind. Other types of limes are equally useful. Unsweetened frozen lime juice may be used with good results, but please do not substitute bottled lime or lemon juice. Lemons may be substituted if limes are not available or are prohibitively expensive.

LIMES (PICKLED)—can be found in bottles in Thai or Oriental markets. They are whole limes that have been preserved in a mixture of soy sauce, sugar, salt, and vinegar.

MELONS (WINTER)—are a large, greenish white variety of squash. They taste a little like zucchini and are available in Thai and Oriental markets. The flesh is always cooked before being eaten, and the rind is frequently carved with ornate designs and used as a serving container for preparations containing the flesh. The whole fruit is large, about 20 pounds, but usually it is cut into smaller pieces before being sold.

MINT—as found in Thailand has a different flavor from that found here, but our mint works very well. Any kind of fresh mint is acceptable. In addition to being widely available, mint is extremely easy to grow and adapts to a wide variety of growing conditions. Do not substitute dried or prepared mint.

MUNG BEANS—are small, round, green beans, which may be found dried in Thai or Oriental markets and in health food stores. We use them in desserts. They may also be sprouted. (See page 59 for growing your own bean sprouts.) They are rich in protein and minerals and when cooked are very bland. Yellow mung beans are the dried form from which the green skins have been removed, and they cannot be sprouted. Our recipes call for the yellow beans. There is no substitute for whole beans for sprouting. Substitute yellow split peas for peeled mung beans.

MUSHROOMS (FRESH)—are not widely used in our recipes; we rely instead principally on Oriental or straw mushrooms, which have a different texture and flavor. Fresh mushrooms can be substituted.

MUSHROOMS (ORIENTAL)—are available dried, usually come in 1-ounce cellophane packages, and may be labeled Dried Forest Mushrooms, or with the Thai name HED HOM. They must be soaked or cooked, then stemmed as directed in the recipes. You may substitute standard fresh mushrooms, recognizing that the flavor and texture will be quite different.

MUSHROOMS (STRAW)—are available in cans in Oriental or Thai markets. If unavailable, substitute canned button mushrooms.

NAM NOMMAO—is a clear liquid flavoring used in desserts. It comes in small bottles and smells something like bananas with a medicinal odor. It is frequently labeled Amyle Essence. Although there is no substitute, it is an optional ingredient.

NAPA CABBAGE—See Cabbage (Napa).

NOODLES—are second only to rice as a mainstay of Thai meals. They come in several sizes and are made of rice or wheat flour or ground mung beans, and water. A few of our recipes call for fresh rice noodles. For these there is, we regret, no completely adequate substitute, but an approximation of the texture and flavor can be obtained by following substitution instructions in the individual recipes. Unfortunately, the names of noodles are not uniform and the same kind of noodle may be labeled differently depending on the manufacturer or country of origin. Noodles made without eggs may be labeled "imitation noodles" or "alimentary paste." Thus, you will need to rely as much on appearance and ingredients as names in some cases. The best procedure is to check the ingredients on the package, and look for noodles of the approximate size we describe.

Egg Noodles—also known as BA MEE, are made from wheat flour and eggs. They are about the size of Italian vermicelli and are medium brown in color. They are sold fresh or frozen and may be found in the refrigerated or freezer section of Thai or Oriental markets. In addition to their use in SARONG (page 148), they may be added to soups or stir-fried on their own as a side dish.

Fresh Rice Noodles—known as GUAYTIO, come in sheets about ¼ inch thick, and are packed in plastic. They are made fresh daily, and the best are those that are still warm when purchased. Fresh rice noodles must be purchased locally because they are very perishable. Some manufacturers produce fresh rice noodles that are presliced into strips ½ to ¾ inch wide, and others produce unsliced noodle sheets. Either may be used. They may be refrigerated for several days, but must be refreshed by dipping them briefly in boiling water to reconstitute the texture and to help keep them from sticking together when cooked. They can be frozen, but lose their fine, smooth texture. You can also make your own (see page 101).

Japanese Noodles—are made from wheat flour and water and are opaque white. They are about the size of vermicelli in diameter and length, and come packaged in ½-pound or 1-pound cellophane packages.

Narrow Rice Noodles—are about ⅛ inch in width, come packed in 1-pound cellophane packages, and may be labeled BANH PHO. Various brands are available; the best ones come from Thailand, although the ones from China are acceptable.

Rice Chips—are thin dried rice noodles that have been cut into 2-inch triangles. They may be found in Thai and Oriental markets in 8-ounce cellophane packages.

Rice Sticks—are very small noodles about the size of Italian vermicelli or bean threads. They are made from ground rice and water, and are usually sold in 1-pound cellophane packages.

Transparent Noodles—are very thin noodles made from mung beans and water. They are known by various names such as "cellophane noodles," "bean threads," WUN SEN, SAIFUN, or SOTANGHON depending on the manufacturer and the country of manufacture. (The Thai name is WUN SEN.) They resemble nylon fishing line in appearance, are very tough when dry, and must be soaked thoroughly before they can be cut easily. For that reason we suggest buying them in 2-ounce packages. The small packages are a little more expensive than larger bulk sizes, but this is an instance where the slight additional expense is clearly justified by convenience, unless you routinely use large quantities at one time.

OIL—is used a great deal in preparing curries and in stir-frying and deep-frying. In Thailand, lard was used traditionally, but vegetable oils have become more prevalent in recent years. Any flavorless light vegetable oil such as peanut, soy, or safflower oil may be used, but you should use a good brand to avoid any "off" flavor in the finished food. If you prefer the flavor, substitute an equal amount of lard in any of the stir-fried recipes.

ONIONS—are used less extensively in Thailand than are shallots. We have substituted yellow onion in all our recipes in which shallots would be used, because shallots are less widely available and are usually quite expensive in the United States. If shallots are available and you prefer their flavor, by all means substitute them in any of the recipes in equal quantity. In some recipes we call for red onions because they have a slightly more subtle flavor than that of yellow onions, but you may use yellow or white onions with excellent results. However, when we call for yellow onion we suggest that you do not substitute red onion. Green onions should be used whenever called for without substitution.

OYSTER SAUCE—is a thick, dark-brown sauce prepared from oyster extract. A staple item in Oriental and Thai markets, it is available in many supermarkets nowadays. There is no substitute.

PEANUTS—are used frequently to add texture and a subtle flavor. Our recipes call for unsalted roasted peanuts, and salted or raw peanuts should not be substituted.

PEPPER (GROUND)—called for in the recipes in this book refers to standard white or black ground pepper. If possible, use freshly ground pepper because it has a richer flavor. We have specified one or the other in each recipe. We suggest that you do not substitute the opposite one, although no great damage will be done if you do. Pepper was the source of all the "hotness" in Thai food for centuries until chilies were introduced, probably by Portuguese traders, sometime in the sixteenth century.

PINEAPPLE—is available fresh in many sections of the country, for at least part of the year. We recommend using fresh pineapple whenever possible, because the canned version lacks the necessary texture and tang. For instructions on peeling pineapple, see the recipe for Galloping Horses (page 145).

PLUM (SALTED)—has a slightly sour and salty taste, and is used principally in sauces and curries. It may be found in bottles in Oriental and Thai markets, and is sometimes labeled "Pickled Plum." There is no substitute.

PORK BELLY—is the same cut of meat used for making bacon. It is frequently available in supermarkets as well as in most butcher shops. If it is not your butcher can probably obtain it on request.

PORK SKINS (COOKED)—are available in Thai and Oriental markets, usually in the frozen food section. They are pork skins that have been sliced into strips about 4 to 6 inches long and ⅛ inch wide.

RADISH (SALTED)—is packed in small (3.5 or 5 ounces) plastic packets and can be found in Thai or Oriental markets. It is radish which has been preserved in brine and should be rinsed lightly to remove any sand that may remain from processing. You may find it either sliced or julienned. The Thai name is HYA PAK GOD KEM.

RED LIME—known as POON DANG in Thailand, is a finely ground red mineral paste found in Thai markets. The paste form is used in some desserts; the liquid form is used primarily in batters for deep-frying. See the section on Preparing Ingredients for a description of the way to prepare and store red lime liquid (page 66).

RICE—is available in several varieties. Each kind is used for a different purpose or effect. The most common type is the traditional long-grain rice, which is the one usually served with soup and main-course dishes. Jasmine rice is a form of long-grain rice that has a very faint aroma of jasmine when cooked. It is available in Thai and Oriental markets, and we recommend it highly because it has a subtle and pleasing aroma. The taste of jasmine is not quite perceptible, but you sense that the rice is pleasingly different. Glutinous (sweet) rice, which is used more often as the main rice in the northern and northeastern provinces of Thailand, is used principally in desserts in other provinces. Glutinous rice in Thailand is long-grain, but the variety available in the United States usually has shorter, plumper grains and has been grown in Japan. (There is another variety in Thailand called "black sweet rice," which is a dark, almost black–purple color. It is not widely available in the United States, but can be found in some Thai markets.) The rice itself is not sweet and the name "sweet rice" comes from the fact that its principal use is in desserts in most of Thailand. It is available in Thai and Oriental markets. Totally acceptable substitutes are California Blue Rose, Italian Arborio, or any other type of short-grain rice that becomes gummy when cooked.

SAUSAGE (CHINESE)—is sold in plastic packages or loose in units of two, connected with a string. They are about 6 inches long and ¾ inch wide, and have a rough, bumpy skin that looks oily and dried out. They are usually made of pork or beef; we prefer the pork variety because it has a richer flavor.

SESAME OIL—is prepared from roasted sesame seeds and has a sharp, nutty, not-quite-hot flavor. Generally used as a flavoring, it is not used extensively for frying because of its cost and because it scorches very easily. (A notable exception is its use in Stir-Fried Transparent Noodles.) It is significantly more expensive than regular cooking oil, but a little goes a long way. Be sure to get the dark-colored variety made from roasted sesame seeds because the lighter-colored oil often sold in health food stores has virtually none of the taste that is prized in good sesame oil. There is no substitute.

SESAME SEEDS—are widely available in many markets and in all health food stores. They may be purchased with or without hulls. We prefer those that have been hulled; they have a rich, nutty flavor and are full of protein and minerals.

SHALLOTS—are used extensively in Thailand, where they are readily available. Because they are generally less available in the United States and are usually expensive, we have substituted yellow onion in our recipes. If you can get shallots easily, please substitute them wherever we have called for yellow onion.

SHRIMP BALLS—see Fish Balls.

SHRIMP (DRIED)—are small shrimp that have been salted and dried in the sun. In Thailand they are known as KUNG HAENG and are available in Thai or Oriental markets. They are packed in plastic bags and are sometimes found on open shelves, but more frequently they are in the refrigerated or frozen section. If you have a choice, purchase refrigerated or frozen ones because they usually have a fresher flavor. Fresh ones are an orange–pink color, which fades to gray as they get older. Do not buy dried shrimp that have even a hint of gray in them. When you first begin to cook them they produce a strong odor, but this will subside as the cooking continues. If dried shrimp are unavailable, you may substitute tiny fresh shrimp, but the salty, sharp flavor will be sacrificed.

SHRIMP PASTE—is known in Thailand as KAPEE. It is a puree of fermented, salted shrimp. When you open the package it will smell even stronger than you thought such a concoction might, but don't despair—the odor and flavor become mild and blend with the other ingredients when cooked as directed. Do remember, however, to cook it as long as the instructions in our recipes recommend. If, after cooking it, you find that the taste is too strong for you, reduce the amount you use very slightly. Do not omit it altogether, because shrimp paste, like fish sauce, is an essential contributor to the unusual flavors of Thai cuisine. There is no substitute.

SOY SAUCE—is a widely available thin, brown liquid made from fermented soybeans, usually with the addition of wheat in some form. It is used less extensively in Thai cooking than fish sauce. The version without wheat is called "Tamari" and is less widely available and more expensive. Either is acceptable. Black soy sauce is slightly thicker and faintly sweet, but less sweet than the type known as sweet soy sauce. Light or "white" soy sauce is almost clear and resembles fish sauce in appearance. Unless otherwise specified, our recipes call for standard soy sauce.

SOYBEANS (FERMENTED)—may be labeled TAO JIEW (or a similar spelling) in Thai markets or DOW SEE in Oriental markets and are packed in bottles. The English label may indicate "yellow bean sauce." They are yellow, very salty and strongly flavored, so they should be rinsed thoroughly before use.

SPRING ROLL WRAPPERS—are available in Thai and Oriental markets and in some larger supermarkets. They are sometimes labeled "spring roll skins" and may be found in the refrigerated or frozen food section. The traditional shape is round, but square ones work equally well. Spring roll wrappers are made without egg, and are softer and more delicate than egg roll wrappers; they do not puff up when fried. They may be refrozen after being thawed, provided that you take care to prevent them from drying out. Rather than refreezing the wrappers we suggest that you make enough fried spring rolls to use a whole package, then freeze the prepared spring rolls following the instructions in the recipe. If you are unable to find spring roll wrappers, substitute egg roll wrappers.

SQUASH—is available in fewer varieties in Thailand than in the United States, and the squash that is available there is not available here. We have used standard squash readily available in the United States, and applied traditional ingredients and procedures to its preparation. Banana squash is a large, hard squash with a texture similar to pumpkin. It is usually sold in slices weighing up to 1 pound each. Pumpkin can be substituted for the same effect.

STAR ANISE—provides a delicate flavor similar to licorice, but much milder. The name comes from the shape of the seed pods which look like 8-pointed stars. Star anise usually comes packed in small cellophane pouches, and a little goes a long way. It keeps indefinitely in a closed container. Fennel seed may be substituted.

SUGAR (GRANULATED)—is standard white sugar. Sometimes it is used to add a slight sweet flavor, but more often it serves as a natural flavor enhancer that is almost undetectable.

SUGAR (PALM)—is a thick, moist sugar derived from palm trees. It can be found in cans or plastic bags in Thai and

Oriental markets. If possible, get the canned variety, since it is generally of better quality. Store unused portions in a tightly closed jar. It keeps indefinitely and should not be refrigerated. A similar effect can be obtained by mixing equal parts of light-brown sugar and molasses.

TAMARIND—is obtained from the fleshy seed pods of the tamarind tree and is used widely in Thai cooking to add an unusual sour flavor. The Thai name is SOM MA KHAM or MA KHAM PEAK. Whole fresh seed pods are sometimes available in Thai and Oriental markets, but it is not these to which we refer. Our recipes call for processed tamarind seeds, which come in small, flat packages and are usually labeled "Wet Tamarind." Tamarind concentrate is also available, is easier to use, and has the same flavor. Ounce for ounce it is sometimes less expensive because there is no waste from discarding the seeds. One ounce of wet tamarind sieved with ¼ cup water equals 2 tablespoons concentrate. We provide instructions to preparing tamarind in each recipe in which it appears. There is no true substitute; some people use lemon juice. We do not recommend that substitution unless you cannot get tamarind anywhere, because lemon juice has a sharper, less subtle flavor.

TAPIOCA PEARLS—are small balls made from the processed root of the cassava plant. They are widely available in Thai and Oriental markets and sometimes can be found in large supermarkets. They come in several sizes, used for different purposes depending on the recipe. They are not the same as the "instant tapioca" commonly used in making pudding, and that form should not be substituted.

TAPIOCA STARCH—is a fine white powder that resembles cornstarch. It is made from the same root as tapioca pearls and is used as a thickening agent for sauces. It produces a clear, fine-textured sauce somewhat like that produced by arrowroot. Sauce made from tapioca starch holds its consistency better than that made from arrowroot, and is a clearer, finer sauce than any made with cornstarch. Either arrowroot or cornstarch may be substituted.

TEA—may be found in a wide variety of flavors, depending in part on the country of origin, but more on the variety of the tea plant from which it comes. Thai tea is packed in 1-pound cellophane packets; it has a texture somewhat like instant coffee and a faint vanilla aroma. When brewed it assumes a deep orange color. It is mixed with sugar, or sweetened condensed milk, and cream to make a sweet drink. Jasmine tea, which is more commonly available, is served without milk or sugar. Jasmine tea should be made very weak. Cold jasmine tea is used routinely in restaurants in Thailand (and sometimes in the United States) instead of water. If you find a very pale-colored liquid in your water glass in a Thai restaurant it is very likely jasmine tea. In Thailand, the purpose is to show that the water has been boiled. In the United States it is simply a nod to custom.

TENDONS (BEEF)—are white strips of gristly connective tissue, about a foot long, and about 1 inch in diameter. They are usually available in Thai and Oriental markets and may be obtained on request from your butcher.

TOFU—is made from processed soybeans and is high in protein, low in calories, and very inexpensive. Fortunately, it is much more widely available in United States markets than it was a few years ago. It can be found in the refrigerated or delicatessen section of many markets, often near prepackaged processed meats. Fresh tofu is packed in water and usually comes in square or rectangular cakes about 2 inches thick and 3 to 4 inches wide. Unfortunately, some manufacturers package it in 12- or 14-ounce units and others package it in 1-pound units. We have specified 1-pound packages, but no great harm will be done if you use the smaller quantities. Since it is sometimes sliced into thinner pieces, we have described in each of the recipes the approximate shape and size it should have after slicing. It should be used immediately after purchase for the best flavor, but can be kept for up to 1 week in the refrigerator if the water is changed once or twice daily. Do not try to keep it for more than 1 week, because the flavor will deteriorate and it may spoil. If it develops a sour taste, discard it. To insure freshness, check the expiration date on the package just as you would when buying milk. Several types of fresh tofu are available. We recommend the type usually labeled "Chinese tofu" because it is firm and easy to work with, but firm "Japanese tofu" works well, too. Do not substitute the very soft, custardy type known as Kinugoshi, or "silken tofu." If you are very ambitious you can make your own fresh tofu by following the instructions in books devoted to tofu cooking. Freeze-dried and prepressed tofu are also available, but these are not packed in water. There is no substitute.

TREE FUNGUS—See Cloud Ears.

TURMERIC—is native to Southeast Asia, where it is used in curries and sauces. In olden days it was known as "Indian saffron" because of its color and sharp flavor. It comes in powdered form and is widely available in supermarkets and Thai, Oriental, and Indian markets.

VEGETABLES (PRESERVED)—are available in Thai and Oriental markets and many large supermarkets. A variety of vegetables, such as mustard greens, turnips, radishes, and cabbage, are commonly available. They are usually served as a side dish or added to salads and have a strong vinegar or briny flavor that contrasts well with other foods. Preserved vegetables are traditional, but not essential, and fresh vegetables of your choice may be substituted in most cases.

VINEGAR—is used in many of the sauces and some other recipes. Good-quality distilled white vinegar should be used. Rice vinegar should not be substituted, because it is milder and will not produce the sharp tang that white vinegar does.

WINTER MELON—See Melon (Winter).

PREPARING INGREDIENTS

Many of the recipes in this book specify ingredients that can be prepared in advance in quantities larger than needed for any one recipe and then stored in tightly closed containers in the refrigerator, the freezer, or on pantry shelves. Advance preparation of these ingredients will significantly reduce your cooking time and, hopefully, increase the likelihood that you will be tempted to cook Thai food more often. Following are some ways in which staple and often-used ingredients can be prepared and stored for future use.

Growing Bean Sprouts

Bean sprouts can be grown by anyone in a very small space, and they need neither sun nor soil. To grow them, select the freshest mung beans you can find, because old ones may not sprout as readily. Health food stores are good sources because the turnover is rapid and the beans are likely to be fresh. Special sprouting jars with wire screen tops are available in health food stores and some houseware departments, but they are not necessary for good results.

1. Place about 2 tablespoons mung beans in a quart jar (an old mayonnaise jar works well), rinse them thoroughly, and cover them with water. Let them soak overnight.

2. Cover the top of the jar with cheesecloth or a fine mesh screen and secure it in place firmly. Drain the beans, turn the jar on its side, and rotate it until the beans are stuck to the sides and not lying on top of one another. Place the jar in a dark place or wrap it in a towel to keep the light out, and leave it undisturbed overnight.

3. Rinse the beans 2 or 3 times a day with fresh water, drain them thoroughly through the cheesecloth or wire mesh, and put the jar back in the dark place or wrap it with the towel. The sprouts will be ready at the end of the third day. Put them in a colander and rinse them thoroughly to remove any pieces of bean husk. To store the sprouts for up to 3 days, wrap them loosely in a paper towel and place them in a plastic bag in the refrigerator.

Freezing Chilies

Fresh green or red chilies can be frozen for later use. This is particularly useful if you grow your own or if chilies are relatively unavailable in your area and you manage to come upon a supply of them. Place whole chilies, stems and all, in boiling water and boil them about 3 minutes. Drain them in a colander, allow them to cool to room temperature, and dry them thoroughly. Place them in a plastic bag and freeze them immediately. For some reason, they do not stick to one another so you will be able to retrieve them with ease when they are needed. Do not try to freeze fresh chilies without the preliminary cooking because they are likely to lose much of their flavor and "bite."

Handling Chilies

The oils in chilies are very strong; some people are particularly sensitive to them while others can handle them with no special precautions other than routine carefulness. After handling chilies, either fresh or dried, be careful to wash your hands thoroughly, scrub under your fingernails, and avoid putting your fingers in or even near your mouth or eyes until all the chili oils have been washed off. If your skin is particularly sensitive to chilies, wear rubber gloves, then wash the gloves thoroughly before removing them.

Roasting and Grinding Red Chilies

Because roasted dried red chilies store just as well after they have been ground as they do when whole, and the ground form take up less storage space, it makes good sense to grind a supply to have available when needed. We suggest small, hot chilies about 3 to 4 inches long, but you may use any kind you like. You may grind dried red chili flakes in the same way and substitute them if whole chilies are not available. Be very careful while roasting the dried flakes because they burn easily and quickly. You should also keep a supply of whole dried chilies on hand for those occasions when they will be needed in the whole form. Roast whole chilies, stems and all, in a dry wok or skillet until the color changes to dark red or brown depending on the chilies used. Be careful not to let them burn. When the chilies are cool enough to handle, remove the stems and seeds. Place the chilies in a food processor or blender and start to grind using short pulsing actions of the processor or blender. After that you can let the machine run steadily until the chilies are ground into small pieces. Preground chilies are commercially available, but they often lack the "bite" of home-ground ones, often contain stems, and, worst of all, may be more expensive.

Coconuts and Coconut Milk

Fresh coconut is definitely preferable to the dried commercially packaged kind for making coconut milk. However, it is not always available in some parts of the country. If you are unable to find it, refer to the alternate procedure following the instructions for preparing coconut milk (page 62). The pieces of fresh coconut from which coconut milk is made can be prepared in advance and stored in a tightly closed container in the freezer for up to 6 months. You could also make the coconut milk itself and freeze it. For convenience in later use, we suggest freezing coconut milk in units of 1 or 2 cups.

Cracking and peeling coconuts is relatively easy when you use the oven method we describe below. In terms of time and energy, it is more economical to prepare several coconuts at once.

Preparing the Coconut

1. Preheat the oven to 400°.

2. Punch holes in the "eyes" of the coconut and drain and discard the liquid. The easiest method is to use a vegetable peeler to punch a large hole in the one soft eye, in which case you will not need to punch holes in the other two eyes. The soft eye can be located easily by poking each eye with the vegetable peeler until you find the one in which the peeler can be inserted easiest. On most coconuts the soft eye is slightly convex. Or, you may use an ice pick or a large nail and a hammer to punch holes in all 3 of the eyes. Unless you have made large holes, you may have to shake the coconut to get out all the liquid.

3. Place the coconut on the oven's center rack and bake for 15 minutes. The shell will crack in one or more places, but you may not be able to see the cracks until the coconut is removed from the oven and begins to cool. Do not heat it for more than 15 minutes or the flesh will begin to cook and the fresh flavor will be lost.

4. Remove the coconut from the oven and, when cool enough to handle, hit it with a hammer until the shell cracks in several places. It's a good idea to wrap the coconut in a kitchen towel or put it in a paper bag before hitting it to keep the pieces of shell from scattering about on the work surface.

5. Separate the coconut meat from the shell by prying it out with a blunt instrument. Do not use a sharp knife because you may ruin the blade or, worse yet, injure yourself badly if the knife slips.

Discard the shells. It is not necessary to remove the dark skin at this time. If you are going to grate the coconut for desserts, the dark skin can be removed later when you are ready to use it. If you are going to grate the coconut to make coconut milk, the dark skin need not be removed at all.

Cut the coconut meat into pieces about 1 inch square, or smaller if you are preparing it only to extract coconut milk. The exact size is not important, but smaller sizes are easier to measure and to grind in a blender. If you are going to grate the coconut by hand, leave it in larger pieces because it will be easier to grate.

6. Coconut pieces may be frozen in a tightly closed container and kept for several months.

Measuring Coconut

Determine the amount of thick coconut milk you will need and place that much warm water in a large measuring cup. Add enough coconut pieces to bring the water level up to twice what it was. For example, if you need 2 cups thick coconut milk, measure 2 cups warm water and add enough coconut pieces to bring the level of the liquid up to 4 cups. One average coconut will make approximately 2 cups thick coconut milk, and up to 3 cups thin coconut milk.

Making Coconut Milk

1. If you are using frozen coconut pieces, thaw them completely until warm or at room temperature. If you don't, the frozen pieces can cause a blender or food processor to jam, seriously damaging it.

2. *Blender Method.* This is the preferred method, because it works better than the food processor and is easier than grating by hand. Place the coconut pieces and warm water in the blender and blend at high speed (liquefy) until you have a finely ground mush. Most home blenders will accept up to 1½ to 2 cups coconut pieces and 1½ to 2 cups liquid at a time, so you may need to repeat the process. Strain the mush through a fine sieve or double thickness of cheesecloth, pressing out all the liquid you can. Proceed to Step 3.

Food Processor Method. Drain the coconut pieces from the water you used for measuring. Dry the coconut pieces and set the water aside. Using the metal chopping blade and a pulsing (on-off) action, process the pieces *without* water until they are very finely ground. Scrape down the sides of the container several times during processing to make sure all the pieces are finely ground. Empty the ground coconut meat into a bowl and add the reserved water. If the water has cooled during the grinding process, discard it and use an equal amount of warm water. Stir, and let the mixture stand for 5 minutes. Strain it through a fine sieve or double thickness of cheesecloth and press out all the liquid you can. Proceed to Step 3.

3. The first straining gives you "thick" coconut milk. You can extract "thin" coconut milk by adding more warm water to the residue from the first straining, letting it stand for 5 minutes, and straining it as before. It is not necessary to grind the coconut again for this second extraction. Both the thick and thin coconut milk may be frozen for future use or used immediately, but do not store coconut milk in the refrigerator for more than 72 hours.

Alternate Method. If fresh coconuts are not available you may substitute dried shredded *unsweetened* packaged coconut. This is often available in supermarkets and can almost always be found in health food stores. Follow the instructions for measuring and preparing the milk as they are given above.

Coriander Root

Coriander root may be chopped in advance and kept in a tightly closed container in the freezer for up to 6 months. When frozen, it will lose its original texture, but that makes no difference because it is pounded or ground to a paste in preparing curries, and the flavor will be unaffected by freezing. If coriander root is difficult to find in your area, or if you grow your own, you should try to freeze a large amount to have available when needed. If you can only find fresh coriander without roots, substitute the bottom 1 inch of stem. More often than not, fresh coriander can be found with only very small bits of root left on the plant. Even if coriander root is readily available, it makes sense to freeze some to have on hand for the times when you are in a hurry and don't want to go to the market.

Curries

Most curries can be prepared in advance and stored up to 2 weeks in a tightly closed container in the refrigerator or for several months in the freezer. Except for those containing coconut milk, curries will keep longer than 2 weeks in the refrigerator without spoiling, but after 2 weeks the flavor begins to deteriorate rapidly. For comments on advance preparation, see each curry recipe. If you freeze curry, you will probably find it more convenient to use if frozen in 1-recipe units per container.

Chopped Garlic

Garlic can be chopped and stored in the refrigerator for up to 6 weeks. It retains its freshness and color better if you coat it lightly with oil, as directed below. If it becomes dark in color and strong smelling, discard it. At first thought, it may seem like a chore to chop a lot of garlic at one time, but it's usually easier to do that than to chop it each time you begin to cook, because of the large amounts needed for some dishes. Furthermore, knowing that you have good chopped garlic on hand may prompt you to use Thai recipes more frequently. Bottled chopped garlic can be found in many supermarkets and may be substituted.

The following method will make garlic preparation fairly easy:

1. Wrap a head of garlic loosely in a kitchen towel, or put it in a paper bag, to keep the cloves from scattering about on the tabletop. Give it a sharp rap with your fist or slam it down on the tabletop. The cloves will separate easily. Remove and discard the outer skin.

2. Place the cloves in a single layer on a flat surface and give them a sharp rap, or press them firmly, with the flat side of a cleaver or wide knife. You can then slip the skins off easily.

3. Remove the skin from the cloves and cut away any brown spots. Keeping your hands wet will help prevent the garlic and skins from sticking to your fingers.

4. *Manual Chopping Method.* Lay the cloves on a cutting surface and press them very hard with the flat side of a cleaver or wide knife until each clove is crushed completely. Scrape them all into a pile. Using an up-and-down motion with a large knife or a cleaver, chop all the crushed cloves finely. The work will go much faster if you use two knives or cleavers, one in each hand.

Food Processor Method 1. Assemble the food processor with the metal chopping blade and cover in place. Drop the cloves through the feed tube a handful at a time. If you are chopping more than about 1 pound, repeat the procedure for each pound to avoid pureeing the chopped pieces. A blender does not work for this procedure.

Food Processor Method 2. Place the whole cloves in the processing container and turn the machine on and off repeatedly and quickly, opening the lid and scraping down the sides as necessary to keep the garlic bits from sticking to the bowl. Be careful not to puree them. A blender does not work for this procedure.

5. Place the chopped garlic in a mixing bowl and add 2 to 3 tablespoons vegetable oil for each pound (2 cups) of chopped garlic. Mix the garlic and oil thoroughly, and store it in an airtight container in the refrigerator. It will keep quite well up to 6 weeks.

6. To remove the strong smell of garlic from your hands, rub them thoroughly with salt before washing them. If a slight smell remains rub with salt again.

Crisp-Fried Garlic

Crisp-fried garlic and its oil may be kept in a closed container on the pantry shelf for a month or two. For each ¼ cup (2 ounces) finely chopped garlic, use 1 cup oil to fry it over moderate heat to a light golden color. When the garlic turns light golden, remove it from the heat immediately and let it continue to cook in the hot oil off the heat. Sometimes the garlic alone is used in a recipe, and sometimes it is used with the oil in which it was cooked. Each recipe specifies the correct procedure.

Growing Lemon Grass

Lemon grass grows like a weed in mild or moderate climates. In cold-winter climates it should be grown in pots and moved to a sunny indoor location in the winter. In mild climates it grows well outdoors all year round. To get it started, cut off the bottom ¼ or ½ inch of several stalks of lemon grass purchased at the market, and put them upright in a small container with just enough water to keep the bottom tips moist. Small roots will form in a few days. When they do, plant the pieces in rich, moist soil and water them frequently. They will grow rapidly, and in a few weeks will form full-sized stalks. Lemon grass spreads reasonably quickly, so in a few months you will have a good supply. To harvest it, remove the oldest stalks from the center of the clump by cutting them at the soil surface or about ¼ inch below the surface of the soil.

Ground Peanuts

Ground peanuts may be stored in a closed container on the pantry shelf for up to 6 months. They can be ground using the same methods described above for grinding garlic. Pieces a little larger than large grains of sand are about right. Be sure to check the peanuts frequently while grinding to make sure you don't puree them and end up with peanut butter. If you are distracted for a moment and do end up with peanut butter, don't despair. It is perfectly good to use, and you might even find it tastes better than some of the commercial brands.

Red Lime Liquid

Put a 3.5-ounce package red lime paste into a 1-quart jar and fill the jar with water. Shake or stir to mix well and let it stand for at least 30 minutes before using. The recipes in this book call for only the liquid that remains after the solids settle. You may keep adding water to replace that which has been used. Shake again after each addition of water. This procedure may be repeated until the residue has turned pale, almost white. The liquid keeps indefinitely in a closed jar on the pantry shelf, and a 3.5-ounce package will last a very long time.

Ground Toasted Rice

Ground toasted rice keeps indefinitely in a closed container on the pantry shelf. It is much easier to prepare it in advance and keep a supply on hand than to prepare it each time it's needed. To prepare it, place uncooked rice in a dry wok or skillet and heat over moderate heat until deep golden, stirring frequently to keep from burning and to allow it to develop a uniform color. Watch the rice carefully after it begins to change color and stir constantly, because it can burn easily at this stage. When it is a uniform deep golden color, remove it from the heat and let it cool to room temperature. Grind it to a fine powder in a blender or a spice or coffee grinder. It is more difficult to get a fine powder in a food processor because the rice tends to spin around without grinding well.

Stock

Thai stock is thin and bland compared to that of most Western cuisines. It is intended to be used in place of water if desired, and adds a light flavor of the meat from which it was prepared. It may be prepared from chicken, beef, pork, or fish as desired, and as appropriate for the dish in which it is to be used. It is easy to prepare and can be cooked in large quantities and frozen to be used as needed. Making stock is an excellent way to use bones and non-fatty trimmings. You simply freeze these pieces until you accumulate a large enough quantity to make stock.

1. Place the bones and/or trimmings in a large pot and add enough water to cover them by 2 or 3 inches. Do not add other ingredients, such as vegetables, salt, etc.

2. Put the pot over medium heat and bring it to a simmer. Do not let it boil, or a great deal of foam will form on the surface. Cover the pot and simmer the stock for 2 to 3 hours. Check it occasionally and skim off any foam that may have formed in spite of your best efforts.

3. Strain the liquid through a fine sieve or double thickness of cheesecloth and use it immediately, or place it in plastic containers with tight-fitting lids and freeze it for later use. Discard the bones and trimmings. Stock may be kept for 6 months in the freezer, and may be thawed and refrozen repeatedly.

MEASURING

The weights and measures we use in this book are based on standard measures in use in kitchens and cookbooks in the

United States. In many instances we have indicated both weight and volume in the recipes and either may be used. We do encourage you, however, to form the habit of weighing ingredients. On page 70 we provide the conversion ratios we used to develop our equivalents in case you want to check your own preparation techniques and measurements. Please understand that our measures may differ slightly from what you would obtain if you performed the same tests and comparisons we did. Take garlic, for example: How large is one clove? Those on the outside of the head are always larger than those on the inside. We conducted our tests by taking 2-pound batches of peeled cloves, using all the cloves in each head except the very tiniest ones, averaging the results, and making the tables. Thus, when we refer to "1 clove garlic" it means the mythical average-sized clove that came from our calculations. Similarly, differences may be experienced in volume using chopped garlic. How "finely chopped" does an instruction to "chop finely" mean? For us, it means particles about the size of grains of sand. Fortunately, differences will not be great and are nothing to be concerned about. Without negating the importance of measuring, we advise you not to be overly compulsive about it.

There may be times when you wish to increase or decrease the quantities in recipes either because you are serving more or fewer people or because you wish to serve several dishes at one meal and full recipes of each would provide too much food. The recipes in this book are easy to multiply or divide using the standard values of measures provided in this chapter. Please note, however, that our stir-fry recipes were developed specifically for use in a 14-inch wok. Unless you use a larger wok, the stir-fried dishes should be cooked in two batches if you double a recipe. This is particularly important if you are using an electric range because it tends to heat more slowly than a gas stove, even under the best of circumstances.

Some conversions are very straightforward—e.g., ¾ cup is one half the amount of 1½ cups. However, suppose you want to reduce a recipe in half and it calls for ¾ cup of some ingredient. How can you measure ½ of ¾ of a cup? Simple. Check the tables and you will find that ¼ cup = 4 tablespoons; thus ¾ cup = 12 tablespoons, and ½ of ¾ cup = 6 tablespoons. In one more simple step you can translate 6 tablespoons into ¼ cup plus 2 tablespoons, which is a little faster to measure than 6 tablespoons. Increasing amounts works exactly the same way in reverse, and a little fore-thought can make some measuring more convenient. For example, suppose that a recipe calls for 2 tablespoons of an ingredient and you wish to double the recipe, keeping in mind our warning about doubling stir-fried dishes. You could, of course, measure 4 tablespoons, but recognizing that 4 tablespoons = ¼ cup would mean that you could measure once instead of 4 times. The same relationships apply to measures using teaspoons and tablespoons. For example, suppose that a recipe calls for 1 tablespoon of an ingredient and you wish to reduce it in half. You could estimate ½ tablespoon, and that would be fine. But if you are compulsively precise, remember that 1 tablespoon = 3 teaspoons, thus ½ table-spoon = 1½ teaspoons and there will be no guessing about when the tablespoon measure is ½ full.

Clearly, there is no way we can anticipate all the possible changes and combinations you may need. We hope the examples above and the tables that follow will provide you with guidance to make your own adjustments in the recipes. We have chosen to give only basic equivalents rather than provide intricate tables of substitutions and conversions. These few basic combinations should be all that are necessary to multiply or divide with ease and accuracy.

GENERAL MEASURES
Volume

1 tablespoon = 3 teaspoons
4 tablespoons = ¼ cup
5 ⅓ tablespoons = ⅓ cup
8 tablespoons = ½ cup
16 tablespoons = 1 cup

1 cup = ½ pint
2 cups = 1 pint
2 pints = 1 quart
4 cups = 1 quart
4 quarts = 1 gallon

Weight

1 pound = 16 ounces

SPECIFIC INGREDIENTS
Chilies

Note: The chili equivalents are approximate, based on taste, and are suggestions only. Please use your own taste as the final criterion.

1 ounce = 7 Serranos
4 very small Thai chilies = 1 Serrano

Chives

¼ cup finely chopped = 1 bunch
2 tablespoons finely chopped = ½ bunch

Coriander Leaves

1 cup = 1 bunch

Coriander Root

¼ cup finely chopped = 1 bunch
2 tablespoons finely chopped = ½ bunch

Garlic

All measures are for peeled, finely chopped cloves.
96 cloves = 8 ounces = ½ pound
48 cloves = 4 ounces = ¼ pound
12 cloves = 1 ounce
12 cloves = 2 tablespoons
8 ounces = 1 cup
4 ounces = ½ cup
2 ounces = ¼ cup
1 ounce = 2 tablespoons
2 cloves = 1 teaspoon

Kaffir Lime Leaves

1 leaf = ¼ teaspoon powdered

Kah

one ⅛-inch dried slice = ½ teaspoon powdered

Lemon Grass

1 stalk fresh = 1 teaspoon powdered

Limes

1 lime = 3 tablespoons juice

Onion

1 ounce = ¼ cup

Tamarind

1 ounce wet + ¼ cup water = 2 tablespoons concentrate

4
Curries, Sauces, and Dressings

THIS CHAPTER CONTAINS much of the heart of Thai cuisine, and frequent references are made to these recipes throughout the book. In particular, the curries provide the unique combinations of flavors that distinguish Thai cuisine from the cuisines of other countries of Southeast Asia. The term "curry" is sometimes confusing because it is often associated with the curry powder used in the cuisines of India. It is, however, a generic term applicable to any dry or liquid preparation made from certain ground herbs and spices. The term may come from the word "kari," which translates as "seasoned sauce," but the exact origin of the word is not known. Although traditional Thai curries, which have been developed over centuries, are prepared according to definite principles, they still allow for variations in ingredients according to individual taste. The one aspect all have in common is that the ingredients must be pounded or ground to a paste in order to blend them so that no sharp bits of individual flavor can distract from the overall effect of the curry. In general, those curries containing dried chilies are ground or pounded to a smoother paste than those containing fresh chilies because unground bits of dried chilies are sharper to the tongue. Some curries are cooked before being combined with other ingredients and some are not, as is indicated in the individual recipes.

Often, the final sauces prepared from Thai curries are thinner than those of other cuisines because thickening agents such as tapioca starch or cornstarch are used in smaller amounts in Thai cooking. Because one curry paste may be used in a number of recipes, we have grouped all of them here and provided references to this chapter elsewhere. Several of the curries may be prepared in advance and stored as directed, and we recommend that procedure to save time and effort when you are ready to cook. You may wish to modify the proportions of some ingredients to suit your own taste or to provide interesting variations. However, we suggest that you first use the recipes as given and then modify them as you wish, using your own "kitchen common sense."

Curries

The volume we list as produced by each curry recipe is approximate. The quantity will differ if you add more or less liquid during grinding, which may be necessary due to some particular characteristic of your blender. The traditional procedure is to pound the ingredients in a mortar, in which case no liquid is added. Pounding in a mortar produces a smoother texture and flavor because the plant fibers are mashed rather than cut, as they are by the blades of a blender, but nonetheless a blender works perfectly adequately.

✳✳✳ ─────────────────────────────

Panang Curry
NAM PRIG GANG PANANG

This uncooked curry contains a large assortment of ingredients that blend together so that no one taste predominates. It can be used equally well with either beef or chicken dishes that are cooked in coconut milk, which aids in blending the flavors. It is easy to prepare and keeps well in a tightly closed jar in the refrigerator for up to 2 weeks, or in the freezer for 6 months. The amount of small red chilies called for below will produce a hot curry. For a milder curry, reduce the number of chilies or substitute New Mexico or California chilies, which are less hot.

MAKES ½ CUP (1 CUP IF GROUND WITH WATER)

7 small dried red chilies or 2 dried New Mexico
    chilies or California chilies
2 pieces Kaffir lime rind
2 pieces kah
½ cup warm water
1 stalk lemon grass, bottom 6 inches only

¼ cup finely chopped coriander root
2 tablespoons (1 ounce) finely chopped garlic
¼ cup (1 ounce) finely chopped yellow onion
2 teaspoons coriander seed
1 teaspoon fennel or cumin seed
1 teaspoon shrimp paste

1. Remove the stems and seeds from the chilies. Soak the chilies, Kaffir lime rind, and *kah* in the warm water at least 15 minutes. After soaking, drain and discard the soaking water. Chop the Kaffir lime rind, chilies, *kah,* and lemon grass finely.

2. Combine all ingredients and pound or grind to a smooth paste in a mortar or blender. (If you use a blender, you may need to add water to aid in grinding.)

✳✳✳ ━━━━━━━━━━━━━━━━━━━━━━━━━━━━━━

Green Curry
NAM PRIG GANG KIEW WAN

This is an uncooked curry, which may be stored in a tightly closed container in the refrigerator for up to 2 weeks, or frozen for up to 6 months.

MAKES ¼ CUP (½ CUP IF GROUND WITH WATER)

2 pieces kah
2 pieces Kaffir lime rind
¼ cup warm water
7 (1 ounce) Serrano chilies
1 stalk lemon grass, bottom 6 inches only
¼ cup finely chopped coriander root
¼ cup (1 ounce) finely chopped yellow onion
2 tablespoons (1 ounce) finely chopped garlic
1 teaspoon shrimp paste

1. Soak the *kah* and Kaffir lime rind in the warm water for 15 minutes. Drain before using. Discard the soaking water.

2. Remove the stems, but not the seeds, from the chilies, and chop the chilies finely. Chop the *kah*, Kaffir lime rind, and lemon grass finely. Add the remaining ingredients and pound or grind to an almost smooth paste in a mortar or blender. (If you use a blender, you may need to add water to aid in grinding.)

✳✳✳ ━━━━━━━━━━━━━━━━━━━━━━━━━━

Red Curry 1
NAM PRIG KING

This curry is hot, rich, and very fragrant when cooked. It may be stored in a closed container in the refrigerator for up to 2 weeks, or in the freezer for up to 6 months.

MAKES ¼ CUP (½ CUP IF GROUND WITH WATER)

7 small dried red chilies
2 pieces kah
2 pieces Kaffir lime rind
¼ cup warm water

1 stalk lemon grass, bottom 6 inches only

2 tablespoons (1 ounce) finely chopped garlic
¼ cup (1 ounce) finely chopped yellow onion
1 teaspoon shrimp paste

1. Remove the stems and seeds from the chilies. Soak the chilies, *kah,* and Kaffir lime rind in the warm water at least 15 minutes. After soaking, drain and discard the soaking water.

2. Chop the chilies, *kah*, Kaffir lime rind, and lemon grass finely.

3. Combine all ingredients and pound or grind to a smooth paste in a mortar or blender. (If you use a blender, you may need to add water to aid in grinding.)

✳✳✳ ————————————————————————————

Red Curry 2
NAM PRIG GANG PED

This curry is similar to Red Curry 1, but is hotter and has the additional flavor of coriander root. It may be stored in a closed container in the refrigerator for up to 2 weeks, or in the freezer for up to 6 months.

MAKES ¼ CUP (½ CUP IF GROUND WITH WATER)

9 small dried red chilies
2 pieces kah
2 pieces Kaffir lime rind
¼ cup warm water

1 stalk lemon grass, bottom 6 inches only

2 tablespoons (1 ounce) finely chopped garlic
¼ cup (1 ounce) finely chopped yellow onion
1 teaspoon shrimp paste
¼ cup finely chopped coriander root

1. Remove the stems and seeds from the chilies. Soak the chilies, *kah*, and Kaffir lime rind in the warm water at least 15 minutes. After soaking, drain and discard the soaking water.

2. Chop the chilies, *kah*, Kaffir lime rind, and lemon grass finely.

3. Combine all ingredients and pound or grind to a smooth paste in a mortar or blender. (If you use a blender, you may need to add water to aid in grinding.)

••• ————————————————————————————

Roasted Red Curry
NAM PRIG PAO

This version is very mild by Thai standards. The New Mexico chilies are only slightly hotter than the California chilies and either may be used. If you prefer a spicier curry, feel free to substitute other, more potent dried chilies. If you do, however, bear in mind that this curry may be used in dishes that contain additional chilies, so that the "heat" will be additive.

The recipe we're presenting has a distinct flavor of shrimp paste, which is the authentic, traditional flavor. If you prefer, reduce the amount of shrimp paste to 1 or 2 tablespoons, but do not omit it altogether. A very strong odor will develop when you are frying the dried shrimp and shrimp paste, so we suggest you prepare this curry when no guests are expected. The most effective way to avoid the odor in your house is to cook the curry on an outdoor barbecue by placing the wok directly on a bed of red-hot coals; let the curry come to room temperature before storing it.

This curry keeps well for 6 months in a closed container in the refrigerator. After it stands for a few days, the oil will rise to the surface. To use the curry, stir it, or simply dip through the oil, allowing some to adhere to the portion being used. An interesting and unusual way to serve this curry is to spread a thin layer on toast, and serve it as a cocktail snack, side dish, or even by itself as a snack.

MAKES 3 CUPS

3 ounces wet tamarind or ¼ cup + 2 tablespoons
    tamarind concentrate
½ cup granulated sugar
¾ cup warm water

¼ pound (about 12) dried New Mexico or California chilies
1 cup vegetable oil

½ cup (¼ pound) finely chopped garlic

1 cup (¼ pound) finely chopped yellow onion

1¼ cups (3 ounces) dried shrimp
¼ cup shrimp paste

1. (Omit this step if you are using tamarind concentrate.) Soak the wet tamarind in ¾ cup warm water for 15 minutes or until it is soft. Press it through a sieve, making sure to press through all the pulp you can. Scrape the outside of the sieve carefully to get all the pulp, and discard the residue inside the sieve.

2. Place the tamarind solution and sugar in a saucepan and bring it to a boil. (If you have used tamarind concentrate, add ¾ cup warm water.) Remove it from the heat immediately, and let it cool to room temperature.

3. Remove the stems and seeds from the chilies, and tear the chilies into pieces about 1 inch square or smaller. Heat a wok, add ½ cup of the oil, and swirl it over the surface of the wok. Stir-fry the chilies over moderate heat until they are a deep red color and lightly fragrant, being careful not to let them burn. Remove the chilies, but not the oil, from the wok and set them aside in a bowl.

4. Add 2 tablespoons more oil to the wok and stir-fry the garlic until it is light golden. Remove the garlic, but not the oil, from the wok and add it to the chilies.

5. Add another 2 tablespoons oil to the wok and stir-fry the onion until it is light golden. Remove the onion, but not the oil, from the wok and add it to the chilies and garlic.

6. Add ¼ cup more oil to the wok. Add the dried shrimp and cook for about 1 minute. Then add the shrimp paste and stir-fry until the color becomes uniform and the strong odor has subsided, about 1 to 2 minutes. Remove the mixture, including the oil, from the wok and add it to the previously fried ingredients. Allow the fried ingredients to cool to room temperature.

7. Place the fried mixture and the oil is a food processor or blender and grind it to a smooth paste. If it seems dry and crumbly, add more oil to form a smooth, thick paste.

8. Add the cooked tamarind mixture from Step 2 to the ground chili mixture and stir to combine it well.

9. Store the curry in a closed jar in the refrigerator for up to 6 months. It may be frozen, but since it keeps so well that is unnecessary.

●●● ────────────────────────────────

Musman Curry
NAM PRIG GANG MUSSAMAN

Musman Curry is rich, flavorful, not very hot, and contains several spices not used routinely in Thai curries. Cloves and cumin suggest an Indian influence. Similarly, the name is thought to be derived from the word "Muslim," further suggesting the influence of Indian traders and merchants.

MAKES ½ CUP (¾ CUP IF GROUND WITH WATER)

7 small dried red chilies
2 pieces kah
½ cup warm water

1 tablespoon coriander seeds
1 teaspoon cumin or fennel seeds
1 teaspoon whole cloves

1 stalk lemon grass, bottom 6 inches only
2 tablespoons (1 ounce) finely chopped garlic
¼ cup (1 ounce) finely chopped yellow onion
1 teaspoon shrimp paste
½ teaspoon ground black pepper
1 teaspoon ground nutmeg

1. Remove the stems and seeds from the chilies. Soak the chilies and *kah* in the warm water for 20 minutes. After soaking, drain and discard the soaking water.

2. Place the coriander seeds, cumin (or fennel) seeds, and the cloves in a dry skillet and roast them over moderate heat until the cumin seeds have darkened, the cloves have turned a green-gray color, and the mixture is very fragrant, about 2 minutes.

3. Chop the chilies, *kah*, and lemon grass finely. Combine with the remaining ingredients and pound or grind to a smooth paste in a mortar or blender. (If you are using a blender, you may need to add water to aid in grinding.)

4. Use immediately or store in a closed container in the refrigerator for up to 2 weeks or in the freezer for up to 6 months.

••• ▬▬▬▬▬▬▬▬▬▬▬▬▬▬▬▬▬▬▬▬▬▬▬▬▬▬

Peanut Curry
NAM JIM TOOA

This curry is used primarily for preparing Saté, but it may be used to marinate and baste chicken as well. It can also be used as a dipping sauce any time a mildly hot peanut flavor is desired.

3 tablespoons coriander seeds
2 tablespoons cumin seeds

3 small dried red chilies
2 pieces kah
¾ cup warm water

1 stalk lemon grass, bottom 6 inches only
¼ cup (1 ounce) finely chopped yellow onion
2 tablespoons (1 ounce) finely chopped garlic
1 teaspoon shrimp paste
1 tablespoon ground white pepper

2 tablespoons vegetable oil
4 cups thick coconut milk

3 tablespoons fish sauce
¼ cup granulated sugar
1½ cups ground roasted unsalted peanuts (page 66)

1. Put the coriander seeds and cumin seeds in a dry wok or skillet and roast them over moderate heat until they are light brown, about 5 minutes. Stir them frequently to allow them to roast evenly and to prevent burning. Set them aside.

2. Remove the stems and seeds from the chilies. Soak the chilies and *kah* in the warm water for 15 minutes. After soaking, drain and discard the soaking water.

3. Chop the chilies, *kah*, and lemon grass finely. Pound or grind the roasted seeds, chilies, *kah*, lemon grass, onion, garlic, shrimp paste, and pepper in a mortar or blender until they are finely ground and smooth. (If you are using a blender, add just enough of the coconut milk to aid in grinding.)

4. Add just enough water or coconut milk to the ground mixture to form a thick paste. (If you ground the ingredients with coconut milk in Step 3 it may not be necessary to add more here.)

5. Heat a wok, add the oil, and swirl it over the surface of the wok. Add the paste from Step 3 and stir-fry until it turns dark and is fragrant. Add the fish sauce, sugar, and ground peanuts. Stir to mix well. Add ¼ cup of the coconut milk and stir over moderate heat until the mixture is thick. Repeat with the rest of the coconut milk, adding about ¼ cup at a time.

6. Use immediately or store in a closed container in the refrigerator for up to 2 weeks, or in the freezer for 6 months.

Sauces

The sauces in this section can be used to accompany many different foods and often are used to flavor rice when you are serving dishes which have little or no sauce of their own. Some of them, like Vinegar Sauce, Spicy Fish Sauce, and Lime Sauce are all-purpose sauces which are usually served as condiments at all meals in much the same way that salt and pepper would be in Western cuisines or that soy sauce would be in Chinese. Some of them, like Won Ton Sauce, are intended for special uses and are mentioned within recipes for specific dishes. They may, however, be used with other dishes if you like, and that is why they are in this separate section.

Cucumber Sauce 1
NAM JIM TANG QUA I

This sauce is intended to be used with Fish Cakes.

MAKES ABOUT 3 CUPS

1 pound (2 medium) cucumbers
2 Serrano chilies
½ medium red onion

½ cup granulated sugar
1 cup white vinegar
½ teaspoon salt

1. Peel the cucumbers and slice them crosswise into slices ⅛ inch thick. Remove the stems, but not the seeds, from the chilies and slice them crosswise into thin slices. Peel the onion and remove the root portion. Slice the onion vertically into thin slices.

2. Combine the cucumbers, chilies, and onion with the remaining ingredients and mix until the sugar is dissolved. If allowed to stand for more than 2 hours, the cucumbers will start to become soggy.

Cucumber Sauce 2
NAM JIM TANG QUA II

For serving with Saté.

MAKES ABOUT 1¾ CUPS

¼ cup granulated sugar
½ cup white vinegar
¼ cup boiling water
¼ teaspoon salt
1 teaspoon ground chili paste

½ pound (1 medium) cucumber
Coriander sprigs to taste

2 tablespoons ground roasted unsalted peanuts (page 66)

1. Combine all ingredients except the cucumber, peanuts, and coriander. Stir until the sugar is dissolved. Allow the mixture to cool to room temperature.

2. Peel the cucumber and slice it crosswise into pieces ⅛ inch thick. Chop the coriander sprigs coarsely.

3. Add the cucumber slices, peanuts, and coriander leaves to the liquid mixture. If allowed to stand for more than 2 hours, the cucumbers and peanuts will start to become soggy.

•••

Cucumber Sauce 3
NAM JIM TANG QUA III

Serve with Deep-Fried Bread and Pork.

MAKES ABOUT 3½ CUPS

2 Serrano chilies
½ cup coriander sprigs
½ pound (1 medium) cucumber

1 cup granulated sugar
2 cups white vinegar
1 teaspoon salt

½ cup (2 ounces) coarsely chopped red onion

1. Remove the stems, but not the seeds, from the chilies and slice the chilies crosswise into ⅛-inch pieces. Chop the coriander sprigs coarsely. Peel the cucumber and slice it crosswise into pieces ⅛ inch thick.

2. Mix the sugar, vinegar, and salt, and stir until the sugar and salt are dissolved. Add the chilies, coriander sprigs, cucumber, and onion. If allowed to stand for more than 2 hours, the cucumbers will start to become soggy.

✳✳✳ ——————————————————

Vinegar Sauce
PRIG DONG

This is a simple all-purpose sauce that may accompany various dishes, including soups and salads, and is usually found on Thai tables no matter what dishes are being served, although it is usually eaten primarily with noodle dishes. It will keep for 3 or 4 days at room temperature or about 2 weeks in the refrigerator before the chilies become soft. The chilies are intended to be eaten, and add a crunchy texture and fiery flavor. If you find the chilies too hot to eat, use just the liquid for flavoring. The proportions are not at all critical, so vary them at will.

MAKES ABOUT ¼ CUP

3 Serrano chilies
¼ cup white vinegar

1. Remove the stems, but not the seeds, from the chilies. Slice the chilies crosswise into pieces ⅛ inch thick. Place the sliced chilies and vinegar in a small serving bowl.

2. Let stand for 15 minutes to allow the flavors to develop.

✳✳✳ ——————————————————

Spicy Fish Sauce
PRIG NAM BLA

This sauce is very popular in Thailand but is less commonly served in the United States because of the strong taste of fish sauce. It is an all-purpose sauce which can be served with most foods and can be used instead of Vinegar Sauce. It should be made fresh each time it is used.

MAKES ABOUT ½ CUP
4 Serrano chilies
½ cup fish sauce

Remove the stems, but not the seeds, from the chilies. Chop the chilies finely. Mix the chilies and fish sauce and place in a serving bowl.

✳✳✳ ─────────────────────────

Lime Sauce
PRIG MANOW

This is a simple, all-purpose sauce which can be served with most foods and is particularly good with seafood dishes. It does not keep well for more than one day, so should be made fresh each time it is served.

MAKES ABOUT ½ CUP
4 Serrano chilies
¼ cup + 2 tablespoons lime juice
3 tablespoons fish sauce

Remove the stems, but not the seeds, from the chilies. Chop the chilies finely. Combine all the ingredients in a small serving bowl.

••• ─────────────────────────

Garlic Sauce
NAM JIM GRATIEM

This is a very popular sauce that can be used for dipping any fried food that is not sweet itself. The ingredients may seem strange when you first read the recipe, but they blend beautifully and produce an elusive flavor. It will keep for up to 2 months in a closed jar in the refrigerator, but it may not last that long because of its popularity. It is so tasty that some people have been known to eat it plain by the spoonful. If you prefer a smooth sauce, grind the ingredients in a blender to the desired consistency before cooking.

MAKES ¾ CUP

½ cup water
½ cup white vinegar
½ cup granulated sugar
1 teaspoon ground chili paste
2 teaspoons (4 cloves) finely chopped garlic
½ teaspoon salt

1. Combine all the ingredients in a stainless-steel or enamel saucepan and boil slowly until the mixture is reduced by about one half. It will become a little thicker as it cools. You may make it any consistency you like, but we suggest that at room temperature it should have a consistency slightly thinner than unwhipped heavy cream. If it gets too thick, it may be thinned easily by adding warm water, and if it is too thin it may be thickened by additional boiling.

2. Use immediately, or store for up to 2 months in a closed jar in the refrigerator. Allow it to come to room temperature before serving.

● ● ● ━━━━━━━━━━━━━━━━━━━━━━━━━━━━━━━━━━━

Plum Sauce
NAM JIM GIM BOI

This sauce is similar to Garlic Sauce, but the plums add a slightly sour flavor. It is used with foods such as Stuffed Squid, which have their own hint of sweetness. If you prefer a smooth sauce, grind all the ingredients to the desired consistency in a blender before cooking them.

MAKES 1 CUP

4 salted plums

¾ cup white vinegar
½ cup water
1 cup granulated sugar
2 teaspoons ground chili paste

1. Remove the pits from the salted plums and chop the plums finely.

2. Combine all the ingredients in a saucepan and cook on medium-high heat until the sauce thickens and is reduced to 1 cup. It will thicken more on cooling.

3. Use immediately, or store in a closed jar in the refrigerator for up to 2 months. Allow it to come to room temperature before serving.

•••━━━━━━━━━━━━━━━━━━━━━━━━━━━━━━

Sweet-and-Sour Topping
NAM PRIEW WAN

This topping is intended primarily for Sweet and Sour Crepes, but it could also be poured over roasted chicken or poached fish. It is best when made within 2 or 3 hours of serving. Longer storage in the refrigerator causes the tomatoes and onions to lose their texture. It should not be frozen for the same reason.

MAKES 3 CUPS

¼ pound (1 medium) yellow onion
½ pound (about 2) tomatoes

2 teaspoons tapioca starch
2 tablespoons water

1 tablespoon vegetable oil

¼ cup white vinegar
¼ cup fish sauce
¼ cup granulated sugar
1 cup water

1. Peel the onion, remove the root portion, and slice the onion vertically into thin slices. Remove the stem portion from the tomatoes, and slice them vertically into wedges about ¼ inch thick at their widest part. Set these ingredients aside.

2. Mix the tapioca starch with 2 tablespoons water and set the mixture aside.

3. Heat a wok, add the oil, and swirl it over the surface of the pan. Stir-fry the tomato and onion over moderate heat until the onions are crisp-tender.

4. Add the vinegar, fish sauce, sugar, and water. Stir until the sugar is dissolved.

5. Stir the tapioca starch mixture, add it to the wok, and stir over moderate heat until the mixture thickens.

6. Keep the sauce warm while you prepare other dishes.

✳✳✳ ━━━━━━━━━━━━━━━━━━━━━━━━━━━━━━

Ground Chili Sauce
NAM JIM PRIG BOD

This is another all-purpose sauce that can be used for dipping or for adding additional spicy flavor to prepared dishes. It keeps indefinitely in a closed jar in the refrigerator or for 2 months at room temperature.

MAKES ¾ CUP

¾ cup white vinegar
1 tablespoon ground chili paste

Stir the ingredients together.

•• ━━━━━━━━━━━━━━━━━━━━━━━━━━━━━━

Won Ton Sauce
NAM JIM SE-EIEW 1

To be served with Steamed Won Tons.

MAKES ABOUT 1 CUP

2 tablespoons white vinegar
1 tablespoon sweet soy sauce
1 tablespoon black soy sauce
1 teaspoon ground black pepper
1 tablespoon crisp-fried garlic with its oil (page 65)

Combine all ingredients and stir to mix them well. Can be kept for a month at room temperature in a closed container.

Sweet-and-Sour Sauce
NAM JIM SE-EIEW 2

MAKES ABOUT ¾ CUP

2 tablespoons white vinegar
¼ cup granulated sugar
¼ cup black soy sauce
2 teaspoons ground chili paste

Combine all ingredients and stir until the sugar is dissolved. Can be kept for a month at room temperature in a closed container.

Ginger Sauce
NAM JIM KING

This is a rich, thick, dark, spicy sauce that goes very well with bland foods, such as fried tofu or poached or boiled chicken or fish. It should be used within 6 hours of preparation, because it becomes very strong if allowed to stand longer than that.

MAKES ABOUT ¾ CUP

1 tablespoon (½ ounce) finely chopped garlic
2 tablespoons brown bean paste
¼ cup (2 ounces) finely chopped ginger root
1 Serrano chili, stemmed but not seeded, and chopped finely
2 tablespoons white vinegar
1 tablespoon granulated sugar
1 tablespoon black soy sauce
3 sprigs coriander leaves and stems, chopped finely

Mix all the ingredients thoroughly.

Sweet Sauce
NAM JIM PAW PEAH

Serve with Steamed Spring Rolls. This sauce should be made fresh each time it is used because it does not keep well.

1 tablespoon fish sauce
1 tablespoon water
3 tablespoons granulated sugar
1 teaspoon black soy sauce

3 teaspoons tapioca starch
2 tablespoons water

1. Mix the fish sauce, 1 tablespoon water, sugar, and black soy sauce in a saucepan and bring it to a slow boil. Boil gently, and stir until the sugar is dissolved but the sauce is not reduced.

2. Mix the tapioca starch and water. Add it to the boiling liquid and stir until the mixture thickens. Remove it from the heat and let it cool to room temperature.

• • •

Tofu Sauce
NAM JIM TOHOO

Intended to be served with Deep-Fried Tofu. Until the peanuts and coriander are added it will keep for up to 2 months in a closed jar in the refrigerator.

MAKES ABOUT 2½ CUPS

1 cup (8 ounces) palm sugar
¾ cup white vinegar
½ cup water
¼ teaspoon salt
2 Serrano chilies, stemmed but not seeded, and chopped finely
3 tablespoons ground roasted unsalted peanuts (page 66)
3 sprigs coriander, chopped very finely

Mix the first five ingredients in a saucepan and bring them to a slow boil over moderate heat. Cook uncovered until the mixture thickens slightly, about 15 minutes. When ready to serve, pour the mixture into a small serving bowl and sprinkle the peanuts and coriander over the top.

Salad Dressings

Like other preparations, Thai salad dressings provide pleasing contrasts in taste and texture. For example, our Peanut Salad Dressing is something like a curry and combines a large variety of ingredients to produce an unusual effect. The other two dressings we describe introduce hot, sweet, and sour tastes which accent the flavors of the salad ingredients.

• • •

Lime Salad Dressing
NAM SOM TAM

This dressing is intended for Green Papaya Salad. It does not keep well because the lime juice loses its flavor on long standing, so it should be made fresh each time it is to be used.

MAKES ABOUT 1¼ CUPS

4 Serrano chilies
2 teaspoons (4 cloves) finely chopped garlic

¼ cup fish sauce
½ cup lime juice
¼ cup + 1 tablespoon granulated sugar

1. Remove the stems, but not the seeds, from the chilies and chop the chilies finely. Pound the garlic and chilies to a smooth paste in a mortar.

2. Add the remaining ingredients and stir until the sugar dissolves.

• • •

Peanut Salad Dressing
NAM SALAD KAK

In some respects this recipe reads more like a curry than what one would expect for a salad dressing, but it works well with mixed salads, and illustrates how the Thai people have utilized a variety of ingredients and procedures in developing their unique cuisine. This recipe produces a mild version of the dressing; you may make it hotter by substituting more potent chilies.

MAKES 3 CUPS

2 dried California or New Mexico chilies
1 piece kah
Warm water

1 ounce wet tamarind or 2 tablespoons tamarind concentrate
½ cup warm water

1½ teaspoons coriander seeds
1 teaspoon cumin seeds

½ stalk lemon grass, bottom 6 inches only
1 tablespoon finely chopped yellow onion
1 tablespoon (½ ounce) finely chopped garlic
½ teaspoon shrimp paste

2 cups thick coconut milk

2 tablespoons vegetable oil

1½ cups ground roasted unsalted peanuts (page 66)

1½ tablespoons fish sauce
¼ cup granulated sugar

1½ cups thin coconut milk

1. Remove the stems and seeds from the chilies. Soak the chilies and *kah* for 15 minutes in warm water. After soaking, drain and discard the soaking water.

2. (Omit this step if you are using tamarind concentrate.) Soak the tamarind in ½ cup warm water for 15 minutes or until it is soft. Press it through a sieve, being sure to press through all the pulp you can. Scrape the outside of the sieve to get all the pulp. Discard the residue left in the sieve.

3. Put the coriander seeds and cumin seeds in a dry wok or skillet and roast them over moderate heat until they are golden brown. Stir them frequently and watch them carefully to prevent burning. Grind them to a fine powder in a blender or a coffee or spice grinder.

4. Chop the chilies, *kah*, and lemon grass finely. Pound or grind the chilies, *kah,* lemon grass, onion, garlic, shrimp paste, and powder from Step 3 to a smooth paste in a mortar or blender. If using a blender, add ¼ cup water to help the grinding, and grind on low speed.

5. Pour the thick coconut milk into a saucepan and bring it to a boil. Remove it from the heat immediately.

6. Heat a wok, add the vegetable oil, and swirl it over the pan. Add the paste from Step 4, and stir-fry until it is darker in color and fragrant. Add 1 cup of the warm thick coconut milk, ¼ cup at a time, stirring after each addition until the mixture becomes thick.

7. Add the ground peanuts and stir while adding the rest of the thick coconut milk gradually. Cook over moderate heat, stirring frequently, until the mixture becomes slightly thick.

8. Add the fish sauce, sugar, and tamarind solution or concentrate and mix them in well. Add the thin coconut milk and bring the mixture to a boil quickly. Remove the mixture from the heat and cool it to room temperature.

9. Use the dressing immediately, or store it in a closed jar in the refrigerator for up to 2 months or in the freezer for 6 months. If you refrigerate the dressing, bring it to room temperature before pouring it over a salad. The dressing may become thicker if refrigerated because the peanuts will absorb some of the liquid. If so, add just enough warm water to bring it to a consistency that is easy to pour and which will flow over the salad, but still thick enough to adhere to the salad ingredients.

Thai Salad Dressing
NAM YAM YAI

This dressing is developed for Thai Salad, and it is an all-purpose dressing good on any green or mixed salad.

MAKES ABOUT ¾ CUP

¼ cup white vinegar
¼ cup granulated sugar
¼ cup boiling water
¼ teaspoon ground chili paste
¼ teaspoon salt

1. Combine all the ingredients and stir until the sugar is dissolved.

2. Use immediately, or store the dressing in a closed jar in the refrigerator for up to 2 months.

Variation: One teaspoon mashed or very finely chopped garlic may be added.

5
Rice

RICE IS TRULY the "staff of life" in Thailand, and it is consumed in large quantities. A Thai meal without large bowls of steaming rice is inconceivable and we have inserted gentle reminders of that fact by ending appropriate recipes with the instruction to "serve with rice." In addition to being nutritious and filling, rice serves as a perfect foil for spicy or hot foods, moderating the intensity of the chilies, pepper, and spices while allowing the flavor to be experienced. The northern and northeastern provinces of Thailand use glutinous ("sweet") rice more than long-grain rice, while the long-grain variety is used more in the central and southern provinces. We suggest that you use jasmine rice if available because it produces a faint, pleasant aroma and has a subtle flavor. For information on types of rice, see the section on ingredients (page 52).

If you should find your mouth burning from food that is too hot or spicy for you, just eat some plain rice—it's much more refreshing and cooling than taking a drink of water, which often intensifies the hot effect. Rice is relatively low in calories, so unless you are on an exceptionally strict diet it will be harmless to the waistline.

Steamed Rice
KAO SOOK

An unnecessary mystique surrounds the procedure for cooking rice. The fact is that rice is one of the simplest foods to cook when done the Thai way. First, forget all you've heard about measuring in cupsful of rice and water, boiling the water first or last, etc. Those "rules" make a straightforward procedure into a chore. Try it the way we outline and you'll be amazed at the simplicity. Unfortunately, it takes longer to read these instructions than to perform the actions. So, bear with us, and after you do it once or twice, you may wonder why you haven't always cooked rice this simple, foolproof way. We suggest allowing about ½ to ¾ cup uncooked rice per person, but the amount need not be measured precisely.

1. Select a pot with a tight-fitting lid that will accommodate the amount of rice you are going to prepare. The amount you select should cover the bottom of the pot at least two grains deep. It can be as deep as you like, but two grains is the minimum. Remember to allow for expansion, because rice triples in volume when cooked. If your smallest pot seems too big, just cook extra rice. It keeps wonderfully well for 2 or 3 days in the refrigerator and can be reheated easily, used to make fried rice or crisp rice, served at room temperature, or made into desserts.

2. Put the rice into the pot. You may rinse it or not, depending on your preference and the cleanliness of the raw grains. Traditionally, it is rinsed in several changes of water until the water runs clear, but that is because rice in Southeast Asia is sold in bulk or in large cloth bags, and may contain numerous impurities. Most rice in the United States is prewashed and packed in plastic bags, so it is already clean. If the rice has been enriched with vitamins, washing it will remove them.

3. Add water to cover the rice by *about* 1 inch. (Remember, there are no precise amounts.) It's easy to measure—just put the tip of your index finger on top of the rice. The water should come *about* to the point where your first joint begins. This amount of water will produce the traditional soft and slightly sticky rice. If you prefer firmer rice, reduce the water to the amount that will come about halfway to the first joint of your finger. After doing this once or twice you won't even need to use your finger—a glance into the pot will do.

4. Bring the rice and water to a rapid boil, uncovered, over high heat.

5. Reduce the heat to simmer and stir the rice quickly with a fork to loosen any grains that may have stuck to the pot. Cover the pot immediately with a tight-fitting lid.

6. Cook for 20 minutes on simmer. Do not lift the lid during this time no matter how curious you may be!

7. Remove the pot from the heat and allow it to stand, covered, about 10 minutes. Remove the cover, fluff the rice quickly with a fork, and replace the cover.

8. If the rice gets cold it can be reheated in a sieve over, not in, hot water or in a non-metallic container in a microwave oven.

9. Serve the rice in a warm covered bowl or rice server, letting each diner take his/her own portions.

Note: If rice is left on low heat while it steams, a crisp crust will form, which is considered a delicacy by many Asian people. It can be deep-fried and eaten along with the soft rice, but it is even better if used as a special accompaniment. One way to use it is to break it up in pieces, deep-fry it and use it to make Ground Pork and Shrimp (NA TANG, see page 191.) You may also deep-fry it until light golden and sprinkle it over any dishes to which you want to add a crisp texture.

●●● ━━━━━━━━━━━━━━━━━━━━━━━━━━━━━━━

Glutinous (Sweet) Rice
KOA NEOW

Glutinous rice requires preliminary soaking, then steaming *over* boiling water rather than cooking *in* water as described in the recipe for steamed rice.

1. Soak the rice for at least 2 hours or, preferably, overnight in enough room-temperature water to cover it. Drain the rice thoroughly in a fine, or cloth-lined colander and discard the soaking water.

2. Put the rice in a covered steamer and cook it over, not in, boiling water for about 25 minutes. It will be soft and sticky. Traditionally it is cooked "until it smells like cooked sweet rice." That is impossible to describe with words, but 25 minutes is about right.

Soft Rice
KAO TOM

Soft rice is the easiest of all rice preparations. It requires no measurement of water or rice and no timing during cooking. Depending on the amount of water and rice you cook, it will be like a mush or like a soup. The choice is yours and depends on your own taste. The amount of water we suggest is an average. Use more or less, according to your own taste. Soft rice is frequently served for breakfast, particularly if it is cooked in stock rather than water.

For medium-soft rice: Put 1 cup cooked long-grain rice in a saucepan. Add 3 cups water or broth and cover the pan. Cook over medium heat for about 15 minutes until it is soft.

For very soft rice: Put 1 cup cooked long-grain rice in a saucepan with 6 cups water or broth and cover the pan. Cook over medium heat for about 30 minutes until it is very soft.

Crisp Rice
KOA KUA

There are two methods for preparing crisp rice. The first one we describe is the traditional method and requires more effort than the easier, short-cut, second method. Either produces good results, but the second method has the advantage of being a good way to use leftover rice. Deep-fry before serving.

Traditional Method

1. Put at least 3 cups raw long-grain rice in a pot and cook it according to the instructions for steamed rice, but cook it until a crust forms in the bottom of the pan, about 30 minutes instead of 20.

2. Remove the soft rice from the center of the pot carefully, and leave the stuck portions in the pot. Heat the pot over the lowest possible heat until the layer of rice is dry. Remove the layer of rice from the pot, breaking it as little as possible, and set it aside to dry at room temperature overnight. Or, place it on a baking sheet in a 200° oven for 1 or 2 hours, until it is completely dry and crisp.

Short-Cut Method

1. Place a thin (not more than ¼ inch) layer of cooked rice on an ungreased baking sheet and press it firmly so the grains stick together. If you prefer a smoother layer of crisp rice, grind the cooked rice to a coarse paste in a food processor before placing it on the baking sheet.

2. Put the baking sheet in a 150° oven and leave it for 3 or 4 hours, or until the rice is dry and crisp.

• • • ─────────────────────────────

Rice with Coconut Milk
KAO MUN

This rice provides a pleasant change from plain steamed rice, and it is particularly good with hot, spicy dishes that do not contain coconut milk themselves. It may, of course, be used at any time you would ordinarily serve steamed rice. The procedure for cooking is the same as for steamed rice, and we provide quantities of ingredients simply because it is easier to make coconut milk when you know how much you will need.

> *2 cups uncooked rice*
> *1½ teaspoons salt*
> *3½ cups thick coconut milk*
>
> *1 teaspoon granulated sugar*

1. Put the rice, salt, and coconut milk in a pot for which you have a tight-fitting lid. Cook the rice as you would steamed rice (see page 95).

2. Following the 10-minute standing time, add the sugar

and mix it in well by fluffing the rice with a fork. Replace the cover and let the rice stand until served. It may be reheated in a non-metallic container in a microwave oven or by placing it in a collander over, not in, gently boiling water.

●●●━━━━━━━━━━━━━━━━━━━━━━━━━━━━━

Chicken Fried Rice
KAO PAD GAI

This is a popular dish in many restaurants as well as homes. It is easy and fast to prepare, and can serve as a meal-in-one if served at a luncheon or as a late supper. At other times it can be served as a separate dish in a complete Thai meal. It is not intended to substitute for steamed rice, so if other dishes are served, steamed rice should be served as usual. Be sure to cook the rice well in advance so that it can cool to room temperature before beginning this recipe. Freshly cooked, warm rice tends to get gummy. This is an excellent way to use leftover rice.

SERVES 6 TO 8

1 pound boned skinned chicken breast
½ pound (2 cups sliced) yellow onions
1 bunch green onions

2 tablespoons vegetable oil
2 tablespoons (1 ounce) finely chopped garlic

¼ cup + 2 tablespoons fish sauce
¼ cup granulated sugar
6 to 8 eggs

8 cups steamed rice, at room temperature or chilled

1 cucumber, sliced diagonally ⅛ thick
6 green onions
2 tomatoes, cut into wedges

Lime Sauce (page 84)

1. Slice the chicken across the grain into strips ⅛ inch thick and 1 to 2 inches long. Peel the yellow onions, remove the root portion, and slice the onions vertically into thin strips. Set the chicken and onions aside in separate containers. Slice the white and green parts of the green onions diagonally into ⅛-inch pieces and set them aside in a separate container.

2. Heat a wok, add the oil, and swirl it over the surface of the pan. Add the garlic and stir-fry until light golden.

3. Add the chicken and stir-fry until the pink color disappears. Add the yellow onions and stir-fry until the slices are barely translucent.

4. Add the fish sauce and sugar, and mix them in thoroughly. Stir while you add the eggs, 1 at a time, breaking the yolks. Continue stirring until the eggs begin to set.

5. Add the rice and stir until the eggs are almost dry and the mixture is well combined. Remove the mixture from the heat, add the sliced green onions from Step 1, and mix them in well.

6. Transfer the mixture to a warm serving platter and serve immediately or keep it warm while you prepare other ingredients.

7. Arrange sliced cucumbers, green onions, and tomato wedges over the rice in a decorative pattern. Serve with Lime Sauce for each diner to add as desired.

6
Noodles

NOODLES ARE CONSUMED in large quantities in Thai households and there is an almost unlimited variety of ways in which they may be prepared. They are second only to rice in relative importance in the Thai diet. In fact, many noodles are prepared from rice, which serves to further emphasize the importance of rice in the diet. The many varieties of noodles range from tiny transparent noodles made from mung beans to large sheets of fresh rice noodles. Please read about noodles in the section on ingredients (page 49) to become familiar with the more popular and common types specified in the recipes.

••• ────────────────────────────────

Fresh Rice Noodles
GUAYTIO

MAKES 1 POUND

1¼ cups uncooked long-grain rice
1¼ cup water

Vegetable oil

1. Soak the rice overnight in the water. After soaking, grind the rice and water for 5 to 10 minutes in a blender to form a very smooth thin batter. (A food processor does not work well for this procedure because the mixture tends to spin around and not grind.) When it is finished you should be able to feel no more than the *barest* hint of solid particles if you rub the batter between your fingers. It is better to overgrind it than to grind it too little.

2. Lightly coat an 8 x 8 x 2-inch baking pan with oil and heat it for about 3 minutes in a steamer. Pour in ½ cup batter in an even layer and replace the steamer lid. Steam for 5 minutes. From this point on, check periodically to make sure there is water in the steamer and add more if it is low.

3. After 5 minutes, coat the top of the first layer lightly with vegetable oil and pour ½ cup batter on top of it. Steam for 5 minutes. Repeat with the remaining batter. After adding the last layer, steam for 8 minutes. When sliced, the layers will separate into thin noodles.

4. Use immediately in any recipe calling for fresh noodles or wrap the noodles tightly in plastic wrap and store in the refrigerator for up to 2 days. They can be frozen for up to six months but will be grainy when thawed.

●●● ──

Thai Noodles
PAD THAI

This is a very popular classic Thai dish often served alone for a luncheon or late supper. It is truly a meal-in-one and needs no accompaniment, although it may be served with other foods if desired. Shrimp, pork, or a combination of meats may be used according to availability and your taste preference. The traditional home recipe, particularly in the provinces, uses dried shrimp and tofu rather than fresh meat. This version is in the variation following the main recipe. In the cities, particularly in Bangkok, pork is the preferred meat. In deference to American tastes, Thai restaurants in the United States often use fresh shrimp and omit the tofu. If you cannot obtain the rice noodles we recommend, substitute smaller ones, but recognize that the texture of the dish may be softer.

SERVES 6 TO 8

½ pound dried rice noodles ⅛ inch wide
Warm water

½ pound shrimp, chicken, pork, or a combination

¼ cup fish sauce
¼ cup + 2 tablespoons granulated sugar
¼ cup + 2 tablespoons white vinegar
1 teaspoon paprika or 1 tablespoon tomato paste or
    1 tablespoon catsup (all are optional)

4 green onions

½ cup vegetable oil (more if needed in Step 6)
1 teaspoon (2 cloves) finely chopped garlic

2 eggs

¾ pound bean sprouts

2 tablespoons ground roasted chilies (page 60)
¾ cup ground roasted unsalted peanuts (page 66)

Lime wedges

1. Soak the noodles for 20 to 25 minutes in enough warm water to cover them. They should be flexible and soft, but not so soft that they can be mashed easily with the fingers. Later cooking in liquid will soften them more. Drain them thoroughly in a colander while preparing the other ingredients. Traditionally they are left in full-length strands, but you may cut them into 8-inch lengths if you find it easier to stir-fry them that way.

2. Peel and devein the shrimp, leaving the tails intact, or slice the chicken or pork across the grain into strips not more than ⅛ inch thick and 1 to 2 inches long.

3. Mix the fish sauce, sugar, vinegar, and optional paprika, tomato paste, or catsup in a bowl, and stir until the sugar is dissolved. Set the mixture aside. Slice the green onions, both white and green parts, diagonally into pieces 1½ inches long and ¼ inch thick. Set aside.

4. Heat a wok, add the oil, and swirl it over the surface of the pan. Add the garlic and stir-fry until light golden. Add the meat and stir-fry until the pink color disappears completely. If you are using shrimp, stir-fry until they turn pink. Add the noodles and toss lightly to coat them with oil and to distribute the meat and garlic.

5. Add the liquid from Step 3 and bring it to a boil rapidly, gently folding the noodles without breaking them. Reduce the heat to medium and boil the mixture, folding frequently, until the noodles have absorbed the liquid.

6. Using a wok scoop or a stiff spatula, lift the noodles gently from one side of the wok. Pour a little oil along the side of the wok, then break 1 egg and slip it into the oil. Break the yolk, and cover the egg with the noodles immediately. Repeat this on the opposite side of the wok with the remaining egg. Allow the eggs to cook undisturbed, over moderate heat, until they are set and almost dry. Additional oil may be added if the eggs or the noodles begin to stick to the wok.

7. When the eggs are set and almost dry, fold them gently but rapidly into the noodles. Try not to break the noodles, which will be soft and fragile at this point. An effective way is to insert the scoop under the eggs, lift it through, and fold the mixture over. Continue the lifting and folding motion until the eggs are broken up and well distributed.

8. Add the bean sprouts and sliced green onions and toss the entire mixture quickly and gently, still avoiding breaking the noodles. Cook for about 2 minutes, or until the bean sprouts and green onions are crisp-tender.

9. Place the mixture on a large warm platter. Sprinkle the ground chilies and peanuts over the top and squeeze lime juice over that, or serve these garnishes separately, for each diner to add according to taste.

Variation: Omit the shrimp, pork, or chicken from the list of ingredients, and ignore any instructions for them. Substitute ½ pound tofu and ¼ pound dried shrimp. Put the tofu on a triple layer of paper towels, cover it with another triple layer, put a plate on top of that, and put a 2-pound weight, e.g., a can of tomatoes, on top of the plate. Let stand for 20 to 30 minutes to press out the excess water. Put the dried shrimp in a sieve, rinse them quickly under hot running water, and set them aside to drain. After the tofu has been pressed, slice it into ¼-inch cubes. Add the tofu and shrimp in Step 5 of the instructions and proceed with the main recipe. *Note:* In Thailand, dried shrimp are available in a smaller size than is generally available in the United States. If you would like to simulate that, chop the dried shrimp very coarsely after they have been rinsed.

Noodles with Broccoli and Beef
PAD SE-EIEW NUE

This noodle dish is smooth, slightly creamy, and has a mild flavor. If fresh rice noodles are not available, substitute medium-wide dried noodles or "rice chips," and soak them in warm water about 30 minutes before using them.

SERVES 6 TO 8

½ pound flank steak
1 pound broccoli
1 pound fresh rice noodles
½ pound bean sprouts

¼ cup vegetable oil
1 teaspoon (2 cloves) finely chopped garlic

2 teaspoons soy sauce

2 tablespoons vegetable oil

3 tablespoons fish sauce

1½ teaspoons vegetable oil (more if needed in Step 6)
3 eggs

¼ teaspoon ground black pepper

Vinegar Sauce (page 83)

1. Slice the beef across the grain into strips ⅛ inch thick and 1 to 2 inches long. Remove the florets from the broccoli, slice the stems diagonally into pieces about ¼ inch thick, and set the stems and florets aside. Slice the noodles into strips about ¾ inch wide and 5 to 6 inches long. Then heat them by tossing them about 10 seconds in boiling water. Drain them in a colander. Place the bean sprouts in a bowl of ice water and let them soak while you cook the other ingredients.

2. Heat a wok, add ¼ cup vegetable oil, and swirl it over the surface of the pan. Add the garlic and stir-fry until it is light golden.

3. Add the beef and stir-fry until the red color disappears. Add the noodles and soy sauce and stir-fry until the noodles are coated evenly with soy sauce and oil. Remove and set aside.

4. Heat the wok again, add 2 tablespoons oil, and swirl it over the surface of the pan. Stir-fry the broccoli until it is crisp-tender. Add the noodle mixture from Step 3 and the fish sauce. Stir gently to mix all the ingredients thoroughly without breaking the noodles.

5. Lift the noodles from one side of the wok. Pour ½ teaspoon vegetable oil into the wok at that point and break 1 egg onto the oiled surface, breaking the yolk. Cover the egg with the noodles and repeat with the other 2 eggs at different points in the wok, using ½ teaspoon oil each time. Let the eggs cook undisturbed over moderate heat until they are set. If the noodles or eggs begin to stick, add a little more oil. When the eggs are set, fold the noodle mixture gently to distribute the eggs evenly.

6. Drain the bean sprouts and add them to the wok. Fold the mixture until the bean sprouts are just crisp-tender about 2 minutes. Scoop the dish out onto a warm serving platter and sprinkle with the ground pepper.

7. Serve immediately with Vinegar Sauce, for each diner to add as desired. Or keep the mixture warm while you prepare other dishes.

• • •

Noodles with Chicken and Broccoli
RAD NA GAI

This is hearty fare suitable for the main course of a luncheon or late supper. It is fast, easy, tasty, nutritious, and filling.

Fresh noodles are highly desirable, but other types of rice noodles may be substituted if fresh ones are not available. For example, "rice chips" may be used if soaked about 30 minutes in warm water. (See page 50.) Very small rice noodles the size of vermicelli also work well.

> SERVES 6 TO 8
>
> ¾ pound fresh rice noodles or ⅓ pound dried noodles
> Boiling water, if needed, in Step 1
>
> ½ pound boneless skinned chicken breast
>
> ¾ pound broccoli
>
> 3 tablespoons tapioca starch
> ½ cup water
>
> 2 tablespoons fish sauce
> 2 tablespoons oyster sauce
> 1¾ cups chicken stock (page 67)
>
> 2 tablespoons vegetable oil
> 1 teaspoon black soy sauce
>
> 2 tablespoons vegetable oil
> 1 teaspoon (2 cloves) finely chopped garlic
>
> ¼ teaspoon ground white pepper
>
> Vinegar Sauce (page 83)

1. Slice the fresh noodles into strips about ¾ inch wide and 5 to 6 inches long. If the noodles aren't soft and moist, dip them quickly in boiling water. They should be soft and moist when added to the wok to help prevent them from sticking together, or to the wok. If you are using dried noodles, soak them in hot water to cover for 30 minutes, then drain them in a colander.

2. Slice the chicken breast across the grain into strips not more than ⅛ inch thick, and set aside.

3. Remove the florets from the broccoli and peel the stems. Slice the stems diagonally into pieces ¼ inch thick and blanch the florets and stems in boiling water or in a microwave oven until they are not quite crisp-tender. Set them aside.

4. Mix the tapioca starch and water in a small container. Set aside.

5. Combine the fish sauce, oyster sauce, and chicken stock. Set aside.

6. Heat a wok, add 2 tablespoons of the oil, and swirl it over the surface of the pan. Add the warm noodles and black soy sauce. Stir-fry until the noodles are hot and well mixed. Place the noodles in a serving bowl, cover them, and keep them warm.

7. Heat the wok again, add the remaining 2 tablespoons oil, and swirl it over the surface of the pan. Add the garlic and stir-fry until it is light golden. Add the chicken and stir-fry until the pink color disappears. Add the broccoli and the mixture from Step 5. Bring to a boil, stirring constantly. Stir the tapioca starch mixture, add it to the wok, and stir until it thickens lightly.

8. Pour the topping over the warm noodles in the serving bowl and sprinkle with ground pepper. Serve with Vinegar Sauce for each diner to add as desired.

•••————————————————————————

Stir-Fried Transparent Noodles
PAD WUN SEN

The procedure for preparing this dish is similar to that of PAD THAI (page 102), but the result is quite different. This recipe uses very small noodles made from mung beans, which become transparent when soaked and have a firmer, chewier texture than rice noodles. The vegetables add a crisp texture, which contrasts nicely with the noodles. These noodles may be served as part of a main meal or used effectively alone as a luncheon dish or late supper.

SERVES 4 TO 6

¼ pound transparent noodles
Warm water

¼ pound Napa cabbage
¼ pound celery
¼ pound carrots
4 green onions
½ pound boneless pork chops or pork loin

¼ cup sesame oil

1 tablespoon (½ ounce) finely chopped garlic

3 tablespoons fish sauce
1 tablespoon granulated sugar

2 eggs
½ teaspoon vegetable oil

Ground black pepper

Lime Sauce (page 84)

1. Soak the noodles in warm water to cover for 20 minutes. Drain them thoroughly, cut them into pieces 3 inches long, and set them aside.

2. Slice the cabbage crosswise into pieces 2 inches long. Slice the celery diagonally into ¼-inch pieces. Slice the carrots diagonally into ¹⁄₁₆-inch pieces. Put all the vegetables in a bowl and set aside. Slice the green onions diagonally into pieces 2 inches long and put them aside in a separate bowl. Slice the pork across the grain into pieces ⅛ inch thick and 1 to 2 inches long. Set aside.

3. Heat a wok, add the sesame oil, and swirl it over the surface of the pan. Add the garlic and stir-fry until it is light golden. Add the pork and stir-fry until the pink color disappears completely. Add the cabbage, celery, and carrots and stir-fry until they are crisp-tender, 3 to 5 minutes.

4. Add the noodles and fish sauce. Stir-fry until the ingredients are mixed well, adding the sugar as you stir.

5. Using a wok scoop or stiff spatula, push the noodles away from one side of the wok. Pour ¼ teaspoon vegetable oil into the wok at that point, and break an egg onto the oiled spot. Repeat at another point with the other ¼ teaspoon vegetable oil and the remaining egg. Break the yolks of the eggs. Cover the eggs with the noodles and allow the eggs to become firm and almost dry before stirring them into the noodles. If the eggs or noodles begin to stick, a little more vegetable oil may be added; do not add more sesame oil.

6. Fold the noodles gently to distribute the eggs evenly. Add the green onions and fold the mixture quickly, over moderate heat, to distribute them. Cook until the onions are crisp-tender.

7. Transfer the noodles to a warm platter and serve immediately. Serve with Lime Sauce for each diner to add as desired.

•••

Stir-Fried Rice Noodles with Sauce
RAD NA MOO

These noodles have a rich, nutty flavor which is produced by the bean paste, and they are economical, easy to prepare, and filling. They can serve as a one-dish-meal when you are in a hurry or have unexpected last-minute guests. Vinegar Sauce is essential to enhance the flavor and to provide a hot and sour accent to the noodles, which are otherwise fairly bland. Small rice noodles the size of vermicelli may be substituted if you prefer.

SERVES 6 TO 8

1 pound dried rice noodles, ⅛ inch wide
Warm water

½ pound boneless pork chops or pork loin

3 tablespoons tapioca starch
½ cup water

1 pound broccoli

3 tablespoons vegetable oil
1 tablespoon soy sauce

2 tablespoons vegetable oil
1 teaspoon (2 cloves) finely chopped garlic

¼ cup + 2 tablespoons fish sauce
¼ cup brown bean paste

3 cups boiling water, or pork or chicken stock

⅛ teaspoon ground black pepper

Vinegar Sauce (page 83)

1. Soak the noodles for 20 minutes in enough warm water to cover them. Drain them briefly in a colander. They should still be wet when stir-fried, to help prevent them from sticking to one another or to the wok.

2. Slice the pork across the grain into strips ⅛ inch thick and 1 to 2 inches long. Set aside.

3. Dissolve the tapioca starch in ½ cup water and set aside.

4. Remove the florets from the broccoli and peel the stems. Slice the stems diagonally into pieces ¼ inch thick and 1 inch long. Put 1 cup water in a wok and bring it to a rapid boil. Add the broccoli and toss it in the boiling water about 2 minutes, until it is bright green and crisp-tender. Drain the broccoli in a colander and dry the wok thoroughly.

5. Heat the wok, add 3 tablespoons of the vegetable oil, and swirl it over the surface of the pan. Add the wet noodles and stir-fry briefly just to coat them with oil. Add the soy sauce and stir-fry to distribute it evenly. Scoop the noodles into a large covered serving bowl and keep them warm. Clean the wok and dry it thoroughly.

6. Heat the wok again, add 2 tablespoons oil, and swirl it over the surface of the pan. Add the garlic and stir-fry until it is light golden. Add the pork and stir-fry until the pink color disappears.

7. Add the broccoli, fish sauce, and bean paste. Mix all the ingredients thoroughly. Add the boiling water, bring the mixture to a boil rapidly, and reduce the heat to moderate. Stir the tapioca starch mixture, add it to the wok, and stir until the mixture thickens.

8. Pour the mixture over the noodles and sprinkle with ground pepper. Serve with Vinegar Sauce, for each diner to add as desired.

•••———————————————————————

Noodles with Coconut Milk, Pineapple, and Ginger
KANOM JEEN SAU NAM

This dish is not often made at home in Thailand, but rather is purchased from street vendors. It is served at room temperature, and the flavors provide an interesting sweet, tart, and sharp contrast with the semisoft, bland noodles. If you wish the sharp flavor of the ginger to be milder, soak the ginger for about 15 minutes in lightly salted room-temperature water after it has been sliced. You may also reduce the amount of dried shrimp if you find the quantity we list too strong. For the best effect, the noodles should be very thin, about the size of vermicelli.

SERVES 10 TO 12 (35 TO 40 PIECES)

½ pound ginger root
4 Serrano chilies
2 cups finely chopped fresh pineapple

½ pound dried shrimp

1 cup thick coconut milk

4 quarts water
1 pound small Japanese noodles

2 tablespoons (1 ounce) finely chopped garlic
¼ cup + 2 tablespoons fish sauce
¼ cup granulated sugar
¾ cup lime juice

1. Peel the ginger root and slice it lengthwise into very thin julienne strips. Remove the stems, but not the seeds, from the chilies and chop the chilies finely. Set these ingredients aside in separate bowls. Set aside the chopped pineapple.

2. Put the dried shrimp in a sieve and rinse them thoroughly under running hot water. Set them aside to drain. When they have drained completely, chop them finely.

3. Bring the coconut milk to a boil, remove it from the heat, and let it cool to room temperature.

4. Bring the 4 quarts water to a full boil, add the noodles, and cook them until tender, about 5 minutes. Plunge them into room-temperature water to stop the cooking, and drain them in a colander. Form the noodles into 35 to 40 small oval patties about 2 inches wide and 6 inches long. Put the patties on a double layer of paper towels to absorb the excess moisture. Let them stand until the surface is almost dry and the noodles have stuck together, about 10 to 15 minutes.

5. Put each of the ingredients, including the garlic, fish sauce, sugar, and lime juice, in separate serving bowls, and put the noodles on a serving platter. Allow each diner to select ingredients as desired to top the noodles. Traditionally, each diner would put a layer of pineapple on a noodle patty, then add a layer of dried shrimp, then a little garlic, and top it off with a layer of chilies. Over that, he or she would pour the individually desired amount of fish sauce, lime juice, sugar, and coconut milk.

Non-traditional variation in serving: Mix the fish sauce, sugar, lime juice, and garlic, and stir until the sugar is dissolved. Put the mixture in a serving pitcher. Put the coconut milk in a separate serving pitcher. Mix the solid ingredients and place them in a serving bowl. Allow each diner to put the desired amount of solid ingredients on his/her portions of noodles and pour the desired amount of fish sauce mixture and coconut milk over that.

• • •

Noodles with Coconut Milk
MEE GATI

SERVES 4 TO 6

½ pound rice stick noodles
Warm water

¾ pound raw shrimp
1 bunch green onions

1 package fresh tofu (16 ounces)

½ pound bean sprouts

¼ cup + 2 tablespoons white bean paste
½ cup granulated sugar
2 tablespoons fish sauce
3 tablespoons white vinegar

1 small tomato
¾ cup thick coconut milk

2 teaspoons vegetable oil
4 eggs

2 limes cut into wedges
Ground roasted chilies (page 60)
White vinegar

1. Soak the noodles in warm water for 20 minutes. They should be pliable and soft, but not so soft that they can be mashed easily with the fingers. Drain them in a colander while you prepare the remaining ingredients.

2. Place the fresh tofu on 4 layers of paper towel and cover it with 4 more layers. Put a plate on top and let stand for 15 minutes or more to press out the excess water. Cut the tofu into ¼-inch dice and set aside.

3. Peel and devein the shrimp, leaving the tails intact. Set aside. Slice the onions diagonally into 1-inch pieces and set aside.

4. Place the bean sprouts in a bowl of ice water and let them stand while you complete the rest of the preparations.

5. Remove any stones that may be in the bean paste and pound the beans to a smooth paste in a mortar. Mix the sugar, fish sauce, vinegar, and bean paste thoroughly in a small container and set aside.

6. Remove the stem portion of the tomato and slice the tomato vertically into pieces ⅛ inch thick. Cook the tomato slices in the coconut milk over medium heat until the slices are soft but still hold their shape. Add the mixture from Step 5 and cook over low heat for 15 minutes. Set the mixture aside.

7. Pour about ½ teaspoon of the vegetable oil into a small wok or large skillet and, using a paper towel, spread it evenly over the surface. Heat it over medium heat until a drop of water splashed on the surface sizzles and evaporates immediately. One at a time, break each egg into a small bowl and beat lightly with a fork until the white and yolk are thoroughly mixed but not frothy. Pour the beaten egg into the hot wok and swirl it around to form a thin sheet. Cook until it is completely set and dry, then remove it from wok and set aside. Repeat with the other eggs.

8. Slice the egg sheets into strips ⅛ inch wide and set them aside. Drain the bean sprouts in a colander.

9. Put half of the cooked mixture from Step 6 in a wok and bring to a boil quickly. Lower the heat to moderate, add the shrimp, and cook until they turn pink. Stirring constantly, add the noodles and stir to mix them in well. Add the rest of the tomato–coconut milk mixture and continue to stir gently while you add the tofu. Continue to stir gently while you add half the bean sprouts, half the green onions, and half the egg strips. Stir until all the ingredients are thoroughly mixed and hot. The green onions need not be cooked, just hot.

10. Place the mixture on a serving platter and garnish with the remaining egg strips and green onion. Serve immediately with wedges of lime, ground dried chilies, a bowl of white vinegar, and the remaining bean sprouts. Or, keep it warm while you prepare other dishes.

• • •

Rice Sticks with Ground Beef
RAD NA NUE SAB

This richly flavored and easily prepared dish can be completed in just a little more time than it takes to soak the noodles, and it is made from readily available ingredients. It serves well as a luncheon or as part of a main meal.

SERVES 4 TO 6

½ pound rice stick noodles
Warm water
2 ounces (½ cup sliced) yellow onions

3 tablespoons tapioca starch
¼ cup + 2 tablespoons water
2 teaspoons curry powder
2 tablespoons fish sauce
1 teaspoon black soy sauce
2 cups chicken stock or water

¼ cup + 1 tablespoon vegetable oil
2 teaspoons black soy sauce

¼ cup vegetable oil
1 teaspoon (2 cloves) finely chopped garlic
½ pound ground beef

Vinegar Sauce (page 83)
Ground roasted chilies (page 60)

1. Soak the noodles in warm water for 20 minutes and drain them thoroughly in a colander. Peel the yellow onion, remove the root portion, and slice the onion vertically into slices about ⅛ inch thick. Set the onions aside.

2. Mix the tapioca starch and ¼ cup + 2 tablespoons water and set aside. Mix the curry powder, fish sauce, 1 teaspoon black soy sauce, and stock or water. Set aside.

3. Heat a wok, add ¼ cup + 1 tablespoon oil, and swirl it over the surface of the pan. Add the noodles and remaining 2 teaspoons black soy sauce. Stir-fry until the noodles are hot and coated with soy sauce and oil, then scoop them out to a serving platter and keep them warm.

4. Heat a wok, add ¼ cup oil, and swirl it over the surface of the pan. Add the garlic and stir-fry until it is light golden. Add the ground beef and stir-fry until the pink color disappears completely. Add the onions and stir-fry until the onion is translucent.

5. Add the curry powder and fish sauce mixture from Step 2 and stir in thoroughly. Stir the tapioca starch mixture and add it to the wok. Toss and stir until the mixture thickens, then pour it over the noodles.

6. Serve immediately with Vinegar Sauce and ground roasted chilies, for each diner to add as desired.

7
Soups

IN THAILAND, soup is eaten anytime during the day, and it is difficult to imagine a traditional Thai meal without it. The Thai are frugal with food and little goes to waste. What better way to use relatively expensive meat products than in a soup, where a little meat will go a long way? Soups also provide a marvelous vehicle for incorporating "innards," such as fish maw, which otherwise might not be used. Rice should always be served with soup so that diners may add it to the soup or eat it separately in a small bowl, after flavoring it with some of the soup or sauce from one of the other dishes. In Thailand, soup is not a separate course and is served right along with everything else. Traditionally it is served in the soup server described in the section on equipment (pages 9–19), but a large covered bowl or tureen works just as well. In any case, it is served piping hot and each diner helps himself or herself.

Hot and Spicy Shrimp Soup
KUNG DOM YAM

As the name suggests, this soup is for those who love spicy food. In fact, it can be one of the spiciest, hottest recipes in this book, but it is easy to modify the hot and spicy flavors to your own taste. It is rich with the taste of fresh shrimp, lemon grass, coriander, and chilies, and is one of the most popular soups in Thailand and in Thai restaurants in America. You may reduce the spiciness by reducing the amount of lemon grass, coriander, Roasted Red Curry, or chilies. Medium or large uncooked shrimp give the best flavor, and if you must use precooked frozen shrimp, be sure to use chicken broth as the soup base. We give two variations to indicate the flexibility of ingredients. You may wish to develop variations of your own to suit your taste and the availability of ingredients. The flavor of the chilies becomes stronger as the soup stands, so allow for that in the number of chilies you use and the length of time you allow the soup to stand before serving.

SERVES 6 TO 8

1½ pounds raw shrimp
1 pound canned straw mushrooms or fresh or
*   canned button mushrooms*

6 stalks lemon grass, bottom 6 inches only
2 quarts water

10 Serrano chilies

¾ cup fish sauce
¼ cup Roasted Red Curry (page 76)

½ cup lime juice
1 cup coriander sprigs

1. Shell and devein the shrimp, leaving the tails intact. Wash the mushrooms and slice them in half lengthwise. Add them to the shrimp and set aside.

2. Slice the lemon grass in half lengthwise. Crush the

pieces with the side of a cleaver or wide-bladed knife and place them in a saucepan with the 2 quarts water.

3. Remove the stems, but not the seeds, from the chilies. Crush the chilies with the side of a cleaver or wide-bladed knife until they split in several places, and set aside.

4. Boil the water and lemon grass, covered, for 5 minutes. Add the shrimp, mushrooms, fish sauce, and Roasted Red Curry. Cover the pot, bring to a boil rapidly, and cook only until the shrimp turn pink. Do not overcook, or shrimp will become tough. If you have used precooked frozen shrimp, heat the mixture only until the shrimp are warm, about 1 minute or less, depending on the size of the shrimp.

5. Remove the soup from the heat, and add the lime juice and chilies. Stir to mix the ingredients thoroughly, put the soup in a serving container, and garnish the top with coriander sprigs.

6. Serve with rice for each diner to add as desired.

Variation 1: Omit the Roasted Red Curry.

Variation 2: Use chicken stock instead of water. This can be particularly effective if it is necessary to substitute precooked frozen shrimp for fresh shrimp.

••• ────────────────────────────

Coconut Chicken Soup
GAI DOM KAH

This is a smooth, creamy soup rich with the taste of coconut and chicken, made light with a touch of lime. It has only a hint of chilies and is excellent for people who are not yet accustomed to the hot chili flavor found in much of Thai food. It also serves as a marvelous accompaniment to some of the hotter dishes, in order to refresh the palate. If you prefer a hotter soup, increase the number of chilies, but be sure they do not overpower the delicate combination of chicken and coconut. Good coconut milk is essential. If you cannot find fresh coconuts in your local market, frozen coconut milk may be substituted. Canned coconut milk is less desirable unless you find a good brand. (We have found Chef's Choice to be very good.)

SERVES 4 TO 6

1 pound white or dark chicken with bones left in

3 cups thick coconut milk
5 pieces kah
3 Kaffir lime leaves

2 Serrano chilies
½ cup coriander sprigs

2 tablespoons fish sauce
2 tablespoons lime juice

1. Slice or chop the chicken into ¾-inch pieces or thin strips. Traditionally, the bones are left in for extra flavor, but they may be removed if you prefer.

2. Put the chicken, coconut milk, *kah,* and Kaffir lime leaves in a saucepan. Cover the pan and bring the mixture to a boil slowly. Reduce the heat and simmer for 15 minutes, or until the chicken is done.

3. Remove the stems, but not the seeds, from the chilies and crush the chilies with the side of a cleaver or large knife until they split open in several places. Chop the coriander sprigs coarsely.

4. Add the fish sauce, lime juice, coriander, and chilies to the soup, remove it from the heat, and stir to mix the ingredients thoroughly. Taste the soup for seasoning and add more lime juice if necessary. You should add enough to reduce the sweetness of the coconut, but not enough to produce a strong taste of lime.

5. Serve with rice, for each diner to add as desired.

••• ─────────────────────────────────────

Beef Noodle Soup
GUAYTIO NUE SOD

This is a rich, hearty soup, perfect for a fall or winter evening, and it can be served as a meal in itself or with other foods. It demands good beef, and no other meat should be substituted. To be at its best, it should be made with fresh rice noodles, but rather than forego it altogether you may substitute any kind of dried rice noodles that have been soaked in hot water about 30 minutes, until they are soft and pliable. In some locales "rice chips," triangular pieces of dried rice noodles about 2 to 3 inches on a side, are available. These are a good substitute if soaked as directed in Step 1.

SERVES 4 TO 6

1 pound fresh rice noodles or ½ pound dried noodles
1 cup coriander sprigs
1 bunch green onions, white and green parts
¼ cup finely chopped coriander root
¾ pound tender beef, e.g., sirloin

5 cups thin beef stock (see Note following recipe)
1 piece cinnamon stick about 2 inches long
2 whole star anise
½ teaspoon (1 clove) crushed garlic
3 slices kah.
1 tablespoon black soy sauce

3 tablespoons fish sauce
1 teaspoon granulated sugar

½ pound bean sprouts
2 tablespoons crisp-fried garlic, with or without
   its oil as desired (page 65)

¼ teaspoon ground black pepper

Ground Chili Sauce (page 87)

1. If you are using dried noodles, soak them about 30 minutes in hot water before cooking them. Or, preferably, slice fresh noodles into strips about ¾ inch wide and 5 to 6 inches long. Bring 2 cups water to a rapid boil in a wok, add the noodles and toss them about 1 minute, until they are heated through. Drain them in a colander and set aside in a covered bowl to keep them warm and moist. Chop the coriander sprigs coarsely and set them aside. Slice the green onion diagonally into pieces 1 inch long and set aside. Crush the chopped coriander root firmly with the side of a cleaver or wide-bladed knife and set aside. Slice the beef across the grain into strips 1 to 2 inches long and not more than ⅛ inch thick and set aside.

2. Put the beef stock, cinnamon, anise, crushed garlic, coriander root, *kah,* and black soy sauce in a 2-quart saucepan. Cover the saucepan and bring the mixture to a boil.

3. Add the beef, fish sauce, and sugar to the saucepan. Cook over moderate heat for 5 minutes, or until the beef is done. Remove the soup from the heat and keep it hot until time to serve. Add the green onions just before serving.

4. Divide the noodles evenly in individual soup bowls and top them with bean sprouts. Pour the soup over them. Top each serving with coriander leaves and crisp fried garlic, including the oil if desired. Sprinkle with ground pepper. Or, serve the noodle-bean sprout mixture, soup, coriander sprigs, and fried garlic in separate bowls for each diner to mix as desired.

5. Serve with Ground Chili Sauce.

Note: The beef stock used in this soup should be light and thin to begin with, like the stock we describe on page 67. Homemade stock is best, but if you use canned stock dilute it with 3 parts stock to 2 parts water. When you cook the beef in it the stock will become strongly flavored.

••• ─────────────────────────────

Fish Maw Soup
GRA PAW BLA

This is a rich, thick, hearty soup. Because tapioca starch is added it is thicker than most Thai soups, and if the diners mix rice with it the soup resembles a thick stew. Before adding it to the soup, the fish maw will have little flavor of its own. But, when cooked with the chicken, it imparts a subtle fish flavor that complements the other ingredients and adds an interesting chewy texture. The fish maw may be omitted, in which case you will have a good, rich chicken soup.

2-ounce package fish maw
Room-temperature water

1 pound chicken breasts, with the bones left in
6 cups water

¼ cup + 1 tablespoon tapioca starch
¼ cup + 2 tablespoons water
10 ounces (½ large can) bamboo shoots, cut in julienne strips

3 tablespoons fish sauce
2 teaspoons black soy sauce

1 cup coriander sprigs
⅛ teaspoon ground white pepper

Ground Chili Sauce (page 87)

1. Soak the fish maw for 15 minutes in enough water to cover it.

2. Place the chicken breasts and 6 cups water in a covered saucepan and boil gently for 20 minutes. Remove the chicken and allow it to cool enough to handle easily. Measure the stock and add enough water to bring it back to 6 cups.

3. Drain the fish maw, discard the soaking liquid, and cut the maw into 1-inch squares. Set them aside.

4. Mix the tapioca starch and water in a small bowl and set aside. Put the bamboo shoots in a colander and rinse them briefly under hot running water to remove the canning liquid. Set them aside.

5. Remove the skin and bones from the chicken and discard. Tear the chicken into thin shreds with your fingers.

6. Bring the chicken stock from Step 2 to a boil, add the bamboo shoots, cover the saucepan, and boil the mixture gently for 5 minutes.

7. Add the fish maw, chicken, fish sauce, and soy sauce. Bring the mixture to a gentle boil. Stir the tapioca starch mixture well, add it to the soup, and stir until it thickens.

8. Remove the soup from the heat and place it in a tureen or serving bowl. Garnish the top with coriander sprigs and sprinkle the pepper over them.

9. Serve with Ground Chili Sauce and rice for each diner to add as desired.

••• ━━━━━━━━━━━━━━━━━━━━━━━━━━━━━━

Stuffed Tofu Soup
GANG JUD TOHOO

SERVES 8 TO 10

1¼ cup finely chopped coriander root
1 tablespoon (½ ounce) finely chopped garlic

1 pound ground pork
¼ teaspoon ground black pepper
1 tablespoon + 1 teaspoon tapioca starch
2 tablespoons fish sauce

1 bunch green onions, white parts only
1 cup coriander sprigs

2 16-ounce packages firm fresh tofu

2 quarts chicken or pork stock (page 67)
15 (½ pound) Fish or Shrimp Balls (page 236)
¼ cup + 3 tablespoons fish sauce

2 tablespoons crisp-fried garlic with its oil (page 65)
⅛ teaspoon ground white pepper

Lime Sauce (page 84)

1. Pound or grind the coriander root and garlic to a coarse paste in a mortar or blender. If you are using a blender, you may need to add the fish sauce to aid in grinding. Place the paste in a mixing bowl with the pork, pepper, tapioca starch, and fish sauce. Stir to mix the ingredients thoroughly. If you are beginning with unground pork, you may put all these ingredients in a food processor and process them until the pork is finely chopped, being careful not to puree it.

2. Slice the green onions diagonally into 1-inch pieces. Chop the coriander sprigs coarsely, and set them aside in a bowl with the green onion.

3. Slice the tofu into 32 pieces of equal size, square or triangular according to your preference. Insert a knife through the end of each piece and cut a pocket the full width of the tofu, going almost to the other end. Stuff the tofu with up to 1 teaspoon of the pork mixture from Step 1 and press the top down lightly to compress the mixture without forcing it out the open end or sides. The stuffed tofu will look something like a well-filled small sandwich.

4. Put the stuffed tofu in a steamer and steam it for 5 minutes, or until the stuffing is completely cooked.

5. Pour the stock into a large pot and add the shrimp or fish balls, stuffed tofu, and fish sauce. Bring the liquid to a slow boil and cook for 5 minutes, until the stuffed tofu and the shrimp balls are heated through. Remember, they are already cooked.

6. Add the coriander sprigs and green onion and pour the soup into a tureen or serving bowl. Sprinkle the top with crisp-fried garlic, and its oil, and the ground white pepper.

7. Serve with Lime Sauce and rice.

••• ─────────────────────────────

Chicken Soup with Pickled Limes
GAI TOON

Be sure to leave preserved limes whole. If sliced, they will impart a bitter taste to the soup.

Serves 6 to 8

8 to 10 dried Oriental mushrooms
Warm water

2 pounds chicken breasts
4 cups water
1 pickled lime, left whole
1½ teaspoons black soy sauce
¼ cup + 2 teaspoons light soy sauce

2 pounds winter melon, cut into 1-inch squares

1 teaspoon granulated sugar
2 cups water

1. Soak the mushrooms in warm water for 15 minutes.

Remove the stems. Chop the chicken, bones and all, into pieces about 1½ to 2 inches square, or remove the bones, use them to make stock for another purpose, and slice the meat into 1½- to 2-inch squares. Traditionally, the bones are left in for additional flavor. Place the water and chicken in a large saucepan and bring the liquid to a boil rapidly. Reduce the heat to a simmer.

2. Add the soaked mushrooms, pickled lime, and both types of soy sauce. Cover the pan and simmer for 10 minutes.

3. Add the winter melon and simmer, covered, for 10 minutes.

4. Add the sugar and the 2 cups water. Bring the mixture to a boil over high heat and stir until the sugar is dissolved. Remove from heat immediately.

5. Place the soup in a serving container and serve it with rice.

✳✳✳ ─────────────────────────────

Hot-and-Spicy Chicken Soup
DOM YOM GAI

This recipe produces a moderately spicy and hot soup with a rich chicken flavor. You may make it milder by reducing the number of chilies or hotter by increasing the number. It is best if the chicken is chopped into small pieces with the bone left in, for added flavor. It is inexpensive, quick to prepare, and delicious.

SERVES 4 TO 6

3 stalks lemon grass, bottom 6 inches only
4 cups water or chicken broth
3 Kaffir lime leaves

1 pound chicken breasts

¼ cup + 2 tablespoons fish sauce

¼ cup + 2 tablespoons lime juice

3 Serrano chilies

½ cup coriander sprigs

1. Slice the lemon grass in half lengthwise. Crush the slices with the side of a knife or cleaver, and place them in a saucepan with the water or chicken broth and Kaffir lime leaves.

2. Chop the chicken into ¾ inch long pieces, leaving the bone in or removing it according to your preference. Traditionally, the bones are left in for flavor. Set the chicken aside.

3. Bring the water with the lemon grass and Kaffir lime leaves to a gentle boil and boil for 5 minutes, covered. Add the chicken and fish sauce and boil gently until the chicken is done, about 15 minutes.

4. Remove the soup from the heat and add the lime juice.

5. Remove the stems, but not the seeds, from the chilies. Crush the chilies with the side of a knife or cleaver until they split in several places. Add them to the soup.

6. Place the soup in a tureen or serving bowl and garnish with coriander sprigs.

7. Serve with rice.

✳✳✳ ━━━━━━━━━━━━━━━━━━━━━━━━━━━━━━━━

Hot-and-Sour Seafood Soup
PO TAK

This soup is rich, spicy, and moderately hot. It contains enough solids to serve as a main course when accompanied by rice and a vegetable dish of your choice. In some locales "artificial crab legs" are available and may be substituted for the crab claws. They do not have shells, so ignore the instruction to crack the shells.

½ pound firm fish fillets
¼ pound raw shrimp
4 squid (see page 215 for cleaning instructions)
½ pound (about 4) small or medium crab claws
20 shelled mussels, shucked clams, or bay scallops

6 cups water
12 pieces kah
10 Kaffir lime leaves

2 tablespoons Roasted Red Curry (page 76)
¼ cup + 2 tablespoons fish sauce

¼ cup + 2 tablespoons lime juice
1 teaspoon ground roasted chilies (page 60)

1 cup coriander sprigs

1. Slice the fish fillets into pieces about 1 inch square. Peel and devein the shrimp, leaving the tails intact. Slice the squid into pieces about 1 inch square. Crack the crab claws by hitting them with a hammer or the side of a cleaver, but do not remove the meat from the shells. Place all the seafood in one bowl and set aside.

2. Put the water, *kah,* and Kaffir lime leaves in a large pot and bring to a boil rapidly. Reduce the heat to moderate and boil gently for 5 minutes.

3. Add the seafood, Roasted Red Curry, and fish sauce to the liquid in the pot. Bring to a gentle boil again and cook until the shrimp turn pink and the fish is firm and opaque, about 3 to 4 minutes. Remove from the heat.

4. Add the lime juice and ground chilies and mix them in well. Place the soup in a tureen or serving bowl and garnish the top with coriander sprigs.

5. Serve with rice.

Spicy Sweet-and-Sour Noodle Soup
YEN TA FOAU

This soup has a rich, smooth flavor and the thin broth is packed full of vegetables, meat, and noodles. It has so many solid ingredients that it is almost not a soup, and could serve well as a complete luncheon or late supper dish.

SERVES 6 TO 8

1 pound dried narrow (⅛ inch) rice noodles or rice stick noodles
   or 1½ pounds fresh rice noodles
Hot water

¼ pound boneless pork chops or pork loin
6 cups water
½ pound squid (see page 215 for cleaning instructions)
½ pound bok choy

1½ tablespoons fish sauce
½ pound (about 15) Fish or Shrimp Balls (page 236)
1 tablespoon granulated sugar
1 teaspoon tomato paste

1 tablespoon crisp-fried garlic and its oil (page 65)

Vinegar Sauce (page 83)

1. Soak the dried noodles in hot water for 30 minutes, or the fresh noodles for 5 minutes. If you are using dried noodles, they should be soft—try to time this step to be completed at the time the soup is done. If not, drain the noodles and keep them warm and moist until time to serve.

2. Boil the pork in the water until it is done, about 30 minutes. Remove the pork from the broth and set the broth aside. When the pork is cool enough to handle, slice it across the grain into strips ⅛ inch thick and 1 to 2 inches long. Slice the squid into pieces about 1 inch square and add them to the pork. Slice the bok choy diagonally into pieces about 1 inch long and add them to the pork and squid.

3. Bring the broth from Step 2 to a boil and add the pork, squid, bok choy, fish sauce, fish or shrimp balls, sugar, and tomato paste. Bring the mixture to a rapid boil and cook for 2 minutes. Remove it from the heat and add the crisp-fried garlic and oil.

4. Place the noodles in a tureen or serving bowl and pour the soup over them. Serve with Vinegar Sauce.

Beef Tendon Soup
ENN TOON

This is a very thin, richly flavored soup that is spicy but not hot. It is frequently served in Thailand to people who have been drinking a lot of alcohol because the flavor is intense enough to be experienced with taste buds that have been dulled with liquor. Because it is thin and has so few solid ingredients, the soup can be drunk from a cup just as easily as eaten with a spoon. It has a rich, beefy flavor in spite of the small amount of meat.

SERVES 8 TO 10

1 pound beef tendons
10 cups water
2 pieces kah
¼ stick cinnamon
1 star anise
1 tablespoon black soy sauce

3 cups water

¼ cup fish sauce
2 teaspoons granulated sugar

2 green onions, white and green parts
½ cup coriander sprigs

¼ pound bean sprouts
1 teaspoon crisp-fried garlic and its oil (page 65)
¼ teaspoon ground black pepper

Ground Chili Sauce (page 87)

1. Put the tendons, water, *kah,* cinnamon, star anise, and soy sauce in a large pot and bring to a boil rapidly. Reduce the heat, cover the pot, and boil slowly over low heat for 1 hour.

2. Remove the tendons from the liquid. When they are cool enough to handle, slice them crosswise into pieces about ½ inch long. Return them to the pot and add 3 cups water. Simmer, covered, for another hour, or until the tendons are tender.

3. Remove the pot from the heat, add the fish sauce and sugar, and stir until the sugar is dissolved. Cover the pot to keep the soup warm.

4. Slice the green onions crosswise into pieces about 1 inch long and set aside. Chop the coriander sprigs coarsely and set aside.

5. Divide the bean sprouts evenly into 6 soup bowls. Pour the hot soup over them and garnish with green onions and coriander sprigs. Sprinkle crisp-fried garlic and its oil, plus black pepper, over the top. Or, serve the soup, bean sprouts, onions, coriander, and garlic and oil separately for each diner to select according to taste.

6. Serve with Ground Chili Sauce and rice or noodles of any kind.

• • •

Won Ton Soup
GEOW NAM MOO

Won Ton Soup is an all-time favorite soup usually associated with Chinese cuisine. This authentic Thai version is made unique by the addition of fish sauce, two forms of garlic, and coriander. We think you'll be pleased at the difference between this version and the blander Chinese version.

¼ *pound boneless pork chops or pork loin*

¼ *pound ground pork*
1 *teaspoon fish sauce*
1 *tablespoon finely chopped green onions*
½ *teaspoon finely chopped garlic*
½ *teaspoon finely chopped coriander root*
⅛ *teaspoon ground white pepper*
24 *won ton wrappers*

2 *quarts water*

2 *stalks bok choy*

6 *cups chicken broth*
¼ *cup fish sauce*
1 *green onion, finely chopped*
1 *teaspoon crisp-fried garlic without its oil (page 65)*
½ *cup coriander sprigs*
⅛ *teaspoon ground white pepper*

1. Barbecue or broil the pork until it is done, and allow it to cool to room temperature. When it is cool enough to handle, slice it across the grain into strips about ⅛ inch thick and 1 to 2 inches long. Set aside.

2. Mix the ground pork, fish sauce, green onions, garlic, coriander root and ground pepper thoroughly. Place 1 to 1½ teaspoons of the filling in the center of a won ton and fold the skin over to form a triangle. Moisten the inside edges of the wrapper and press them together lightly to seal them. Repeat with the other wrappers, setting them aside under a lightly dampened towel to keep them from drying out.

3. Bring the water to a rapid boil in a large pot and add the won tons. Reduce the heat and boil the won tons gently until they are done, about 5 minutes. Drain them in a colander, discard the water, and cover the won tons with wax paper to keep them soft and moist.

4. Slice the bok choy diagonally into pieces about ¾ inch thick. Blanch them about 2 minutes in enough boiling water to cover. Drain and rinse the bok choy immediately with cool water to stop the cooking.

5. Bring the chicken broth to a rapid boil, stir in the fish sauce, then remove the mixture from the heat. Divide the won tons, green onions, bok choy, and sliced pork equally into individual soup bowls. Pour the hot broth over these ingredients, and sprinkle with crisp-fried garlic, coriander sprigs, and ground pepper.

●●●━━━━━━━━━━━━━━━━━━━━━━━━━━━━━━

Tofu Soup
GANG JUAD TOHOO

SERVES 4

½ pound firm fresh tofu
4 cups water
2 ounces (about 1 stalk) celery
2 ounces (about 2 cups sliced) Chinese or Napa cabbage

4 green onions, white and green parts
3 tablespoons fish sauce
1 teaspoon crisp-fried garlic and its oil (page 65)

½ cup coarsely chopped coriander sprigs
⅛ teaspoon ground white pepper

Lime Sauce (page 84)

1. Cut the tofu into ¾-inch cubes and place them in a large saucepan with the water. Slice the celery diagonally into pieces about ⅛ inch thick and 1 inch long. Slice the cabbage into pieces about ¼ inch wide and 1 inch long. Add the vegetables to the saucepan. Bring the mixture to a gentle boil, and cook until the celery is crisp-tender, about 3 minutes. Meanwhile, slice the green onions diagonally into pieces about ⅛ inch thick and set aside.

2. Add the green onions, fish sauce, and crisp-fried garlic and its oil to the saucepan. Remove the soup from the heat immediately and pour into a tureen or serving bowl. Garnish with the coriander sprigs and sprinkle the ground pepper on top.

3. Serve with Lime Sauce and rice.

8
Salads

SALADS PLAY A DIFFERENT ROLE in Thai cuisine than in most Western diets. Rather than being seen as a separate course they are usually served as part of the main course, and used to refresh the palate during dining instead of before or after. Because of this, they often contain meat. In fact, several of them may be considered meals in themselves, particularly for a luncheon, a late supper, or a summer patio meal.

• • •

Thai Salad
YUM YAI

SERVES 6 TO 8

¼ pound raw shrimp
¾ pound boneless pork chop or pork loin
Boiling water

3 eggs

2 heads romaine or iceberg lettuce
1 medium cucumber
2 medium tomatoes

¾ cup Thai Salad Dressing (page 93)

1. Peel and devein the shrimp, leaving the tails intact. Drop them into rapidly boiling water and cook until they turn pink. Remove them from the water, and set them aside to cool to room temperature. Drop the pork into boiling water and cook until it is done, about 15 to 20 minutes. When it is cool enough to handle, slice the pork into strips ⅛ inch thick and 1 to 2 inches long.

2. Hard-cook the eggs in simmering water. Cool them, peel them, and slice them crosswise into slices ¼ inch thick.

3. Slice the lettuce into strips 1 inch wide. Peel the cucumber and slice it diagonally into thin pieces. Remove the stem portion from the tomatoes and slice the tomatoes vertically into pieces ¼ inch thick.

4. Place the lettuce in a shallow bowl or on a platter. Arrange the shrimp, pork, eggs, cucumber, and tomatoes decoratively on top of the lettuce. Pour the dressing over the salad.

Ahead-of-time note: Complete the salad, except for adding the salad dressing, several hours in advance. Cover it with plastic wrap, and keep it refrigerated until serving time. Add the salad dressing just before serving.

• • • ──────────────────────────────

Green Salad
SALAD KAK

SERVES 4 TO 6

2 eggs

1 head romaine lettuce
½ medium cucumber
¼ pound bean sprouts
1 or 2 medium tomatoes

1 medium potato or 1 small package unsalted potato chips
Vegetable oil for deep-frying

*Peanut Salad Dressing (page 90) to taste**

* If the salad dressing has been stored in the refrigerator, allow it to come to room temperature and dilute it with a little warm water if it has become too thick to pour easily.

1. Hard-cook the eggs in simmering water.

2. Wash the lettuce and slice it crosswise into pieces 1 inch long. Peel the cucumber and slice it crosswise into pieces about ⅛ inch thick. Peel the eggs and slice them crosswise into pieces about ¼ inch thick. Remove the stem portion from the tomatoes and slice the tomatoes vertically into small wedges or thin strips.

3. (If you are using commercial potato chips, omit this step.) Slice the potato crosswise into paper-thin strips without peeling them. Heat about 1 inch oil to 375° in a wok or skillet and deep-fry the potato until the pieces are crisp and light golden. Drain them thoroughly on paper towels, but do not salt them.

4. Place the lettuce in a serving bowl and arrange the other ingredients in a decorative pattern over it, with the potato chips on top.

Ahead-of-time note: May be prepared ahead to this point except for adding the potato chips. Cover the salad with plastic wrap and store in the refrigerator until ready to serve. Just before serving, add the potato chips and the dressing.

5. Just before serving, pour peanut salad dressing over the salad.

✳✳✳ ───────────────────────────────

Pickled Vegetables
PAK DONG

SERVES 4 TO 6

¼ cup boiling water
¼ cup white vinegar
¼ cup granulated sugar
½ teaspoon salt

1 cup coarsely chopped cauliflower florets or stems,
   or a combination
1 cup shredded cabbage
1 cup shredded carrot
2 Serrano chilies, stemmed but not seeded,
   and sliced thinly lengthwise

1. Combine the water, vinegar, sugar, and salt. Stir until the sugar is dissolved, and let the mixture cool to room temperature.

2. Add the vegetables to the liquid and let them marinate, covered, for 1 day at room temperature or 2 to 3 days in the refrigerator.

•••———————————————————————————————

Transparent Noodle Salad
YUM WUN SEN

SERVES 4 TO 6

¼ pound transparent noodles
Warm water

2 ounces (2 cups sliced) Napa cabbage
1 medium carrot
1 stalk celery
2 green onions, white and green parts
2 Serrano chilies or 1 teaspoon ground roasted chilies (page 60)

2 tablespoons vegetable oil
1 teaspoon (2 cloves) finely chopped garlic
¼ pound ground pork or ground chicken

3 tablespoons fish sauce
3 tablespoons lime juice

Green lettuce leaves
½ cup coriander sprigs

1. Soak the noodles for twenty minutes in warm water to cover. Drain them well, cut them into 2-inch lengths, and set them aside in a colander to continue draining.

2. Slice the cabbage into paper-thin shreds. Shred the carrot finely. Slice the celery and green onions diagonally into thin strips. If using Serrano chilies, slice the chilies into thin lengthwise strips. Set the vegetables aside in one bowl, and mix in the chilies.

3. Heat a wok, add the oil, and swirl it over the surface of the pan. Add the garlic and stir-fry until it is light golden. Add the pork or chicken and stir-fry until the pink color disappears completely. Add the noodles and toss them gently over moderate heat until all the ingredients are mixed well.

4. Scoop the meat and noodles into a mixing bowl and add the raw vegetables, fish sauce, and lime juice. Mix thoroughly and allow the salad to cool to room temperature.

5. Put a single layer of lettuce leaves on a serving platter and arrange the salad over them. Garnish the salad with coriander sprigs.

Variation: When the pink color has disappeared from the pork or chicken, add ¼ pound peeled, deveined raw shrimp with the tails intact. Cook until they have turned pink.

✳✳✳ ——————————————————————

Beef Salad
YUM NUE

SERVES 6 TO 8

¼ cup finely chopped coriander root
2 tablespoons (1 ounce) finely chopped garlic
¼ teaspoon ground black pepper
1½ teaspoons salt
1 pound flank steak

4 Serrano chilies
1 medium (½ pound) cucumber
1 cup (¼ pound) red onion
1 head romaine or iceberg lettuce

¼ cup + 2 tablespoons lime juice
1 tablespoon fish sauce
2 teaspoons granulated sugar

1 bunch green onions, white and green parts
1 cup coriander sprigs

1. Pound or grind the coriander root, garlic, pepper, and salt to a coarse paste in a mortar or blender. If using a blender, add just enough water to aid in grinding. Spread the paste evenly over the beef and marinate the beef for 1 hour at room temperature or, preferably, cover it and refrigerate it overnight.

2. Grill or broil the beef to the doneness you prefer. Slice it across the grain into strips ⅛ inch thick and 1 to 2 inches long. Set it aside.

3. Remove the stems, but not the seeds, from the chilies, and chop the chilies finely. Peel the cucumber and slice it diagonally into pieces ⅛ inch thick. Peel the red onion, remove the root portion, and slice the onion vertically into paper-thin slices. Slice the lettuce into pieces about 1 inch wide.

4. Mix the lime juice, fish sauce, and sugar in a small bowl. Stir until the sugar is dissolved.

Ahead-of-time note: The ingredients may be prepared to this point several hours ahead of time and stored, covered, in the refrigerator.

5. Place the lettuce on a serving platter. Arrange the other ingredients decoratively over the lettuce. Pour the liquid from Step 4 over the salad.

6. Slice the green onions diagonally into pieces about ⅛ inch thick, and chop the coriander sprigs coarsely. Garnish the salad with them.

7. Serve with rice.

●●●————————————————————————

Green Papaya Salad
SOM TAM

This salad has a crisp texture and a tart flavor accented by the salty shrimp. In reading the recipe, you may think it calls for too much dried shrimp, but that amount is necessary to produce the traditional flavor. You may, of course, reduce the dried shrimp, but we suggest you try it with the full amount first. Traditionally, this salad is made with green (unripe) papayas, but because these are often difficult to get in the United States, you may substitute carrots or cabbage with no loss in the quality of the dish. If green papayas are available, please try them.

SERVES 4 TO 6

½ pound dried shrimp

2 pounds green papayas
¼ pound green beans
1 tomato

¼ cup ground roasted unsalted peanuts (page 66)

½ cup Lime Salad Dressing (page 90)
Green lettuce leaves

1. Place the dried shrimp in a sieve and rinse them thoroughly under hot running water. Set them aside in the sieve to drain.

2. Peel and seed the papayas and shred them into long julienne strips. Slice the green beans lengthwise into thin strips. Slice the tomato vertically into very thin slices. Place these ingredients in a mortar or sturdy bowl and pound them with a pestle or large wooden spoon to soften them so they will absorb the flavor of the dressing more easily.

3. Grind the dried shrimp to a powder in a blender or food processor and set aside. If you use a blender, it will be necessary to grind them in two or more batches.

Ahead-of-time note: The salad may be prepared up to this point several hours before serving. Store the vegetables in a covered container in the refrigerator. Add the shrimp, peanuts, and dressing when you are ready to serve the salad.

4. When you are ready to serve, add the shrimp and peanuts to the salad and toss with Lime Salad Dressing.

5. Put a single layer of lettuce leaves on a serving platter and arrange the salad on top of them.

Ground Pork Salad
NAM SOD

SERVES 4 TO 6

4 cups water
½ pound cooked pork skins

1 pound ground pork

5 Serrano chilies
¼ pound red onion
3 ounces ginger root

2 teaspoons salt
½ cup lime juice
½ cup ground roasted unsalted peanuts (page 66)

Green lettuce or Napa cabbage
Assorted raw vegetables (broccoli, green beans,
*   eggplant, zucchini, etc.), cut into serving size pieces*

1. Bring the water to a rapid boil in a saucepan. Add the pork skins and remove the pan from the heat. Let the pork skins stand in the water for 3 minutes, then drain in a colander.

2. Heat a wok and add the ground pork without oil. Stir-fry until the pink color disappears completely. Remove the pork from the wok and set it aside to cool to room temperature.

3. Remove the stems, but not the seeds, from the chilies and chop the chilies finely. Place them in a mixing bowl. Peel the onion, removing the root portion, and slice it vertically into paper-thin slices. Place the slices in the bowl with the chilies. Peel the ginger and slice it lengthwise into very thin julienne strips. Add the strips to the bowl with the onion and chilies.

Ahead-of-time note: The ingredients may be prepared to this point several hours in advance. Cover and store them in the refrigerator until ready to serve. Bring to room temperature before serving. Add the salt, lime juice, and peanuts just before serving.

4. Add the salt, lime juice, and peanuts to the bowl and toss lightly to mix the ingredients thoroughly.

5. Place a single layer of lettuce or cabbage leaves on a serving platter and arrange the salad on top of them.

6. Serve with assorted raw vegetables and rice.

✳✳✳ ────────────────────────────────

Ground Beef Salad
LAB NUE

SERVES 4 TO 6

1 pound lean ground beef

¼ cup fish sauce
½ cup lime juice
1 tablespoon ground kah powder (page 47)
2 tablespoons ground toasted rice (page 66)
1 bunch green onions, white and green parts

1 teaspoon ground roasted chilies (page 60)

½ cup mint leaves

Romaine lettuce or Napa cabbage leaves
Assorted raw vegetables (broccoli, green beans,
   eggplant, zucchini, etc.), cut into serving size pieces

1. Heat a wok and add the ground beef without oil. Stir-fry until the beef is done to your taste.

2. Mix the fish sauce and lime juice in a small bowl and set aside. Mix the ground *kah* powder and ground rice and set aside. Slice the green onions diagonally into pieces about ⅛ inch thick.

Ahead-of-time note: The separate ingredients may be prepared to this point several hours in advance. Refrigerate the beef if it is prepared more than 2 hours in advance. Bring the ingredients to room temperature before serving.

3. Mix all the ingredients except the lettuce or cabbage leaves and assorted vegetables, tossing lightly.

4. Place a single layer of lettuce or cabbage leaves on a serving platter and arrange the salad on top of them.

5. Serve with assorted vegetables and rice.

9
Appetizers and Snacks

THE PEOPLE OF THAILAND love to eat throughout the day, and a large repertoire of snacks and appetizers has been developed to accommodate this custom. The street vendors are legendary, and advertise their products with loud, lyrical cries. They are found everywhere; some follow crowds to special events, while others have daily routes through residential neighborhoods, arriving pretty much on schedule every day from morning to night. Imagine for a moment how pleasant it would be to have these snacks available all day long no matter where you are, at sports events, parades, the theater, etc. Then remember your most recent lukewarm, tasteless hot dog smothered in bland mustard. Because appetizers and snacks play such a large role in everyday Thai life we have provided a large assortment of them in this separate chapter. They may also be served as main dishes if you prefer.

Galloping Horses
MA HOA

This is an unusual tart–sweet preparation with a hint of garlic and coriander. It is especially attractive if coriander sprigs and red chilies are used as garnishes to provide red and green contrasts to the yellow pineapple and beige pork mixture. For those who may not like pineapple, or are unable to find it fresh, we have provided two variations. We do not recommend using canned pineapple, because it lacks the necessary tang and crisp, fresh flavor.

SERVES 8 TO 10

2 tablespoons (1 ounce) finely chopped garlic
¼ cup finely chopped coriander root
3 tablespoons vegetable oil

1 pound ground pork

¼ cup fish sauce
½ cup granulated sugar
1¼ cups ground roasted unsalted peanuts (page 66)
⅛ teaspoon ground white pepper

1 fresh pineapple

Green lettuce leaves
Fresh red chilies
Coriander sprigs

1. Pound or grind the garlic and coriander root to a smooth paste in a mortar or blender. Since the small amount may be difficult to grind in a blender, use the 3 tablespoons oil to aid in grinding.

2. Heat a wok, add the oil, and swirl it over the surface of the pan. (If you ground the coriander root and garlic with oil, do not add more here.) Add the ground paste from Step 1 and stir-fry until it is light golden. Add the ground pork and stir-fry until the pink color disappears.

3. Add the fish sauce and sugar and cook until the mixture is dry and crumbly. Add the ground peanuts and pepper, mix them in well, and stir-fry about 1 minute. Remove the mixture from the wok and set it aside to cool to room temperature.

4. Peel the pineapple according to the instructions following this recipe. Cut the pineapple lengthwise into 4 to 6 wedges depending on the size of the pineapple and the size you want the final pieces to be. Cut each wedge into slices ¼ inch thick.

5. Prepare a bed of lettuce leaves on a platter. Arrange the pineapple slices decoratively on the lettuce and top the pineapple with the pork mixture. It is not necessary to mound the pork mixture carefully on top of each pineapple slice. Garnish the arrangement with coriander sprigs and small strips of red chilies or chili "flowers" (page 29).

Variation 1: Substitute orange or tangerine wedges for the pineapple. Be sure to remove all the white membrane and seeds from the wedges.

Variation 2: Omit the fruit wedges and increase the amount of lettuce. Each diner may take a little pork mixture and roll it in a lettuce leaf. Or, you may prepare the rolls in advance. Allow 1 to 2 tablespoons mixture for each lettuce leaf depending on the size of the leaf. For this variation, we recommend soft lettuce, such as Boston lettuce, so the leaves can be rolled easily. Place the pork mixture 1 inch from the base of a leaf and roll the leaf about one third of the way toward the tip. Fold the sides over toward the middle and continue to roll it toward the tip in much the same way as you would roll a spring roll. Without the fruit, the dish is technically not "Galloping Horses" but it is quite good nonetheless.

Peeling Pineapple

The peeling method we describe here results in minimum waste and produces an attractive spiral pattern on the surface of the pineapple.

1. Cut off the leaves just below the point where they join the pineapple. Discard the leaves or, if they are in good condition, place the intact piece in the center of a serving platter and arrange the MA HOA around it.

2. Using a sharp knife, remove the tough brown skin by cutting down from the top of the pineapple, taking as little flesh as possible. A spiral pattern of brown "eyes" will remain in the flesh of the pineapple.

3. Examine the pattern of "eyes," and you will see that they form spiral lines down the pineapple. With a sharp knife follow one spiral, cutting shallowly into the pineapple at a 45° angle above and toward one spiral of "eyes." Repeat the action on the same spiral, cutting from below the "eyes." This will result in a V-shaped spiral down the pineapple. The eyes and a small amount of adjacent flesh will fall out.

4. Repeat for the remaining spirals. Discard the eyes.

5. Slice or chop the pineapple, depending on the recipe you are following.

●●● ───────────────────────────────

Ground Pork Wrapped in Noodles
SARONG

These tasty little morsels are simple in concept, easy and fun to prepare, and delightfully pleasing to both eye and palate. Unless your dinner guests or family are terribly jaded, be prepared for exclamations of delight. You may substitute ground chicken, beef, shrimp, or a combination of these meats depending on availability and your own taste. The noodles are about the size of Italian vermicelli and are made of wheat flour and eggs. They are usually found in the refrigerated section of Oriental and Thai markets.

MAKES 24 PIECES

1 tablespoon (½ ounce) finely chopped garlic
2 tablespoons finely chopped coriander root

½ pound ground pork
1 teaspoon fish sauce
1 egg yolk
⅛ teaspoon ground white pepper

Small fresh round egg noodles

Vegetable oil for deep-frying

Garlic Sauce (page 84)

1. Pound or grind the garlic and coriander root to a coarse paste in a mortar, blender, or food processor. A mortar is particularly useful, because the small amount of coriander root and garlic tends to fly around in a machine without grinding well. This can be avoided in a food processor, but not a blender, by partially grinding the coriander root and garlic, then adding unground meat and grinding it along with the coriander and garlic. If you use this procedure, be sure not to grind the meat to a puree. It should be chopped finely, but still have texture. If you use a blender, add the fish sauce to aid in grinding.

2. Mix the ground meat, fish sauce, paste from Step 1, egg yolk, and pepper in a small bowl. (If you ground the coriander root and garlic with fish sauce, do not add more here.) Shape the mixture into small balls, using about 2 tablespoons mixture for each. Do not make them large, or the wrapping may burn before the inside is done. This is most important if you are using pork, less important if you are using beef.

3. Wrap each ball with 6 to 8 full-length strands of noodles. The meat will be covered, but you may still be able to see it in a few spots. Try not to break the noodles when removing them from the package because small pieces are virtually impossible to wrap. Wrap the balls only moderately tightly, so the oil will penetrate to cook the meat and the noodles will puff slightly. Don't worry if there are a few loose ends after wrapping. They can be broken off after cooking or left on if they are attractive. With experience, there will be no loose ends.

Ahead-of-time note: The SARONG may be prepared to this point up to 1 day ahead and stored, covered, in the refrigerator. Bring them to room temperature before frying. They may also be frozen, uncooked, for up to 1 month if wrapped tightly in aluminum foil or heavy-duty plastic wrap. Thaw them well in advance and let them come to room temperature before frying.

4. Heat 1 to 1½ inches oil to 375° in a wok. Fry only a few SARONG at a time, to keep the oil from cooling too quickly and to avoid overcrowding the pan, which might prevent them from browning well. Fry until the noodles are light golden brown and the meat is done but not dry.

5. Serve hot, warm, or at room temperature with a small bowl of Garlic Sauce for dipping.

Tapioca with Stuffing
SAKU SAI MU

This is an unusual preparation, in terms of both the ingredients used and the final texture and flavor. The tapioca wrappers provide a chewy, smooth, bland contrast to the savory filling and garlic coating. The wrapper dough is very sticky, and it is essential to keep your hands wet to prevent it from sticking to your fingers and creating a big mess. In all honesty, we must let you know that SAKU SAI MU is not easy to prepare and may take some practice, but the end result is worth it. Be sure to use small tapioca pearls about the size of coriander seeds. The pork should be as lean as possible, because the mixture should be cohesive and fat will cause it to be crumbly.

MAKES ABOUT 75 PIECES

The Filling

¼ cup finely chopped coriander root
1 tablespoon (½ ounce) finely chopped garlic
1 tablespoon vegetable oil
1 package (3½ ounces) salted radish, rinsed

2 ounces very lean ground pork

2 cups (½ pound) finely chopped yellow onion
¼ teaspoon ground black pepper
2 teaspoons salt

⅓ cup palm sugar
1 tablespoon ground roasted unsalted peanuts (page 66)

The Wrappers

¾ pound small tapioca pearls (about the size of coriander seeds)
1½ to 2 cups boiling water

½ cup crisp-fried garlic and its oil (page 65)

Red lettuce leaves
Coriander sprigs
Red chili "flowers" (page 29)

The Filling

1. Pound the coriander root and garlic to a coarse paste in a mortar, or grind it with the oil in a blender. Chop the salted radish finely and set aside.

2. Heat the wok, add the oil, and swirl it over the surface of the pan. (Do not add more oil if you ground the garlic and coriander root in oil.) Stir-fry the paste from Step 1 until it is light golden. Add the ground pork and stir-fry until the pink color disappears. Add the chopped onion, salted radish, and black pepper. Mix these ingredients well, then add the salt. Stir-fry over moderate heat about 3 minutes, until the onion is translucent.

3. Add the palm sugar and stir until the mixture thickens. Add the ground peanuts, and stir them in well. Remove the mixture from the heat and set it aside to cool to room temperature. It will be dry, but cohesive.

Final Preparation

1. Place the tapioca pearls in a large mixing bowl. Add 1½ cups boiling water gradually, stirring the tapioca constantly until a paste is formed. About half of the pearls will dissolve and form a paste; the rest will still be solid but partly or completely translucent. If necessary, add up to ½ cup more boiling water gradually. The dough should be a firm, sticky mass and you will be able to see and feel the undissolved tapioca pearls.

2. Wet your hands with water and keep a large bowl of water handy to use from this point on. It is essential that your hands be wet to keep the dough from sticking to them.

3. Form about 1½ tablespoons dough into a smooth ball. Press the ball with your fingers until it is a flat, thin circle about 2 inches in diameter.

4. Place about ¾ teaspoon pork mixture in the center of the circle of dough and fold the dough around it, forming a small ball. Seal the edges by pressing lightly with your fingers, and smooth the edges so the seams do not show.

5. Place the balls ½ inch apart on a steamer rack. If you are using a metal steamer, it should be oiled lightly to keep them from sticking. (Traditionally, the steamer would be lined with banana leaves.)

6. Steam the balls for 10 minutes without lifting the lid.

7. Remove the balls from the steamer and coat them immediately with crisp-fried garlic and the oil in which it was fried.

8. Arrange the balls decoratively on a single layer of whole lettuce leaves and garnish with coriander sprigs and red chili flowers.

9. Serve warm or at room temperature.

Shrimp with Crisp Skins
GOONG GRA BOG

These shrimp are a real treat for an appetizer or snack. Like other preparations in this chapter they may be served as a main course. They are easy to prepare and may be made at a moment's notice if you omit the marinating time. In that case the flavor will not penetrate the shrimp as well, but the taste will still be good. Cooked shrimp should not be substituted, because frying may make them tough. The dish is best if the shrimp still have the tails attached, but it is good even if they do not.

SERVES 6 TO 8

1 pound (about 30) raw medium shrimp

¼ cup finely chopped coriander root
2 tablespoons (1 ounce) finely chopped garlic
½ teaspoon salt

Won ton wrappers

1 tablespoon tapioca starch (optional)
¼ cup water (optional)

Vegetable oil for deep-frying

Garlic Sauce (page 84) or Plum Sauce (page 85)

1. Peel and devein the shrimp, leaving the tails intact.

2. Pound the coriander root, garlic, and salt to a paste in a mortar. The small amount makes it very difficult to do this in a blender because there is no liquid to aid in grinding.

3. Put the shrimp and paste from Step 2 into a mixing bowl and stir until each shrimp is coated with the mixture. Cover the container and marinate the shrimp for 1 to 4 hours in the refrigerator.

4. Wrap each shrimp in a won ton wrapper (leaving the tail exposed if shrimp have them) and seal the edges with water or the optional tapioca starch mixed with water.

5. Heat 1 inch oil to 375° in a wok. Deep-fry up to 10 pieces at a time to keep from overcrowding the pan.

6. Serve immediately with Garlic Sauce or Plum Sauce. Do not fry the shrimp in advance because the wrappers may become soggy. These are best served hot or warm.

• • •

Barbecued Beef with Peanut Curry
SATÉ

The origin of the term "Saté" is obscure, although it is thought to be derived from the word "steak," and probably originated in Indonesia. Whatever the origin, it is a popular preparation in Thailand, where it is sold on the streets by vendors. It is no less tasty in a restaurant or in your own home. It can be made with either beef or pork, and the latter is preferred by many Thai people. If you don't have access to a charcoal grill you could use the broiler of your stove or even grill them over the flame of a gas stove if you don't mind the drippings messing up the stove top. This dish is an excellent appetizer or cocktail snack; it could also be served as part of the main meal. It would be wonderful for a backyard barbecue, where everyone can cook his or her own portions. It can be prepared for cooking well in advance.

SERVES 6 TO 8

1½ *pounds flank steak*

2 *teaspoons coriander seeds*
1½ *teaspoons fennel seeds or cumin seeds*
2 *teaspoons ground turmeric*
¾ *cup thick coconut milk*

1 *package bamboo skewers*

Peanut Curry (page 79) or Cucumber Sauce 1 (page 81)

1. Slice the beef across the grain into strips not more than ⅛ inch thick.

2. Roast the coriander seeds and fennel (or cumin) seeds in a dry pan until they are light golden, then grind them to a coarse powder in a mortar or electric coffee or spice grinder. Mix the powder, turmeric, and coconut milk thoroughly.

3. Thread the beef lengthwise on the skewers and marinate in the mixture from Step 2, covered, for 1 hour at room temperature or overnight in the refrigerator.

Ahead of time note: The beef can be prepared up to this point in advance and kept covered until cooking time. It should be refrigerated if it is to stand for more than 2 hours. It may also be frozen if wrapped tightly in aluminum foil or heavy-duty plastic wrap.

4. Grill the beef to the doneness you prefer over hot coals, or broil it in a preheated broiler, or cook it over a gas flame. Baste the meat frequently with any remaining marinade.

5. Serve with Peanut Curry or Cucumber Sauce 1 for dipping.

• • •

Steamed Won Tons
KANOM JEEB

Steaming produces very tender wrappers which encase a mild, chewy filling. Do not try to deep-fry these won tons because the flavors will not blend properly.

½ ounce (about 7) dried Oriental mushrooms
½ cup warm water
¼ cup (1 ounce) bamboo shoots
2 green onions, white and green parts
½ stalk celery
½ medium carrot

¼ pound raw shrimp
½ pound ground pork

2 tablespoons (1 ounce) finely chopped garlic
¼ cup finely chopped coriander root

1 tablespoon fish sauce
1 teaspoon granulated sugar
¼ teaspoon ground black pepper
1 egg yolk

40 won ton wrappers

1 teaspoon tapioca starch
2 tablespoons water

¼ cup crisp-fried garlic and its oil (page 65)
Won Ton Sauce (page 87)

1. Soak the mushrooms in the warm water for 20 minutes. Remove and discard the stems, and chop the mushrooms finely. Chop the bamboo shoots, green onions, celery, and carrot finely and mix them with the mushrooms. Set the mixture aside.

2. Peel and devein the shrimp and remove the tails. Grind the shrimp or chop them very finely, then mix with the ground pork.

3. Pound or grind the garlic and coriander root to a smooth paste in a mortar or blender. If you use a blender, add the fish sauce to aid in the grinding. Thoroughly mix the paste, fish sauce, sugar, pepper, egg yolk, and meat mixture from Step 2.

4. Mix in the chopped vegetables from Step 1 and let the mixture marinate for 15 minutes at room temperature.

5. Place 1 to 1½ teaspoons filling in a won ton wrapper and fold the edges over to form a triangle. Seal the edges with a little tapioca starch—water mixture. Repeat for the remaining wrappers.

6. Place the won tons ¼ inch apart on a lightly oiled steaming rack and sprinkle them lightly with room temperature water. Steam them about 10 minutes, until they are firm to the touch.

7. Remove the won tons from the steamer and brush them with crisp-fried garlic and its oil.

8. Serve hot or warm with Won Ton Sauce.

●●●━━━━━━━━━━━━━━━━━━━━━━━━━━━

Chive Dumplings
CHIVE NUNG

These dumplings are delicate, light, and stimulating to the appetite. The chives take on a soft texture and mild flavor, which contrasts well with the relatively sharp taste of crisp-fried garlic. We have presented the traditional procedure for preparing the dough, which is somewhat time-consuming. You may also cook the dough over very low heat, stirring and pounding it constantly and thoroughly until it is completely cooked. We find that "short-cut" procedure much more difficult, because the dough is very thick and difficult to stir unless so much water is added that it ruins the texture. Thorough kneading is essential to allow the dough to form a smooth, even texture.

MAKES ABOUT 30

2 cups uncooked rice
1 cup water

2 quarts water

2 tablespoons tapioca starch

½ pound chives, preferably Chinese chives
1 teaspoon salt
2 tablespoons crisp-fried garlic and its oil (page 65)
¼ teaspoon ground black pepper

½ cup crisp-fried garlic and its oil (page 65)
Sweet-and-Sour Sauce (page 88)

Making the Dough: Step 1

1. Soak the rice in 1 cup water overnight. The exact amount of water is not critical because it will be drained away later.

2. Grind the rice and soaking water to a puree in a blender. Traditionally this is done in a very large mortar, but it is a *very* difficult process. If you use a mortar, drain the water from the rice before pounding and pound small portions at a time. A food processor is less effective for this procedure because the mixture tends to whirl around and grind less efficiently than in a blender.

Ahead-of-time note: The ground rice mixture may be refrigerated in a covered container for 1 to 2 days. Bring to room temperature before straining.

3. Place the puree in a muslin bag or in a large sieve lined with muslin or other fine cloth. A Thai tea strainer works very well. Allow it to drain undisturbed while you prepare the other ingredients.

Making the Filling

Cut the chives into pieces ⅛ inch long, and mix them with the salt, garlic and its oil, and pepper. Set aside.

Ahead-of-time note: This mixture may be refrigerated in a covered container for 1 to 2 days

Making the Dough: Step 2

1. Bring about 2 quarts water to a rapid boil in a large pot.

2. Press the excess water out of the rice dough by massaging the cloth gently. Do not press out all the water. The dough should be soft, pliable, and moist, and it shouldn't fall apart.

3. Remove the dough from the cloth, and knead the dough thoroughly until it is smooth and silky, not less than 5 minutes. If necessary, add more water to keep it pliable and smooth.

4. Divide the dough into 4 pieces, and form each piece into a patty about 3 inches in diameter and ½ inch thick.

5. Drop the patties into the boiling water and cook them for 3 minutes after the water returns to the boil. The patties will be cooked on the outside and raw in the middle.

6. Place the patties in a mortar and pound them firmly with a pestle until the dough is smooth again. This will take several minutes of strong pounding. You may pound the dough on a flat surface with a wooden mallet or use a heavy wooden spoon and a sturdy mixing bowl, but these procedures are *much* more difficult than using a mortar and pestle.

7. Repeat Steps 3 through 6 two more times.

8. After the dough has been boiled and pounded 3 times, add the tapioca starch and knead it in thoroughly, at least 5 minutes. You may need to add more water, about a tablespoon at a time, to keep the dough soft and pliable.

9. Divide the dough into 30 pieces of equal size, and cover them with a damp cloth to keep them from drying out.

Preparing the Dumplings

1. Take a piece of dough and, using your fingers, form it into a circle about 3 inches in diameter and $\frac{1}{16}$ inch thick.

2. Place a rounded teaspoonful of filling in the center of the circle; either bring the edges up to form a small ball with a fluted top or fold the edges over the filling to form a semicircle and seal the edges by pressing with your fingers. Repeat this procedure for each piece of dough.

3. Line a steamer rack with a lightly oiled piece of cheesecloth. (Traditionally, the steamer is lined with banana leaves.) Place the dumplings on the rack ½ inch apart and sprinkle them lightly with water. Steam the dumplings for 10 to 15 minutes, until they are almost translucent and the dough is firm to the touch.

4. Remove the dumplings from the steamer and sprinkle them generously with crisp-fried garlic and the oil in which it was fried.

5. Serve warm, with Sweet and Sour Sauce.

Fried Chicken Curry Won Tons
GARI PUFF GAI

These appetizers are light, crisp, and mildly flavored. The curry powder and potato suggest an Indian influence. Because they are not hot and spicy they may be served to almost anyone and provide a good introduction to Thai cuisine. The texture is particularly interesting because of the contrast of crisp skin and soft potato. They are not filling, and we suggest allowing 8 to 10 per person.

MAKES 4½ DOZEN

1 medium (½ pound) potato

¼ cup vegetable oil
½ pound ground chicken
1 cup (¼ pound) finely chopped yellow onion
1 teaspoon curry powder
4½ teaspoons fish sauce
4½ teaspoons granulated sugar
⅛ teaspoon ground white pepper

54 won ton wrappers

Vegetable oil for deep-frying

Cucumber Sauce 3 (page 82)
Plum Sauce (page 85) or Garlic Sauce (page 84)

1. Boil the potato in enough water to cover until it can be pierced easily with a fork, about 30 minutes. Drain and allow it to cool to room temperature. Peel it, cut it into ⅛-inch dice, and set aside.

2. Heat a wok and add the ¼ cup oil. Stir-fry the chicken until the pink color disappears, then add the onion, curry powder, fish sauce, sugar, and pepper. Stir-fry about 2 minutes, until the mixture is dry, the onion is translucent, and the chicken is light golden. Place the mixture in a bowl, add the potato, mix it in thoroughly, and allow the mixture to cool to room temperature. If the chicken has formed lumps from the cooking, break them up with a fork or your fingers.

3. Place 1 to 1½ teaspoons of the mixture in the center of a won ton wrapper. Fold one corner over to the opposite corner to make a triangle and seal the edges by moistening them and pressing them together lightly. Repeat with the remaining won ton wrappers and filling. As they are finished, set them aside under wax paper to prevent them from drying out.

4. Put about 1 inch oil in a wok and heat it to 375°. Deep-fry 8 or 10 won tons at a time until they are golden, making sure not to overcrowd the wok. Drain them on paper towels.

5. Serve immediately with Cucumber Sauce 3 and Plum Sauce or Garlic Sauce.

Ahead-of-time note: The won tons may be prepared in advance by cooking them in Step 4 until they are lightly colored and the wrappers are partially cooked. Allow them to cool to room temperature, wrap them tightly in plastic wrap or aluminum foil, and freeze them. They should not be frozen without the preliminary frying because the wrappers are likely to dry out and crack. The final deep-frying may be done without thawing the won tons if you cook them long enough to heat them thoroughly. Or, they may be thawed just before frying.

•••────────────────────────────────────

Fried Spring Rolls
PAW PIA TOD

Spring rolls are a perennial favorite in Thailand and are usually purchased from street vendors. It is easy to enjoy them in your own home. They are not difficult to make and can be prepared in advance, partially cooked, and frozen. Regardless of the nation of origin, spring rolls have similar kinds of ingredients and preparation techniques. These are typically Thai because of the bean threads, fish sauce, and coriander root, which add unusual flavors and texture. Egg roll wrappers may be substituted for spring roll wrappers. Please read about the difference between them in the section on ingredients.

MAKES 12

2 ounces bean threads
Warm water

1½ tablespoons finely chopped garlic
¼ cup finely chopped coriander root

1 cup (¼ pound) bamboo shoots
2 ounces mushrooms, fresh or canned
1 stalk celery
2 green onions
¾ cup bean sprouts
1 small carrot

¼ pound ground pork
¼ pound ground raw shrimp

1 egg
2 tablespoons fish sauce
⅛ teaspoon ground white pepper

12 spring roll wrappers

Vegetable oil for deep-frying

Assorted raw vegetables (broccoli, green beans,
  eggplant, zucchini, etc.), cut into serving size pieces
Mint leaves

Garlic Sauce (page 84) or Plum Sauce (page 85)

1. Soak the bean threads in warm water to cover for 10 minutes. Drain thoroughly and set them aside.

2. Pound or grind the garlic and coriander root to a smooth paste in a mortar, blender, or food processor. A mortar is particularly useful because the small amount of coriander root and garlic tends to fly around in a machine without grinding well. (This can be avoided in a food processor, but not a blender, by partially grinding the coriander root and garlic, then adding unground pork and shrimp instead of using ground pork and shrimp as listed in the ingredients, and grinding the mixture some more. If you use this procedure, be sure not to grind the meat to a puree.

It should be chopped finely, but still have texture.) If you use a blender, add the fish sauce to aid in grinding.

3. Chop the bamboo shoots, mushrooms, celery, green onions, bean threads, and bean sprouts into small, coarse pieces. Shred the carrot finely.

4. Mix the ground pork and shrimp, the paste from Step 2, and the chopped ingredients from Step 3. Add the egg, fish sauce, and ground pepper. (If you ground the garlic and coriander root with fish sauce, do not add more here.) Mix the ingredients thoroughly.

5. Place a spring roll wrapper on a flat surface with one pointed edge toward you, unless, of course, you have the traditional round wrappers. Put about 2 tablespoons filling one third the way up the wrapper. Fold the bottom edge of the wrapper over the filling, and form the filling into a lightly packed log-shaped roll. Fold the side edges over, and roll the log up to the end of the wrapper. Seal the edges by wetting them and pressing them together gently. Repeat with the other wrappers.

6. Heat about 1½ inches oil to 375° in a wok. Fry the spring rolls 2 or 3 at a time until they are firm and golden brown and the filling is well cooked but not dry, about 4 minutes.

Ahead-of-time note: The spring rolls may be partially cooked, allowed to cool to room temperature, wrapped tightly in plastic freezer wrap, aluminum foil, or both, and frozen. They will keep perfectly well up to 6 months. They may be fried while still frozen, or you may thaw them first. It is crucial that the spring rolls be cooked partially before freezing. If not, the wrappers are likely to split and dry out.

7. Serve warm, with assorted raw vegetables, mint, and Garlic Sauce or Plum Sauce.

••• ─────────────────────────────────

Deep-Fried Bread and Pork
KANOM PANG NA MOO

This is an unusual preparation that shows the cleverness with which the Thai people approach combinations of ingredients. It has a rich, subtle flavor that is enhanced by the sourness of the vinegar and the cool crunchiness of cucumbers in the accompanying sauce. The bread will not be greasy if it is cooked properly.

MAKES 40 PIECES

¼ cup finely chopped coriander root
1 tablespoon (½ ounce) finely chopped garlic

¾ pound ground pork
1 egg
4 teaspoons fish sauce
¼ teaspoon ground white pepper

10 slices firm white bread, such as French or sourdough

Vegetable oil for deep-frying

Cucumber Sauce 3 (page 82)

1. Pound or grind the coriander root and garlic to a coarse paste in a mortar or blender. If using a blender, you may need to add the fish sauce to aid in grinding.

2. Mix the ground pork, paste from Step 1, egg, and fish sauce thoroughly. (If you ground the coriander root and garlic with the fish sauce, do not add more here.)

Ahead-of-time note: The mixture may be prepared up to 1 day in advance and stored, covered, in the refrigerator. Or it may be frozen and kept for 6 months.

3. Spread the mixture on one side of each piece of bread.

4. Heat 1 inch oil to 375 ° in a wok or deep skillet. Add 2 slices bread to the hot oil at a time, pork side down. Deep-fry until each side is golden, turning only once. Make sure that the oil is hot, so the bread won't be greasy when cooked. Drain the pieces, pork side up, on paper towels. When the bread is cool enough to handle, slice each piece into quarters.

5. Serve warm or at room temperature with Cucumber Sauce 3.

Sweet Thai Noodles
MEE KROB

MEE KROB is a classic Thai dish, a mainstay in any Thai restaurant worth its fish sauce. There are several ways to prepare it, some of which are cloyingly sweet because they use a large amount of caramelized sugar. The traditional version we have presented here may be less sweet than those you have had before, but you may make it as sweet as you like by adding more sugar to taste. There are several steps in the preparation, and they should be followed in sequence for the best results. Plan to discard the oil in which the dried shrimp are fried. If dried shrimp are not available, you may substitute tiny fresh shrimp, but the desirable contrasting salty flavor will be lost. Although the green onions and chilies are mentioned as garnish in the instructions, they are essential ingredients in the traditional version. You may increase or decrease the amount according to taste.

SERVES 6 TO 8

¼ cup water
1 cup granulated sugar
1 cup white vinegar
1 teaspoon salt

¼ pound dried shrimp
8 Serrano chilies
1 bunch green onions, white part only

6 to 8 ounces fresh, firm tofu
3 eggs

Vegetable oil for deep-frying
¼ pound very thin rice noodles (rice vermicelli)

1. Combine the water, sugar, vinegar, and salt in a small saucepan. Bring the mixture to a gentle boil and cook about 10 minutes, until it forms a thin syrup. Set aside.

2. Put the dried shrimp in a sieve and rinse them thoroughly under running water. Set them aside in the sieve to drain. Remove the stems, but not the seeds, from the chilies. Slice the green onions and chilies lengthwise into thin strips and set them aside together.

3. Slice the tofu into ¼-inch cubes and set aside. Beat the eggs lightly, until they are well mixed but not frothy. Strain through a fine sieve and set aside.

4. Pour about 3 inches oil in a wok and heat it to 400°. Dry the tofu with paper towels and deep-fry it until the cubes are firm and light golden, but not dry and hard. Remove them from the oil and set aside to drain on paper towels.

5. Using the same oil, deep-fry the noodles a handful at a time. The noodles will puff up immediately, and begin to brown in about 10 seconds. Be careful not to let them burn. They should be light golden and very puffy. If they do not expand immediately upon touching the oil, the oil is not hot enough. If they turn dark brown immediately, the oil is too hot. Scoop the noodles out to drain on paper towels. Remove about half the oil from the wok and save it for another use.

6. Dribble the beaten, sieved eggs over the surface of the hot oil in the wok, to form narrow strands: holding the bowl of eggs in one hand, dip the other into the eggs, stretch it out about 12 inches over the oil, and let the egg run in a thin, steady stream from your fingertips while moving your hand in a circular motion so the surface of the oil is covered with a thin net of egg. You will need to repeat this procedure about four times. The intent is to form a thin net of egg strands that will cook quickly without massing together. When the strands are set completely and light golden on the bottom, flip them over carefully and brown the other side. Remove from the oil and drain on paper towels.

7. Dry the shrimp thoroughly with paper towels. Using the same oil, deep-fry the shrimp until they are just crisp and light golden, about 3 minutes. Be prepared for the very strong smell they produce as they fry, but don't be concerned, since the shrimp will taste nothing like the smell. (You may wish to do this well in advance of the time your guests arrive and set the fried shrimp aside to drain on paper towels.) They will form a great deal of foam while they are frying, and it will be necessary to use a strainer to lift them up occasionally to see how well they are cooking. Do not overcook them or let them get dry or hard! Remove them from the oil and drain on paper towels. Discard the oil.

8. Clean the wok thoroughly and place half the sugar syrup from Step 1 in it. Heat the syrup almost to boiling, but do not let it boil. Add half the noodles, half the egg nets (see the variation below), half the tofu, and half the shrimp. Mix gently until the syrup is absorbed, being careful to break the noodles as little as possible. Remove the mixture from the wok and place it on a serving platter. Repeat wth the rest of the syrup, noodles, eggs, and shrimp.

9. Garnish the MEE KROB with the green onions and chilies. Serve immediately or hold it at room temperature for up to 2 hours.

Variation: If the eggs have formed attractive nets you may drape them over the MEE KROB as a garnish rather than adding them in Step 8.

•••──

Steamed Spring Rolls
PAW PIA SOD

These spring rolls are a pleasant change from the usual deep-fried ones. They are lightly spiced, and the soft wrappers contrast well with the chewy sausage and crunchy bean sprouts. The only difficult part in their preparation is the initial softening of the wrappers in hot water. Unless you are careful they may tear or stick together. With experience you may be able to soften more than one at a time, but we suggest you do just one at a time until you become skilled. If the wrappers are very thin and delicate (the best ones are) they may soften in the steam before actually touching the water.

MAKES 8

¼ pound (about 3) Chinese sausages

2½ cups (½ pound) bean sprouts

¾ cup (6 ounces) cooked crabmeat
4 green onions, white part only, chopped finely
¼ pound boiled ham

8 spring roll wrappers

8 green onions

Sweet Sauce (page 88)
Vinegar Sauce (page 83)

1. Boil the sausages or fry them in a dry skillet until done, about 5 minutes. Allow them to cool to room temperature and slice them diagonally into long, thin slices. Set aside.

2. Place the bean sprouts in a colander and rinse them under very hot running water. Set them aside to drain.

3. Tear the crabmeat into thick shreds and set them aside. Wash and trim the green onions and set aside. Slice the ham into thin julienne strips and set aside.

4. Place one wrapper on the table with a pointed edge toward you unless, of course, the wrappers are round. Arrange one eighth of the bean sprouts on the wrapper in a sausage-shaped pile one third the way from the edge nearest you. Place one eighth of the ham on top of that, and then one eighth of the crabmeat. Place one eighth of chopped onion on top of the crabmeat. Place one eighth of the sausage on top of that. Fold the near edge of the wrapper over the filling, and roll it up loosely toward the top without folding the sides over it. Repeat with the remaining wrappers and filling.

Ahead-of-time note: The spring rolls may be prepared to this point up to 6 hours in advance. Cover them tightly with plastic wrap to keep them from drying out and store them in the refrigerator. Bring them to room temperature before proceeding with Step 5.

5. Place the spring rolls on a lightly oiled steaming rack, seam side down. Steam them for 5 minutes, or until they are heated through.

6. Serve immediately with whole green onions, Sweet Sauce, and Vinegar Sauce.

*** ─────────────────────────────────

Stuffed Yellow Chilies
PRIG LEANG SOD SAI

These appetizers are for those who love hot food. You may make them milder by using a milder chili, but remember that most small chilies are hot. If you do like hot and spicy food you will very likely love this dish with its contrasting flavors and textures. A short steaming period will result in crisper, much hotter chilies. The steaming time we suggest will result in moderate hotness. You may substitute larger chilies, such as Anaheim chilies, and slice them crosswise into pieces about ¼ inch thick after they are cooked.

SERVES 4 TO 6

1 teaspoon finely chopped coriander root
1 teaspoon (2 cloves) finely chopped garlic
¼ pound lean ground pork
¼ pound ground raw shrimp
1 tablespoon fish sauce
1½ tablespoons tapioca starch

½ pound (about 12) small yellow chilies

Vegetable oil for deep-frying

2 eggs
1 teaspoon all-purpose flour

Lime Sauce (page 84)

1. Pound the coriander root and garlic to a coarse paste in a mortar, or grind them in a blender with the fish sauce. Mix thoroughly with the pork, shrimp, fish sauce, and tapioca starch. (If you ground the garlic and coriander root with the fish sauce, do not add more.) Set the mixture aside.

2. Remove and save the stems from the chilies, and scoop out the seeds without breaking the chilies; *or* leave the stems in place, split the chilies along one side, and remove and discard the seeds.

3. Stuff the chilies with the mixture from Step 1. If you removed the stems, put them back in place and secure them with a toothpick. If you split the chilies along the side, press the sides back together. It is not necessary to secure the sides with toothpicks.

4. Place the chilies on a lightly oiled steaming rack and steam them for 15 to 20 minutes, until the pork mixture is done and the chilies are soft. Remove from the steamer and let them cool to room temperature. At this point they will still have a very hot chili flavor, but this will become milder after frying.

5. Beat the eggs lightly while adding the flour to them. Heat a wok and add about ½ cup of oil. Dip your fingers into the egg mixture and dribble just enough of it over the surface of the hot oil to form a thin, single-layered network of egg strands. Cook the eggs just until set. As soon they are set, but before they dry out, put one stuffed chili in the center of the net and wrap the egg network around it, turning the chili as you do. Continue turning the chili and the wrapping in the oil until the egg is golden. It will not be crisp. Repeat with the remaining chilies.

6. Serve warm or at room temperature, with Lime Sauce for dipping.

Variation: Increase the amount of flour to 1 tablespoon and skip Step 5 of the main recipe. Instead, dip the chilies in the egg batter instead of wrapping them with egg nets, and deep-fry them until they are crisp and golden brown. This non-traditional procedure is a little easier, but produces chilies that are less attractive.

Ahead-of-time note: The fried chilies may be prepared up to 4 hours in advance if they are to be served at room temperature. Do not refrigerate them after they have been fried.

10
Beef

BEEF IS EXPENSIVE in Thailand and a little is made to go a long way. In general, the Thai people do not use beef as extensively as it is used in the United States, and they usually prefer pork. When beef is served, it is often in small quantities or in a dish that has a significant amount of sauce, such as Beef Musman. The recipes in this chapter range from spicy hot to mild. Some have a generous amount of sauce while others have none at all. Those with no sauce should either be served with dishes that have sauce or be accompanied by a separate sauce to flavor the ever-present rice.

✳✳✳ ────────────────────────────────

Grilled Beef with Thai Seasoning
NUE NAM TOK

This is one of those convenient dishes that can be prepared completely in advance. The only last-minute preparation is the final mixing and garnishing. The flavors blend well, and the addition of ground toasted rice adds an elusive texture and flavor. NUE NAM TOK has little sauce of its own.

SERVES 6

1½ pounds flank steak

¼ pound (1 cup sliced) red onion
4 green onions, green and white parts

¼ cup + 1 tablespoon lime juice
2 tablespoons fish sauce
1 teaspoon ground roasted chilies (page 60)
2 tablespoons ground toasted rice (page 66)

Red lettuce leaves
Coriander sprigs
Mint or basil leaves

Vinegar Sauce (page 83)

1. Grill the beef to the desired doneness, preferably over charcoal. Slice it across the grain into strips ⅛ inch thick and 1 to 2 inches long. Put these in a large ceramic or glass mixing bowl.

2. Peel the red onion, remove the root portion, and slice the onion vertically into thin strips. Slice the green onion diagonally into thin pieces. Add both types of onion to the beef.

3. Add the lime juice, fish sauce, ground chilies, and ground rice. Mix well.

Ahead-of-time note: If prepared in advance, keep the dry and liquid ingredients separate. Mix them just before serving.

4. Arrange a single layer of lettuce leaves on a serving platter, and place the beef mixture on top. Garnish with sprigs of coriander and mint or basil leaves.

5. Serve at room temperature, with Vinegar Sauce and rice.

✳✳✳ ━━━━━━━━━━━━━━━━━━━━━━━━━━━━

Stir-Fried Beef with Mint
NUE GRA PAO

This is a rich, hearty dish with plenty of typical Thai flavors. Any kind of beef may be used, but flank steak works particularly well because it is easy to cut it across the grain, which helps keep the meat from falling apart during stir-frying and produces a tender result. Be sure to serve plenty of rice, because it helps moderate the hot chilies without detracting from the flavor. You may reduce the number of chilies by up to one half, but traditionally this dish should have a rich, hot chili flavor.

SERVES 4 TO 6

1 pound flank steak

14 (2 ounces) finely chopped Serrano chilies
¼ cup (2 ounces) finely chopped garlic
½ cup (2 ounces) finely chopped yellow onion

¼ cup + 2 tablespoons vegetable oil

3 tablespoons fish sauce
1 tablespoon granulated sugar
½ cup water (more if needed in Step 5)
½ cup loosely packed mint or basil leaves

Green lettuce leaves

1. Slice the beef across the grain into strips ⅛ inch thick and 2 to 3 inches long. Set aside.

2. Pound or grind the chilies, garlic, and onion to a coarse paste in a mortar or blender. If you use a blender you may need to add the oil to aid in grinding.

3. Heat a wok, add the oil, and swirl it over the surface of the pan. (Do not add more oil if you have ground the chilies, onion, and garlic in oil.) Add the paste from Step 2 and stir-fry until it is light golden.

4. Add the beef and stir-fry until it is a uniform tan color, but do not overcook it.

5. Add the fish sauce, sugar, water, and mint (or basil) leaves. More water may be added if the sauce is too dry. There should be about ½ to ¾ cup sauce, depending on how much water you added.

Ahead-of-time note: The dish may be prepared a day in advance to this point. To do so, proceed through Step 5, omitting the mint or basil leaves. When you are ready to serve, heat the mixture and add the leaves. If the meat has absorbed the liquid, add just enough warm water to bring it back to the original consistency.

6. Arrange a single layer of lettuce leaves in a serving bowl and put the beef mixture over them. Serve the beef immediately or keep it warm while preparing other dishes.

7. Serve with rice.

✳✳✳ ─────────────────────────────

Beef Panang
PANANG NUE

This moderately hot, slightly sweet dish is prepared with coconut milk and an uncooked curry. If you prefer a milder dish, reduce the number of chilies in the curry or in this recipe. In the traditional version we describe here, the beef is cooked in thin coconut milk, which adds flavor and smoothness. If you prefer the beef flavor to be more distinct, use the variation that follows the main recipe. The thick coconut milk should always be added as described, to allow the flavors to develop gradually and the mixture to thicken properly.

SERVES 4 TO 6

5 Kaffir lime leaves
½ cup warm water
3 Serrano chilies

1 pound flank steak
1 cup thin coconut milk

2 cups thick coconut milk

1 recipe Panang Curry (page 73)

2 tablespoons ground roasted unsalted peanuts (page 66)

2 tablespoons fish sauce
2 tablespoons granulated sugar

Paprika (optional)

Green lettuce leaves

1. Soak the Kaffir lime leaves in the warm water for 15 minutes. Drain and discard the water. Slice them lengthwise into thin strips and set them aside. Remove the stems, but not the seeds, from the chilies and slice the chilies lengthwise into thin strips. Set them aside.

2. Slice the beef across the grain into thin strips ⅛ inch thick and 2 to 3 inches long. Boil them slowly, uncovered, with the thin coconut milk until the beef is done, about 15 minutes. Most of the coconut milk will boil away and some will be absorbed by the beef. Very little, if any, will be left in the pan.

3. In a separate container, bring the thick coconut milk to a boil over high heat. Remove it from the heat immediately, and set it aside.

4. Heat a wok, add ½ cup of the thick coconut milk, and stir constantly, over moderate heat, until it thickens, forms large bubbles, and begins to splutter. Add the Panang Curry and Kaffir lime leaves. Stir-fry until the mixture is fragrant and almost dry.

5. Add another ½ cup thick coconut milk. Add the ground peanuts gradually, stirring constantly, until the mixture becomes thick. Add another ½ cup thick coconut milk and continue to stir until it thickens again.

6. Add the beef and coconut milk (if any remains) in which it was cooked, fish sauce, and sugar to the curry paste mixture. Add the final ½ cup thick coconut milk and stir until the mixture thickens slightly. If you prefer a red-colored preparation, add paprika to get the shade of red you like.

7. Serve immediately or keep the dish warm while you prepare others. When ready to serve, put a single layer of lettuce leaves in a serving bowl and pour the beef and sauce over them. Garnish with the sliced chilies, and serve with rice.

Variation

1. Omit the thin coconut milk and ignore the reference to it in Step 2 of the main recipe.

2. Stir-fry the beef in 2 tablespoons vegetable oil until the red color disappears completely. Remove the beef from the wok and set aside. Clean the wok, and proceed to Step 3 of the main recipe.

3. In Step 6, ignore the reference to the coconut milk in which the beef was cooked.

●●●────────────────────────────────────

Thai Dried Beef
NUE SWAN

This beef is popular in Thailand but, unfortunately, is not often found in Thai restaurants in America. It is easy to prepare and, once the initial drying is completed, it cooks extremely quickly. It has a slightly chewy texture but bears no resemblance to commercially dried beef. Thai dried beef is sometimes called "Thai beef jerky," but we have chosen not to use that name to avoid confusing it with the tough, rubbery beef sold in the United States in small plastic bags at an exorbitant price. There is absolutely no resemblance between the two. The flavor of NUE SWAN has a hint of sugar and spices, and it is not tough. It is extremely important to avoid overdrying it, and equally important to fry it very quickly.

SERVES 6 TO 8

1½ pounds flank steak
2 tablespoons coriander seeds
½ teaspoon cumin or fennel seeds
¼ cup + 2 tablespoons granulated sugar
¼ cup fish sauce

Vegetable oil for deep-frying

Green lettuce leaves
Green onions, white and green parts
Radishes

Lime Sauce (page 84) or Spicy Fish Sauce (page 83)

1. Lay the beef flat on a cutting board and slice it horizontally into slices ⅛ inch thick by holding one hand flat on top of the beef to keep it from sliding and cutting parallel to the surface of the cutting board. Each piece will be the length and width of the original piece of beef. Slice each of these pieces across the grain into strips 3 to 4 inches wide.

2. Roast the coriander and cumin (or fennel) seeds in a dry wok or skillet until they are fragrant and golden. Pound or grind them to a coarse powder in a mortar, blender, or coffee or spice grinder. Combine the ground seeds with the sugar and fish sauce, and pour this over the beef. Make sure all parts of the beef are coated.

3. Cover the beef and marinate it for at least 1 hour at room temperature or, preferably, overnight in the refrigerator.

4. Heat the oven to the lowest possible temperature. Place the beef on an ungreased cookie sheet and put it on the center rack of the oven. Close the oven door and let the beef dry about 10 hours. To avoid drying the beef too much, it is imperative that the oven not be too hot. If you have been using the oven for baking or broiling, just put the beef in the oven after it has been turned off; no other heat will be necessary. If your oven has a pilot light, that in itself will be enough heat. After drying, the beef should still be soft, and it will be slightly darker in color than it was in the beginning. In this recipe, drying refers to the surface of the meat being dry, not that the meat is completely dry throughout.

Ahead-of-time note: The beef may be prepared to this point a few days in advance and refrigerated, wrapped tightly in aluminum foil. Bring it to room temperature before proceeding with the final step.

5. Heat ½ inch oil to 375° in a wok. If any moisture has developed on the surface of the beef, dry it thoroughly with a paper towel to insure that it will brown properly. Fry the beef *very quickly* (5 seconds) until the outer surface is crisp and barely brown and the inside is soft, juicy, and tender. Put a single layer of lettuce leaves on a serving platter and arrange the beef on the leaves. Garnish with green onions and radishes, preferably cut into decorative shapes.

6. Serve with Lime Sauce or Spicy Fish Sauce and glutinous rice.

Beef with Broccoli
PAD NUE GOB BROCCOLI

This beef preparation is mild and has none of the typical flavor of chilies associated with Thai food. The oyster sauce and mild flavors suggest a Chinese influence. It is good by itself or as an accompaniment to spicier dishes, in which case it can serve to refresh the palate. The broccoli should be crisp, barely cooked, to add texture.

SERVES 6 TO 8

2 pounds broccoli

1 pound flank steak

2 teaspoons tapioca starch
¼ cup water

¼ cup fish sauce
¼ cup oyster sauce
1 teaspoon black soy sauce
2 cups water

¼ cup vegetable oil
2 tablespoons (1 ounce) finely chopped garlic

Lime Sauce (page 84) or Spicy Fish Sauce (page 83)

1. Peel the stems of the broccoli and remove the tough, bottom ¼ inch of the stem. Remove the florets from the broccoli and slice the stems diagonally into pieces about ¼ inch thick. Blanch stems and florets in boiling water for 1 minute, plunge into cold water to stop the cooking, and set aside in cold water.

2. Slice the beef across the grain into slices 1 to 2 inches long and not more than ⅛ inch thick. Set aside.

3. Mix the tapioca starch and the water in a small bowl and set aside.

4. Mix the fish sauce, oyster sauce, soy sauce, and water in a small bowl. Set aside.

5. Heat a wok, add the oil, and swirl it over the surface of the pan. Stir-fry the garlic until it is light golden. Add the beef to the wok and stir-fry until the pink color disappears.

6. Add the broccoli and the liquid from Step 4. Bring the mixture to a boil rapidly. Stir the tapioca starch mixture, add it to the wok, and stir until the mixture thickens.

7. Serve immediately with Lime Sauce or Spicy Fish Sauce and rice.

••• ─────────────────────────────

Beef Musman
MUSSAMAN NUE

This dish has a smooth, rich, mildly hot, and spicy flavor. It produces a large amount of sauce because of the thin coconut milk, so a little meat goes a long way when served with ample rice. Be sure to add the thick coconut milk in small increments so that it can thicken properly and the flavor can develop gradually. Otherwise, you will simply be boiling the curry in coconut milk and the final product will be less flavorful. Beef Musman is a good example of the influence of other cuisines on Thai cooking, and of how ingredients have been adapted in Thailand. The name is thought to be derived from the word "Muslim" and the ingredients indicate an Indian influence in the use of potatoes, nutmeg, cardamom, and cloves. Even though the dish contains potatoes, it is still served with rice. Chicken may be substituted for beef, in which case the Thai name becomes MUSSAMAN GAI.

SERVES 8 TO 10

2 ounces wet tamarind or ¼ cup tamarind concentrate
½ cup warm water

1 pound flank steak
1 cup (¼ pound) whole roasted unsalted peanuts
3 cups thin coconut milk

1 large (about ¾ pound) potato

2 cups thick coconut milk
1 recipe Musman Curry (page 78)
12 cardamom seeds

¼ cup plus 2 tablespoons fish sauce
¼ cup plus 3 tablespoons sugar

1. (Omit this step if you are using tamarind concentrate.) Soak the wet tamarind in warm water for 15 minutes, or until it is soft. Press it through a sieve, making sure to press through all the pulp you can. Scrape the outside of the sieve carefully to get all the pulp, and discard the residue inside the sieve.

2. Cut the beef into ⅓-inch cubes. Place the beef, peanuts, and thin coconut milk in a large covered saucepan and boil gently over medium heat for 30 minutes.

3. Peel the potato and cut it into ⅓-inch cubes. Add it to the saucepan, stir, and cook the mixture, covered, for 15 minutes more. Remove the mixture from the heat and set aside.

4. Bring the thick coconut milk to a boil in a saucepan, and remove it from the heat.

5. Heat a wok and add ¼ cup of the thick coconut milk and the Musman Curry. Stir the mixture over moderate heat until it is thick and pale tan. Add the cardamom seeds. Add the rest of the thick coconut milk ¼ cup at a time, stirring it over high heat until the sauce becomes slightly thick after each addition.

6. Add the mixture from Step 5 to the beef mixture, and bring it to a boil. Add the fish sauce, sugar, and tamarind solution or concentrate. (If you have used tamarind concentrate, add ½ cup warm water and stir to mix well.)

Ahead-of-time note: This dish may be prepared a day in advance and stored, covered, in the refrigerator. It actually improves in flavor if prepared ahead. We suggest preparing it several hours or a day in advance and heating it thoroughly, without letting it boil, just before serving.

7. Serve with rice.

Salty Dried Beef
NUE KEM

This dish is similar to Thai Dried Beef (NUE SWAN), but has none of the spicy, sweet flavor. Rather, it is slightly salty with a hint of fish sauce, and tastes almost as if it has been smoked. It's unlikely that anyone will be able to guess how easy it is to prepare. Usually it is served with one or more dishes that have sauce.

SERVES 4 TO 6

1 pound flank steak
¼ cup fish sauce

Vegetable oil for deep-frying

Green lettuce leaves
Green onions, white and green parts
Radishes
Lime Sauce (page 84) or Spicy Fish Sauce (page 83)

1. Lay the beef flat on a cutting board and slice it horizontally into slices ⅛ inch thick by holding one hand flat on top of the beef to keep it from sliding and cutting parallel to the surface of the cutting board. Each piece will be the length and width of the original piece of beef. Slice each of these pieces across the grain into strips 3 to 4 inches wide. Put the beef in a bowl and pour the fish sauce over it, making sure that all surfaces are moistened. Let the slices marinate, covered, for 1 hour at room temperature or, preferably, overnight in the refrigerator.

2. Heat the oven to the lowest possible temperature. Place the beef slices on an ungreased cookie sheet and put it on the middle rack of the oven. Close the oven door and let the beef dry about 10 hours. To avoid drying the beef too much, it is imperative that the oven not be too hot. If you have been using the oven for baking or broiling, just put the beef in the oven after it has been turned off; no other heat will be necessary. If your oven has a pilot light, that in itself will be ample heat. After 10 hours, the surface of the beef will be only slightly darker in color than when you began. Do not let the beef get dry and hard.

Ahead-of-time note: The beef may be prepared to this point 1 or 2 days in advance. Wrap it tightly in aluminum foil and refrigerate it. It may also be frozen. Bring it to room temperature before proceeding with the recipe.

3. Heat ½ inch oil to 375° in a wok. Dry the surface of the beef thoroughly with a paper towel to insure that it will brown properly. Fry the beef *very quickly* (5 seconds), until the outside is barely brown and crisp. The inside of the beef should be soft and juicy. Put a single layer of lettuce leaves on a serving platter and arrange the slices of beef on them. Garnish with green onions and radishes, preferably cut into decorative shapes.

4. Serve with Lime Sauce or Spicy Fish Sauce and glutinous rice.

11
Pork

PORK IS VERY POPULAR in Thailand, and many dishes are prepared using it. In many of them, chicken may be substituted if you prefer. Because pork and beef are rather expensive in Thailand, they are often reserved for special occasions or feasts, particularly those dishes that use a relatively large amount of meat in relation to the amount of sauce produced.

*** ─────────────────────────────

Pork with Green Beans
MOO PAD PRIG KING

This is an excellent and very popular dish. The green beans add an interesting, crisp contrast to the texture of the meat, and they are accented by the spiciness of the curry. Please use fresh, young beans whenever possible, because frozen ones do not provide the right texture. Canned beans should never be used. There is relatively little sauce, but you may make more by adding up to ¼ cup additional water in Step 5.

SERVES 4 TO 6

1 pound fresh, young green beans

½ pound boneless pork chops or pork loin

¼ cup vegetable oil

1 recipe Red Curry 1 (page 75)

¼ cup fish sauce
1½ tablespoons granulated sugar

Red lettuce leaves

1. Slice the green beans diagonally into pieces ⅛ inch thick and about 2 inches long, and blanch them for 10 seconds in rapidly boiling water. They should be barely crisp-tender. Place them in cold water to stop the cooking. Drain and set aside.

2. Slice the pork across the grain into strips 1 to 2 inches long and not more than ⅛ inch thick. Set aside.

3. Heat a wok, add the oil, and swirl it over the surface of the pan. Add the Red Curry 1 and stir-fry over moderate heat until it deepens in color, forms a thick paste, and becomes fragrant, about 5 minutes. Add water as needed if it becomes dry and crumbly. When you are finished it should be a smooth, thick paste.

4. Add the pork and stir until the pink color disappears from the meat, about 3 to 4 minutes.

5. Add the green beans and fish sauce, and stir while you add the sugar gradually. Put a single layer of lettuce leaves in a serving bowl, and pour the pork and sauce over them.

6. Serve immediately with rice, or keep it warm while you prepare other dishes.

❋❋❋ ──────────────────────────

Ginger Pork
MOO PAD KING

This preparation is highly spiced and mildly peppery; it produces a moderate amount of richly flavored thin sauce. The cloud ears absorb the flavors of the sauce and add a crunchy, gelatinous texture if they are not overcooked. They may lose this texture if reheated, but the flavor will be just as good. If you do not like the texture of cloud ears, they may be omitted.

SERVES 4 TO 6

1 ounce cloud ears
1 cup warm water

1½ pounds boneless pork chops or pork loin

6 ounces ginger root
6 ounces (1½ cups square-sliced) yellow onion
4 (½ ounce) Serrano chilies (optional)

3 tablespoons fish sauce
2 teaspoons granulated sugar
1 teaspoon black soy sauce
1 cup water

1 bunch green onions, white and green parts

¼ cup vegetable oil
1 teaspoon (2 cloves) finely chopped garlic

¼ teaspoon ground white pepper

1. Soak the cloud ears in the warm water for 15 minutes, until they are soft.

2. Slice the pork across the grain into strips not more than ⅛ inch thick; then slice these strips into pieces about 1 to 2 inches long and ½ inch wide. Set them aside.

3. Peel the ginger root and slice it crosswise into thin pieces. Peel the yellow onion, remove the root portion, and slice it into ½-inch squares. Place the ginger and onion in a bowl. Drain the cloud ears, cut them into pieces about the size of the yellow onion, and add them to the onion and ginger root. Remove the stems, but not the seeds, from the chilies, and slice the chilies lengthwise into very thin strips. Add the chilies to the other ingredients prepared in this step.

4. Mix the fish sauce, sugar, soy sauce, and water in a bowl and stir until the sugar is dissolved. Set aside.

5. Slice the green onions diagonally into pieces 1 inch long and set aside.

6. Heat a wok, add the oil, and swirl it over the surface of the pan. Add the garlic and stir-fry until it is light golden. Add the pork and stir-fry until the pink color disappears.

7. Add the ingredients from Step 3 to the wok and stir-fry until the onion is translucent. Add the mixture from Step 4 and bring to a boil rapidly.

8. Add the green onions and stir briefly. They should be just hot and crisp-tender.

9. Scoop the contents out into a serving bowl and sprinkle with ground white pepper. Serve with rice.

✳✳✳ ─────────────────────────────

Garlic Pork
MOO GRATIEM

This is a rich, hot, spicy dish with the hearty flavors of garlic and pepper. Unlike most other preparations, this one uses white pepper instead of chilies for the hot flavor. It is delicious and of historical significance. Until chilies were introduced to Thailand by Western traders in the sixteenth century, Thai cuisine relied exclusively on pepper for hot flavors. Traditionally, white peppercorns were pounded to a paste with coriander root and garlic and they were then stir-fried together. Because pepper has a tendency to stick to the wok at that early stage of cooking, we have introduced it a little later in the recipe with no difference in the finished product. The amount of pepper listed in the ingredients is not an error—it really does take that much to produce an authentic result. If you prefer a less peppery taste, the white pepper may be reduced by up to one half, but do not reduce it too much or the effect will be lost completely. Similarly, you may add more pepper if you like, but do not add so much that it masks the other flavors. More than others, this recipe benefits from freshly ground pepper, and we suggest that you grind your own if possible.

SERVES 4 TO 6

1 pound boneless pork chops or pork loin

½ cup (¼ pound) finely chopped garlic
¼ cup finely chopped coriander root

2 tablespoons fish sauce
1 tablespoon granulated sugar
¾ cup water

3 tablespoons vegetable oil

1 tablespoon ground white pepper

Red lettuce leaves

1. Slice the pork across the grain into strips 1 to 2 inches long and not more than ⅛ inch thick and set aside. Pound or grind the garlic and coriander root to a smooth paste in a mortar or blender. If you use a blender, add the oil to aid in grinding.

2. Combine the fish sauce, sugar, and water in a small bowl and stir until the sugar dissolves. Set aside.

3. Heat a wok, add the oil, and swirl it over the surface of the pan. (If you used the oil for grinding, do not add more here.) Add the paste from Step 1 and stir-fry until it is light golden.

4. Add the pork and stir-fry until the pink color disappears.

5. Add the white pepper and stir-fry the mixture about 1 minute. Unless you have a very well-seasoned wok, the mixture may begin to stick because of the pepper. To prevent burning, keep it scraped off as well as you can. When the liquid is added the stuck portions will loosen. The mixture will be bitter if it burns, so be careful at this stage.

6. Add the liquid from Step 2 and stir over moderate heat until the sauce begins to thicken and any stuck portions are loosened from the wok surface, about 1 minute. More water may be added if the mixture gets too dry. There should be about ½ cup sauce.

7. Place a single layer of lettuce leaves in a serving bowl, pour the pork and sauce over them, and serve with rice.

Sweet-and-Sour Pork

PAD PRIEW WAN

Sweet-and-sour dishes are found throughout Southeast Asia and the Orient, and Thailand is no exception. Their popularity is easy to understand, because they provide interesting contrasts of seemingly incompatible textures and flavors. This dish is another example of how the Thai people have borrowed from their neighbors and modified basic ingredients to develop a unique dish of their own. It is a colorful, easy-to-prepare mixture of ingredients combining hot, sweet, sour, and salty tastes in a thin sauce. Because the meat and vegetables are sliced into fairly large pieces, the slicing goes quickly and can be done well in advance of the final cooking.

SERVES 6 TO 8

1¼ pounds boneless pork chops or pork loin

1 large cucumber
½ pound (2 cups sliced) yellow onions
1 large (½ pound) bell pepper
3 or 4 medium tomatoes
2 bunches green onions, white and green parts
14 (2 ounces) Serrano chilies

1 cup water
½ cup fish sauce
⅓ cup granulated sugar
2 tablespoons tapioca starch
½ cup water

¼ cup vegetable oil
1 teaspoon (2 cloves) finely chopped garlic
¼ cup white vinegar

1. Slice the pork across the grain into pieces about 1 inch long and not more than ⅛ inch thick. Set aside.

2. Peel the cucumber and yellow onion. Slice the cucumber crosswise into pieces about 1 inch long, and slice each of these sections lengthwise into pieces about ¼ inch thick. Cut the onion in half vertically and lay each piece on its flat side. Slice each half into pieces about ¼ inch thick. Set the cucumber and yellow onion aside in a bowl. Remove the stem and seeds from the bell pepper and cut the pepper into pieces about 1 inch square. Slice each tomato in half vertically and remove the stem portion. Lay each half on its flat side and slice into pieces about ¼ inch thick. Set the bell pepper and tomato aside in a bowl. Slice the green onions diagonally into pieces about 1 inch long and set them aside in a separate bowl. Remove the stems, but not the seeds, from the chilies. Slice the chilies lengthwise into thin strips and add these to the green onions.

3. Mix the water, fish sauce, and sugar in a bowl. Stir until the sugar dissolves and set aside. Mix the tapioca starch and water in a small bowl and set aside.

4. Heat a wok, add the oil, and swirl it over the surface of the pan. Add the garlic and stir-fry until it is light golden. Add the pork and stir-fry until the pink color disappears. Add the cucumbers and onions and stir-fry until the onion is crisp-tender. Add the vinegar and mix it in well. (Adding the vinegar at this point instead of with the other liquids helps keep the vegetables crisp.)

5. Add the chopped bell pepper, sliced tomatoes, and fish sauce liquid from Step 3. Cover the wok and bring the mixture to a full boil rapidly.

6. Add the green onions and chilies and stir frequently until the green onions are hot and crisp-tender. Stir the tapioca starch mixture, add it to the wok, and stir until it begins to thicken.

7. Transfer the contents of the wok to a large, warm serving bowl and serve it immediately, or keep it warm while you prepare other dishes. Serve with rice.

Garlic–Pepper Pork
MOO GRATIEM PRIG THAI

It may come as a surprise to find that this dish is usually eaten for breakfast. It can, of course, be eaten at any other time of day, but early morning is the traditional time for it. When Kamolmal was growing up, her mother served this dish almost every morning for breakfast, accompanied with bowls of steaming hot soft rice.

SERVES 4 TO 6

2 tablespoons (1 ounce) finely chopped garlic
1/4 cup finely chopped coriander root
1 teaspoon ground white pepper
1/2 teaspoon salt

1 pound boneless pork chops or pork loin

Vegetable oil for deep-frying

Green lettuce leaves

Lime Sauce (page 84)

1. Pound or grind the garlic, coriander root, pepper, and salt to a coarse paste in a mortar or blender. If you use a blender, add just enough oil to aid in the grinding.

2. Slice the pork horizontally into pieces about 1/2 inch thick. (See page 175 for horizontal slicing technique.)

3. Spread the ground mixture from Step 1 evenly over both sides of the pork slices and marinate them about 2 hours, covered, at room temperature or overnight in the refrigerator.

4. Heat about 1 inch oil to 350° in a wok. Fry the pork until both sides are golden brown and the center has lost all the pink color but is still moist, about 5 minutes.

5. When the pork is cool enough to handle, slice it across the grain into slices 1/8 inch thick and about 2 inches long. Place these on lettuce leaves in a serving bowl.

6. Serve with Lime Sauce and rice.

Stir-Fried Pork
MOO WAN

This recipe requires no special ingredients, and provides a good introduction to Thai cuisine and cooking procedures. It has a mild flavor and is easy and quick to prepare. It serves well when you have little time to cook. If it is to be served with other dishes, we suggest that at least one of them be highly spiced for contrast.

SERVES 6 TO 8

2 pounds boneless pork chops or pork loin
½ pound (2 cups sliced) yellow onion

¼ cup (2 ounces) finely chopped garlic
½ cup finely chopped coriander root

1 cup water
¼ cup fish sauce
2 tablespoons granulated sugar

½ cup vegetable oil

Red lettuce leaves

1. Slice the pork across the grain into strips ⅛ inch thick and 1 to 2 inches long. Set aside. Peel the onion and slice it vertically into thin strips. Set aside in a separate bowl.

2. Pound or grind the garlic and coriander root to a coarse paste in a mortar or blender and set the paste aside. If you use a blender, add as little oil as possible to aid in grinding.

3. Mix the water, fish sauce, and sugar in a small bowl, stirring until the sugar is dissolved. Set aside.

4. Heat a wok, add the oil, and swirl it over the surface of the pan. Stir-fry the onion until it is dark golden and almost crisp. Watch it carefully when the color begins to change, because it cooks quickly after that. Be careful not to let it burn. Remove the onion from the oil and set aside.

5. Add the paste from Step 2 to the hot oil in the wok and stir-fry until it is light golden. Add the pork and stir-fry until the pink color disappears.

6. Add the liquid from Step 3 and stir over moderate heat until it begins to thicken.

7. Line a serving bowl with a single layer of lettuce leaves and add the cooked pork mixture. Garnish with the fried onions and serve with rice.

●●●————————————————————————

Ground Pork and Shrimp
NA TANG

This dish is delicate, mild, and slightly sweet. The use of fried bread with this dish is an adaptation for the United States. Traditionally, the ground mixture is poured over fried crisp rice. It tastes fine over fried bread, but is much better over crisp rice, which contrasts with the chewy texture of the pork and shrimp. We suggest you go to the extra trouble of making crisp rice.

SERVES 6 TO 8

1 pound firm fresh tofu
2 cups thick coconut milk (½ cup more if needed in Step 7)

¼ cup finely chopped coriander root
2 tablespoons (1 ounce) finely chopped garlic

½ pound ground pork
½ pound ground raw shrimp

2 tablespoons fish sauce
2 tablespoons granulated sugar

6 cups Crisp Rice (page 97) or 12 slices firm white bread

⅛ teaspoon ground white pepper

Coriander sprigs

1. Slice the tofu into ¼-inch cubes and place them in a saucepan with 1 cup of the thick coconut milk. Bring to a simmer over low heat and simmer until oil rises to the surface of the coconut milk, about 5 minutes.

2. Pound or grind the coriander root and garlic to a smooth paste in a mortar or blender. If you use a blender, add just enough coconut milk to aid in grinding.

3. Heat a wok and add 1 tablespoon of the boiled coconut milk and the paste from Step 2. Stir-fry over moderate heat until the mixture begins to thicken and turns light brown, being careful not to let it burn.

4. Add the ground pork and stir-fry until the pink color of the pork disappears. Add the ground shrimp and stir-fry until it turns pink. Add the remaining 1 cup of coconut milk, ¼ cup at a time, stirring after each addition and cooking until the mixture thickens.

5. Add the fish sauce and sugar and mix them in well. Add the tofu and coconut milk from Step 1 and stir it in gently without breaking the tofu. Remove the mixture from the heat and let it cool to room temperature.

6. Deep-fry the crisp rice or bread until it is golden brown. Arrange the rice or bread on a serving platter.

7. Check the consistency of the cooked mixture. It should be thin enough to pour, but thick enough to adhere to the rice or bread. If it is too thick, add more thick coconut milk.

8. Pour the cooked mixture over the bread or rice, sprinkle it with pepper, and garnish the top with coriander sprigs. Or serve the rice or toast and the topping separately, for each diner to select as desired.

✳✳✳━━━━━━━━━━━━━━━━━━━━━━━━

Barbecued Pork with Cucumber
YUM MOO GAB TANG QUA

This dish should be served at room temperature. It makes a perfect summer meal, looking very much like a light, summery salad. The beige pork, red tomatoes, and dark and pale green colors contrast for a very pretty presentation, and the crisp cucumbers and chewy pork and shrimp continue the contrast. If dried shrimp are not available, you may substitute very small shrimp, but the chewy texture and light salt flavor will be sacrificed. Vinegar Sauce is essential to this dish, accenting the existing flavors and adding a new dimension of its own.

SERVES 6 TO 8

¼ *pound dried shrimp*

1 *pound pork loin*

2 *pounds cucumber*
½ *pound (2 cups sliced) red onion*
1 *bunch green onions, white and green parts*
4 *Serrano chilies*

¼ *cup fish sauce*
¼ *cup granulated sugar*
½ *cup lime juice*

Red lettuce leaves
Tomato wedges
1 *cup coriander sprigs*

1. Put the dried shrimp in a sieve and rinse them thoroughly under hot running water. Allow them to drain completely, then chop them into coarse pieces.

2. Barbecue or broil the pork until it is done but still moist. Allow it to cool to room temperature and slice it across the grain into strips ⅛ inch thick and 1 to 2 inches long.

3. Peel the cucumber and red onion. Slice the cucumber diagonally into pieces ⅛ inch thick and 1½ inches long. Slice the red onion vertically into thin pieces. Slice the green onions diagonally into ⅛-inch pieces. Remove the stems, but not the seeds, from the chilies and slice the chilies lengthwise into thin strips. Place these ingredients in a mixing bowl. Add the chopped shrimp and sliced pork.

4. Put the fish sauce, sugar, and lime juice in a small bowl and stir until the sugar is dissolved. Pour the mixture into the bowl with the other ingredients and toss to mix well.

Ahead-of-time note: Prepare the vegetables, meat, and liquid up to 4 hours in advance and keep them covered in separate containers in the refrigerator. Bring the ingredients to room temperature, mix them, and proceed to Step 5 just before serving.

5. Place a single layer of whole lettuce leaves on a serving platter and arrange the "salad" from Step 4 over them. Garnish with tomato wedges and coriander sprigs. Serve with rice.

Pork with Eggplant and Mint

PAD PED MA KAEU YAW

This dish is rich and filling but not hot or highly spiced, and it needs little accompaniment other than rice. You may, of course, make it hotter by adding additional chilies to taste. The final mixture is thick and has approximately equal amounts of pork and eggplant. If you like both pork and eggplant separately, do try this combination for a real treat. This dish was a favorite of Kamolmal's grandmother, from whom she learned to prepare it.

SERVES 6 TO 8

10 (1½ ounces) finely chopped Serrano chilies
½ cup (2 ounces) finely chopped yellow onion
¼ cup (2 ounces) finely chopped garlic

2 pounds eggplant

2 cups water
1 teaspoon salt

¾ cup vegetable oil

1 pound ground pork

¼ cup + 2 tablespoons fish sauce
¼ cup granulated sugar
1 cup water

¼ cup mint leaves
Coriander sprigs

1. Pound or grind the chilies, onion, and garlic to a coarse paste in a mortar or blender. If you are using a blender, add just enough water to aid in grinding.

2. Remove the green "cap" from the stem end of the eggplant, but do not peel the eggplant. Prepare it as follows:

For American eggplant: Cut the eggplant lengthwise into 4 to 6 wedges, depending on the size of the eggplant. Each wedge should be about 2 inches wide at its widest part. Cut each of the long wedges crosswise into pieces about ¼ inch thick.

For Japanese or long green Thai eggplant: Slice the eggplant in half lengthwise, then cut each of these pieces crosswise into two to four pieces. Each piece should be about 4 to 6 inches long and ¼ to ½ inch thick.·

3. Put the water and salt in a wok and bring it to a full boil over high heat. Add the eggplant pieces and parboil them, turning them gently about 6 or 8 times to maximize contact with the water. Parboil the eggplant until cooked, but not soft and mushy, about 2 to 3 minutes. Drain the eggplant in a colander. Discard the water and dry the wok thoroughly.

4. Heat the wok again, add the oil, and swirl it over the surface of the pan. When it is hot enough to form a light haze, add the eggplant pieces, and turn them frequently by inserting a wok scoop or stiff spatula underneath them, lifting it through and folding it over. Do not stir or use force, because the eggplant may fall apart. It will reduce in volume as it cooks. Cook until it is lightly browned, but not crisp, and is reduced to about half its original volume, almost 5 minutes.

5. Remove the eggplant pieces from the wok with a strainer and allow the excess oil to drain back into the wok as you lift the eggplant out. Place the eggplant in a serving bowl and keep it warm.

6. Add the paste from Step 1 to the wok and stir-fry until it is light golden. Add the pork and stir-fry until the pink color disappears.

7. Add the fish sauce and sugar and stir to mix them in thoroughly. Add the water and bring the mixture to a full boil over high heat, stirring frequently. Add the mint leaves and mix them in well. Remove the wok from the heat.

Ahead-of-time note: Prepare the ingredients through Step 7 except for adding the mint leaves. Store the eggplant and pork mixture in separate covered containers for up to 2 hours at room temperature, or overnight in the refrigerator. To serve, heat them separately, add the mint leaves, and proceed to Step 8. Advance preparation and reheating cause the eggplant's texture to suffer, but the flavor is still quite good.

8. If any oil has exuded from the eggplant, pour it off and discard it. Scoop the pork mixture on top of the eggplant pieces, garnish with coriander sprigs and serve hot.

12
Chicken

CHICKEN IS POPULAR in Thailand, a versatile food for the rich, flavorful sauces and curries that distinguish Thai cooking. As in the United States, chicken is generally less expensive than pork or beef. Interestingly, turkey is seldom substituted, although there are turkeys in Thailand. This may seem strange until you realize that turkeys are kept as pets by some Thai families. When Kamolmal and Choompol, her husband, first came to America they were given a turkey at Thanksgiving by a well-meaning American friend. They were quite puzzled about what to do with it, because in Thailand they had kept a turkey for a family pet, and the thought of eating one was just too much to consider. So they gave it away to someone else.

✳✳✳ ━━━━━━━━━━━━━━━━━━━━━━━━━━━━━━━

Chicken with Green Curry
GANG KIEW WAN GAI

This is a popular, rich, hot dish that combines the smoothness of coconut milk, the heat of chilies, and the tang of lime. It has a large amount of thin sauce, so use a serving bowl large enough to accommodate it and serve plenty of rice so you can enjoy every drop of sauce. The main recipe calls for cooking the chicken in coconut milk, which gives it a full, rich, yet subtle coconut flavor. Traditionally the bones are not removed from the chicken and it is simply chopped with a cleaver, but you may remove them if you prefer, keeping in mind that leaving them in will produce a richer, fuller flavor. If you prefer less coconut flavor or less sauce, use the variation that follows the main recipe. In Thailand, this dish is made with tiny green Thai eggplant, which contribute color and crunchy bits of bitter flavor. However, these are rarely available in the United States except where there is a large Thai community, and even then they are very expensive. To obtain a similar effect in color and texture, but not taste, substitute fresh green peas.

SERVES 6 TO 8

5 Kaffir lime leaves
1/4 cup warm water
20-ounce can bamboo shoots
4 Serrano chilies

2- to 3-pounds white and dark chicken pieces or 1½
   to 2 pounds boned chicken breasts
1 cup fresh green peas or, preferably, 1 cup small,
   round, green Thai eggplant
4 cups thin coconut milk

1 cup thick coconut milk
1 recipe Green Curry (page 74)

1/4 cup + 1 tablespoon fish sauce

1/4 cup mint or basil leaves

1. Soak the Kaffir lime leaves in the warm water while preparing the rest of the ingredients. Drain the canning liquid from the bamboo shoots, rinse them with water, and slice them into thin julienne strips if they aren't already in strips. Set them aside in a colander to drain. Remove the stems, but not the seeds, from the chilies and slice the chilies lengthwise into thin strips. Set them aside.

2. Chop or slice the chicken into pieces about 1 to 2 inches long. Traditionally, the bones are left in.

3. Boil the chicken and the green peas (or small Thai eggplant) in the thin coconut milk about 10 minutes. Set aside. Or follow one of the variations described at the end of the main recipe.

4. Heat a wok and add ½ cup of the thick coconut milk. Stir constantly until the coconut milk thickens, forms large bubbles, and begins to turn a pale tan color.

5. Add the green curry and stir until the mixture is almost dry.

6. Add the remaining ½ cup thick coconut milk, stirring constantly until it is slightly thick, but not dry. Add the bamboo shoots and fish sauce. Stir quickly to mix all the ingredients thoroughly. Add the drained Kaffir lime leaves, chilies, and basil or mint leaves.

7. Add the curry mixture from step 6 to the chicken and thin coconut milk and bring it to a boil. Remove the mixture from the heat and serve immediately, or keep it warm while you prepare other dishes. Serve with rice.

Variation: This procedure produces significantly less sauce, and the sauce it does have is much thicker and flavored strongly.

1. Omit the thin coconut milk and green peas (or small Thai eggplant) from the ingredients, and ignore the part of Step 3 in the main recipe that instructs you to boil the chicken. Ignore Step 7 completely.

2. Stir-fry the chicken in ¼ cup oil until the pink color disappears. This will go quickly if you removed the bones from the chicken, and may take 4 to 5 minutes over moderate heat if you have not. Remove the chicken from the wok and set it aside.

3. Proceed with the main recipe, ignoring all references to thin coconut milk.

Stuffed Chicken Wings
PEEG GAI SOD SAI

This is a favorite of almost everyone, and may be served as an appetizer, cocktail snack, or a main course. If you are using it as an appetizer, slice the pieces about half as thick as you would for a main course. Begin this dish well in advance, because boning chicken wings is time-consuming the first few times you do it; after a few times, however, it goes fairly rapidly. We give instructions for boning chicken wings following this recipe, and urge you not to avoid the recipe because of the necessity of boning wings. The effort is well worth it. The red lime liquid adds to the crispness of batter-fried foods, but it may be omitted if unavailable. The batter we suggest here may also be used for deep-frying other meats or vegetables. Water can be substituted for the coconut milk, but coconut milk enhances the flavor.

SERVES 6 TO 8

6 chicken wings

2 ounces bean threads
1 cup warm water

2 tablespoons finely chopped coriander root
1 tablespoon (½ ounce) finely chopped garlic

½ pound ground chicken
1½ tablespoons fish sauce
1 egg yolk
⅛ teaspoon ground white pepper

1 cup all-purpose flour
¾ to 1 cup thick coconut milk
3 tablespoons red lime liquid (page 66)
½ teaspoon salt
¼ teaspoon ground white pepper
1 tablespoon egg white (optional)
Vegetable oil for deep-frying

Garlic Sauce (page 84)

1. Bone the chicken wings as described in the instructions following the recipe.

2. Soak the bean threads in warm water for 10 minutes. They should be pliable but firm.

3. Pound or grind the coriander root and garlic to a coarse paste in a mortar, blender, or food processor. If you use a blender, it may be necessary to add the fish sauce to keep the garlic and coriander root from flying around in the container.

4. Drain the bean threads thoroughly and cut them into pieces about 1 inch long.

5. Mix the ground chicken, paste from Step 3, fish sauce, bean threads, egg yolk, and white pepper thoroughly. (If you gound the garlic and coriander root with the fish sauce, do not add more here.)

6. Divide the mixture into 6 portions and stuff the chicken wings with it, making sure the stuffing goes all the way to the end of the wings. Massaging the wings from the outside helps get the stuffing in completely. If your chicken wings have a few small holes in them don't worry about it, but keep the mixture from poking out. There is no need to tie or skewer the opening at the end.

Optional, recommended, and not traditional: Partially cook the stuffed wings in a microwave oven. For 6 wings, 4 minutes on high is enough.

Ahead-of-time note: The wings can be prepared ahead to this point and kept a few hours or overnight, covered, in the refrigerator. Bring them to room temperature before proceeding with the rest of the recipe.

7. Combine the flour, coconut milk, red lime liquid, salt, and pepper to form a smooth batter. (Beat the optional egg white until stiff but not dry, and fold it into the batter.)

8. Heat 1½ inches oil to 375° in a wok or deep skillet. Dip the stuffed wings in the batter one at a time and deep-fry them until they are crisp and medium golden brown. Do not overcrowd the pan, or the wings will not brown properly. Drain the fried wings on paper towels.

9. Slice the wings diagonally into pieces about ½ inch thick. Serve hot, warm, or at room temperature with Garlic Sauce.

Boning Chicken Wings

Boning chicken wings may seem like an impossible task, but actually it isn't difficult. It can be time-consuming and seem tedious the first few times you try it, but if you practice a little the process can be speeded up considerably. Allow yourself time to perform the task leisurely the first few times or you may become frustrated and give up on it. Since wings with the tips still attached are easier to bone, if your market routinely removes them, ask for wings with tips attached. If they refuse, shop elsewhere.

The following sequence will make the boning easier:

1. If possible, select chicken wings that have relatively loose skins, because loose skin makes it easier to manipulate the bones, skin, meat, and knife.

2. Make sure that your knife is very sharp and, if possible, has a narrow, curved blade. A standard boning knife is perfect.

3. Bring the wings to room temperature, because the meat and skin of cold wings are more difficult to handle.

4. Hold a wing vertically, with the part that was attached to the body pointing up. Cut carefully around the bone to sever all tendons at that point. There are several tendons, so make sure that you get all of them.

5. Scrape the meat from the bone by holding the knife blade close to the bone and working carefully so you do not puncture the skin. Or, push the meat from the bone with your fingers as you work down toward the elbow. As you work down, fold the skin back on the part of the wing you have not yet reached. This process is like turning a balloon inside out. It is easier to continue to turn the skin inside out as you work, to keep it out of the way. When you have finished, the wing will be inside out.

6. When you reach the elbow, examine it to see how the skin is attached. Cut and pull carefully to loosen the skin, meat, and tendons at this point. It is here that the greatest possibility for puncturing the skin exists. After the skin and tendons have been cut and pulled from the bone and elbow, remove the bone by bending the joint gently backwards and pulling out the bone with a twisting motion. Be careful not to break the bones in the second section.

7. Use the same procedure for loosening the skin, meat, and tendons on the next section of bone.

8. When you reach the next joint, remove the bones by twisting as described in Step 6. It is easier to remove the small bone first, because that gives you more room to maneuver the large one, which is attached more firmly than the small one.

9. At this point the chicken wing will be folded inside out. Find the tip of the wing and pull it carefully through the boned wing to position the skin on the outside. Check for tiny holes to see where you may have cut or poked through the skin so you will have an idea of how not to make that mistake on the next wing. If there are some holes, don't worry about them; just resolve to do better next time.

●●● ──────────────────────────────

Chicken and Cashews
GAI PAD MAMUANG HIM MA PAN

This dish may seem more Chinese than Thai, but it is prepared in many Thai homes and demonstrates how the Thai people have borrowed ideas and incorporated them cleverly into their own cuisine with subtle changes. The addition of fish sauce and chilies provides the Thai touch. It is less spicy and hot than many other preparations and is very good as an accompaniment to hotter dishes because it adds an interesting contrast and helps refresh the palate.

SERVES 4 TO 6

½ pound (2 cups sliced) yellow onion
1 large green (bell) pepper
2 stalks celery
1 medium carrot

¾ pound boned skinned chicken breast
10 small dried red chilies

¼ cup oyster sauce
1 tablespoon fish sauce
½ cup water

1 tablespoon tapioca starch
¼ cup water

3 tablespoons vegetable oil
1 teaspoon (2 cloves) finely chopped garlic

¼ pound unsalted cashews

1. Peel the yellow onion and remove the root portion. Remove the stem and seeds from the bell pepper and cut the pepper and onion into ½-inch squares. Slice the celery and carrot diagonally into pieces ⅛ inch thick. Set these ingredients aside in one bowl. Lay the chicken breast flat on a cutting board and slice it in half horizontally. Cut the chicken into ¾-inch squares and set aside. Remove the stems and seeds from the dried chilies and set aside.

2. Mix the oyster sauce, fish sauce, and ½ cup water in a small bowl. In a separate bowl mix the tapioca starch and ¼ cup water.

3. Heat a wok, add the oil, and swirl it over the surface of the pan. Add the chilies and stir-fry until they turn a deep red color, but be careful not to let them burn. Remove the chilies from the wok and set them aside. Add the garlic and stir-fry until it is light golden.

4. Add the chicken and stir-fry until the pink color disappears. Add the vegetables and stir-fry until they are crisp-tender. Add the fish sauce mixture from Step 2 and stir it in well. Stir the tapioca starch mixture from Step 2 and add it to the wok. While stirring, add the cashews and fried chilies. The mixture will be moderately thick.

5. Scoop the contents of the wok out to a warm serving bowl and serve immediately or keep the dish warm while you prepare other dishes.

6. Serve with rice.

•••

Barbecued Chicken 1
GAI YANG I

Thai barbecued chicken combines the distinctive flavors of traditional Thai cooking with a favorite technique of cooking in the United States, but it is not an American adaptation. It is authentically Thai, and an excellent way to begin your venture into Thai cooking, because it uses widely available ingredients and a familiar technique. As with other barbecued foods, it is best if cooked over charcoal, but is also good prepared in the kitchen under a hot broiler. If possible, marinate the chicken overnight in the refrigerator to allow the flavors to penetrate the meat.

SERVES 6 TO 8

1 whole (2½- 3-pound) chicken

3 tablespoons (1½ ounces) finely chopped garlic
1 tablespoon ground white pepper
1 teaspoon salt
2 teaspoons ground turmeric
1 cup thick coconut milk

Garlic Sauce (page 84)

Rice with Coconut Milk (page 98)

1. Cut the chicken into serving pieces of desired size. These may be individual pieces such as leg, thigh, breast, etc., or you may simply cut the chicken in half.

2. Pound or grind the garlic to a smooth paste in a mortar or blender. Mix it with the ground pepper, salt, turmeric, and coconut milk. If you use a blender, it may be necessary to use a little coconut milk to aid in grinding. Pour the mixture over the chicken and marinate it, covered and refrigerated, for 2 hours or overnight. Turn the pieces periodically to allow them to marinate evenly.

Ahead-of-time note: The flavor is best if the chicken is prepared to this point a day in advance and allowed to marinate overnight in a covered container in the refrigerator.

3. Prepare hot coals in your outdoor grill or preheat the broiler. Grill the chicken until juices from the thickest part run clear, about 30 minutes. Baste it frequently with the marinade. Discard any marinade that isn't used. If you use the kitchen broiler, pour the pan drippings over the chicken just before serving it.

4. Chop the chicken into pieces 1 to 2 inches long, using a cleaver or heavy knife (or leave it as is if you prefer).

5. Serve with Garlic Sauce and Rice with Coconut Milk.

• • •

Barbecued Chicken 2
GAI YANG II

This barbecued chicken is spicier and not as sweet as the previous recipe. It has a full, rich flavor and we would be hard-pressed to say which of them we like best.

SERVES 6 TO 8

1 whole (2½- to 3-pound) chicken

¼ cup finely chopped coriander root
2 tablespoons (1 ounce) finely chopped garlic

2 tablespoons fish sauce
2 tablespoons granulated sugar
½ teaspoon five-spice powder
½ cup water
⅛ teaspoon ground white pepper
1 tablespoon light soy sauce
1 teaspoon black soy sauce
Garlic Sauce (page 84) or Plum Sauce (page 85)

1. Cut the chicken into serving pieces or split it in half.

2. Pound the coriander root and garlic to a smooth paste in a mortar or grind them in a blender with the fish sauce and light soy sauce. Mix the paste with the fish sauce, sugar, five-spice powder, water, pepper, and both types of soy sauce (do not add more fish sauce or light soy sauce if you used them in grinding).

3. Pour the mixture over the chicken, making sure that all parts of the chicken are covered. Cover and marinate for 2 hours or, preferably, overnight in the refrigerator. Turn the pieces periodically to make sure they marinate evenly.

Ahead-of-time note: The flavor is best if the chicken is prepared to this point a day in advance and allowed to marinate overnight.

4. Prepare hot coals in your outdoor grill or preheat the broiler. Grill the chicken until juices from the thickest part run clear, about 30 minutes. Baste it frequently with the marinade. Discard any marinade that isn't used. If you have used the broiler, pour the pan juices over the chicken just before it is served.

5. Chop the chicken into pieces 1 or 2 inches long, using a cleaver or heavy knife (or leave it as is, if you prefer).

6. Serve with rice and Garlic Sauce or Plum Sauce.

• • •

Chicken with Richly Flavored Rice
KAO MAN GAI

In this recipe nothing is wasted except the chicken bones. The chicken produces a slightly oily broth, which adds flavor to the rice with which it is cooked. In fact, you could call this dish "Chicken with Oily Rice" if the name didn't sound so unappealing. If possible, select a chicken with a great deal of fat. Or add up to 1 tablespoon chicken fat when simmering the chicken. If you have leftover skins from boning chicken breasts, they may be added for additional flavor. The dish is mild and richly flavored, and is served with a spicy sauce for added flavor.

SERVES 6 TO 8

1 whole (2½- to 3-pound) chicken
Water

3 cups raw long-grain rice
1 teaspoon salt
1 teaspoon (2 cloves) finely chopped garlic
2 cups broth from cooking the chicken in Step 1

1 cucumber
Coriander sprigs

Ginger Sauce (page 88)

1. Put the chicken in a pot with enough water to barely cover it. Do not remove any of the fat or skin, because they are needed to produce the oily broth. You may include the gizzard, heart, liver, and neck if you like these pieces. Traditionally they would be included. Cover the pot, bring it to a slow boil and cook the chicken about 1 hour, or until the chicken is done but not falling off the bones. Periodically remove any foam that rises to the surface.

2. Remove the chicken from the broth. Do not skim the fat from the broth, but do remove any foam that has accumulated. Set the chicken aside in a covered container or under an aluminum foil tent to keep it warm.

3. Place the rice, salt, garlic, and 2 cups of the broth, using as much of the fat as possible, in a saucepan. Bring to a boil, stir briefly to loosen any stuck grains of rice, cover the pan with a tight-fitting lid, and reduce the heat to a simmer. Cook the rice for 20 minutes without lifting the lid. (See page 96 for more detailed instructions.)

4. Slice the chicken, skin and all, into thin slices about 1 inch wide. Cut these into pieces 2 inches long. Peel the cucumber and slice it diagonally into slices ⅛ inch thick. Place the rice on a serving platter and arrange the chicken slices over it. Surround it with cucumber slices and garnish with coriander sprigs.

5. Serve with Ginger Sauce.

✳✳✳ ━━━━━━━━━━━━━━━━━━━━━━━━━━━━━━━

Chicken in Roasted Curry Sauce

GAI PAD NAM PRIG PAO

This is a very popular dish, rich with the full, hearty taste of roasted chilies, fish sauce, and shrimp paste. The spiciness will depend on the chilies used in preparing the Roasted Red Curry and can range from fiery hot to mild. The dish can almost always be found in Thai restaurants.

SERVES 4 TO 6

3 tablespoons fish sauce
1½ tablespoons granulated sugar
½ cup water
¼ cup Roasted Red Curry (page 76)
1 pound boned skinned chicken breasts
6 green onions, white part only

1 tablespoon vegetable oil
1 teaspoon (2 cloves) finely chopped garlic

½ cup whole roasted unsalted peanuts

1. Mix the fish sauce, sugar, water, and Roasted Red Curry in a small bowl and set aside. Lay the chicken breasts flat on a cutting surface, and slice them horizontally by holding one hand flat on top of the chicken to keep it from sliding and cutting parallel to the surface of the cutting board. Each piece will be the length and width of the original piece of chicken. Cut the chicken into 1-inch squares and set aside. Slice the green onions diagonally into pieces about ½ inch long.

2. Heat a wok, add the oil, and swirl it over the surface of the pan. Add the garlic and stir-fry until it is light golden. Add the chicken and stir-fry until the pink color disappears completely. Add the liquid mixture from Step 1 and stir until it boils.

3. Add the peanuts and green onions, stirring until the onions are crisp-tender and the peanuts heated through.

4. Serve immediately or keep it warm while you prepare other dishes.

5. Serve with rice.

Chicken Balls
LOOK CHIN GAI

Chicken balls are easy to prepare and may be made a day in advance and stored in the refrigerator or frozen in tightly sealed containers for up to 6 months. They can be barbecued or broiled and served with a dipping sauce, e.g., Garlic Sauce, added to soups, or used to prepare curry dishes. We suggest you make a full recipe and freeze the ones you are not going to use immediately so they will be available at any time. Chicken balls are sometimes available in Thai markets, but they are so easy to prepare there is really no need to buy them.

MAKES 1 POUND (ABOUT 30 BALLS)

1 pound boned skinned chicken

2 tablespoons fish sauce
¼ cup water
¼ teaspoon ground white pepper
1 tablespoon (½ ounce) finely chopped garlic

2 quarts water

1. Grind all the ingredients except the 2 quarts water in a food processor until a smooth puree is formed.

2. Bring the 2 quarts water to a slow boil in a large pot. Form balls out of the meat mixture, using 1 to 1½ tablespoons meat mixture for each. Drop them into the boiling water and cook until they rise to the surface and are firm. Remove them from the water and drain them thoroughly on a rack.

3. Use them immediately, store them for 1 day, tightly covered, in the refrigerator, or wrap them tightly in aluminum foil or plastic wrap and store them in the freezer for up to 6 months.

∗∗∗ ─────────────────────────────────────

Spicy Ground Chicken
LOB GAI

This is a moderately spiced dish that has relatively little sauce, but what there is adds a marvelous flavor to rice. Because it is served at room temperature it is very well suited for patio meals in the summer.

SERVES 4 TO 6

1 pound ground chicken breast

2 green onions, white part only
1 ounce (¼ cup sliced) red onion

3 pieces kah

2 tablespoons fish sauce
¼ cup lime juice
1½ teaspoons ground roasted chilies (page 60)
1 tablespoon ground toasted rice (page 66)

¼ cup loosely packed mint leaves

Red lettuce leaves
Fresh red chili "flowers" (page 29)

Assorted raw vegetables (broccoli, green beans,
    eggplant, zucchini, etc.), cut into serving size pieces

1. Heat a wok over medium heat and add the chicken without oil. Stir-fry until the pink color disappears. Place it in a mixing bowl.

2. Slice the green onions crosswise into pieces about ⅛ inch thick and add them to the chicken. Peel the red onion, remove the root portion, slice the onion vertically into paper-thin strips, and add these to the bowl.

3. Heat a small skillet and roast the *kah* without oil until it is light golden. Grind it to a powder in a blender or a coffee or spice grinder and add it to the chicken mixture.

4. Add the fish sauce, lime juice, roasted chilies, toasted rice, and mint leaves. Stir to mix the ingredients thoroughly.

5. Arrange a single layer of lettuce leaves in a serving bowl. Place the chicken mixture on them and garnish with fresh red chili "flowers."

6. Serve at room temperature with rice and assorted raw vegetables.

13
Seafood

SEAFOOD IS USED WIDELY in Thai cuisine because of its abundance. Freshwater fish is more widely available in most parts of Thailand than seafood, but they may be used interchangeably. Because most fish markets in America stock more seafood than freshwater fish, we have called for seafood in the recipes, but you may substitute freshwater fish if they are common in your area.

Stuffed Squid
BLA MUK SOD SAI

These stuffed squid have a very thin, crisp crust and a soft, slightly sweet filling. The sweetness comes primarily from carrots and cabbage, and if you prefer something less sweet a stuffing with meat or other vegetables may be substituted, e.g., the stuffing suggested for Stuffed Chicken Wings (page 200). If you have thought you might not like squid, we're willing to bet that you'll change your mind after trying this version. Squid can be found more easily in American markets than they could a few years ago, and are available in either fresh or frozen form, depending on where you live. Either is acceptable. Occasionally you may find squid that are already cleaned, but it really makes little difference, because cleaning them isn't difficult. We have provided instructions immediately following this recipe. The red lime liquid helps make the crust crisper, but it may be omitted if unavailable.

SERVES 6 TO 8

2 pounds squid (about 12 to 15)
1 ounce each (¼ cup each chopped or shredded) carrots,
*   cabbage, and celery*

2 tablespoons finely chopped coriander root
1 tablespoon (½ ounce) finely chopped garlic

½ pound ground pork or chicken
3 tablespoons fish sauce
1 egg yolk
⅛ teaspoon ground white pepper

Vegetable oil for deep-frying

1 cup all-purpose flour
1 tablespoon tapioca starch
¾ cup thick coconut milk
3 tablespoons red lime liquid (page 66)
½ teaspoon salt
⅛ teaspoon ground white pepper

Plum Sauce (page 85)

1. Clean the squid using the instructions that follow this recipe. Set them aside. Chop or shred the carrot, celery, and cabbage finely and set them aside in a bowl.

2. Pound or grind the coriander root and garlic to a smooth paste. A mortar and pestle are best for this small amount, but you may use a blender if you add the fish sauce to aid in grinding.

3. Mix the ground meat, paste from Step 2, fish sauce, egg yolk, chopped vegetables, and pepper thoroughly. (If you ground the coriander root and garlic with fish sauce, do not add more fish sauce at this point.) Stuff the squid with the mixture, making sure the cavity is filled completely but not packed tightly. It is somewhat easier to stuff the squid if you cut off a little of the pointed tip so that air will not be trapped as you push the stuffing in. It is not necessary to skewer or sew the open ends.

Optional and non-traditional, but recommended: Partially cook the stuffed squid in a microwave oven. About 3 minutes on high is enough.

4. Heat 1½ inches oil to 375° in a wok or deep skillet.

5. Thoroughly mix the flour, tapioca starch, coconut milk, red lime liquid, salt, and pepper to form a smooth batter. Dip each stuffed squid in the batter and then place it in the oil; doing the squid one at a time helps keep the oil from cooling too quickly. Do only enough squid to fit comfortably in the pan; if crowded, the squid will not brown well. As soon as you have put them into the oil, puncture each squid with a fork to reduce spattering. (If you have cut off the pointed tip of the squid it is not necessary to puncture them.) Deep-fry until the squid are golden brown, about 5 minutes. Drain them on paper towels and keep them warm while you fry the remaining squid.

6. Slice the squid crosswise into pieces about ½ to ¾ inch wide.

7. Serve with Plum Sauce.

Cleaning Squid

Most squid are frozen immediately after they are caught and then shipped in large frozen blocks. Some markets sell them frozen and others thaw them before putting them out for sale. In either case you will probably find that they have not yet been cleaned. If so, you are in luck, because they will have the tentacles attached. These make tasty accompaniments to the stuffed squid and can be fried right along with them. Cleaning squid is a very simple process. The crucial point is to be sure the body cavity is completely clean.

1. Hold the body of the squid in one hand and grasp the tentacles firmly just above the eyes. With a firm and steady motion pull the body and tentacles apart. Most of the inner parts will come out easily.

2. Remove the long, thin piece of cartilage known as the quill. Reach inside the body cavity and pull out all remaining parts carefully and completely.

3. Wash the inside of the body cavity very carefully, using cold running water, until the water runs clear. Reach in with your fingers all the way to the tip of the body and clean out any remaining residue.

4. Under cool running water, rub the outside of the body gently with your fingers to remove the speckled skin.

5. Place the tentacles on a cutting board and cut at a point just below the eyes. Discard the eye portion and wash the tentacles under cool running water until the water runs clear. While doing this, rub the tentacles gently with your fingers to remove the speckled skin.

6. If the squid are not to be used right away, place them in a bowl of ice water, cover the bowl with a lid or plastic wrap, and store them in the refrigerator for up to 1 day.

✳✳✳ ────────────────────────────────

Deep-Fried Fish
BLA TOD RAD PRIG

This dish is enjoyed by some people who ordinarily do not even like fish. For those who do like fish, it is a real treat. The fish has a crisp skin, even though no batter or coating is used, and it is served with a tangy sauce that enhances the natural fish flavor without masking it. If possible, select a whole fish with the head and tail intact. At the very least the fish should still have the skin attached, because skinned fillets may come apart during the frying. Any firm-fleshed fish that will fit comfortably in a wok or skillet without hanging over the edges may be used. Some successful types are small red snapper and trout. The fish may cook for what will seem to be a long time, but that is necessary to develop the crisp skin. If prepared properly the fish will not disintegrate or dry out.

SERVES 4 OR 6

1 ounce wet tamarind or 2 tablespoons tamarind concentrate
¼ cup warm water

2 ounces (about 14) Serrano chilies
½ cup (1 ounce) finely chopped yellow onion
2 tablespoons (1 ounce) finely chopped garlic

¼ cup vegetable oil
3 tablespoons fish sauce
2 tablespoons granulated sugar
¾ cup water
¼ cup loosely packed mint leaves

1 whole fish, 2 or 3 pounds after cleaning
Vegetable oil for deep-frying

¼ cup loosely packed mint leaves
¼ cup long thin carrot shreds
¼ cup finely shredded cabbage

1. (Omit this step if you are using tamarind concentrate.) Soak the wet tamarind in the warm water for 15 minutes, or until it is soft. Put the mixture in a sieve and press out all the pulp and liquid you can. Discard the seeds and any residue that will not go through the sieve. Scrape all the pulp from the outside of the sieve and add it to the sieved solution. Set the solution aside.

2. Remove the stems, but not the seeds, from the chilies and chop the chilies finely. Pound or grind the chilies, onion, and garlic to a coarse paste in a mortar or blender. If using a blender, add the oil to aid in grinding.

3. Heat a saucepan or skillet and add ¼ cup oil. (If you have ground the chilies, garlic, and onion in oil, do not add more oil.) Add the paste from Step 2 and stir-fry until it is light golden. Add the fish sauce, sugar, ¾ cup water, and tamarind solution. (If you used tamarind concentrate, add an additional ¼ cup water.) Bring the mixture to a boil and remove it from the heat. Add the mint leaves and keep the sauce warm while you cook the fish.

4. If you have a whole, uncleaned fish, clean and wash it thoroughly, as described in the instructions following this recipe.

Make three diagonal slashes on each side, cutting about halfway to the bone. Omit the slashes if you are using a boned fish.

5. Put 1½ inches vegetable oil in a wok and heat it to 375°. Dry the fish thoroughly and slide it into the oil gently to avoid splattering. Fry until it is crisp on the outside and the flesh along the cuts is light golden, about 5 minutes. Thicker fish may take longer. Turn it at least once, being careful not to break it. Do not undercook it, because the skin and the exposed parts of the flesh should be light and crispy. Remove the fish carefully, drain it thoroughly on paper towels, and place it on a serving platter.

6. Pour the sauce over the fish and garnish with mint leaves, shredded carrot, and shredded cabbage.

7. Serve with rice. Do not try to keep the fish warm for more than 15 minutes because it may get soggy.

Cleaning Fish

Most fish markets in the United States sell fish that have already been cleaned, but it is possible in some Thai and Oriental markets to buy them uncleaned, either frozen or alive. In some markets you may find a whole, uncleaned fish that has been frozen immediately upon being caught. In that case we advise that you buy the whole frozen fish, keep it frozen at home, and thaw and clean it when you plan to use it. That way it stays much fresher tasting and you can purchase an ample supply in advance and keep them in your freezer to be available on a moment's notice. Frozen fish can be thawed by placing them in the refrigerator for a day to thaw slowly or they can be thawed more quickly by placing them in a bowl of cool, never warm or hot, water. We find no noticeable difference in flavor or texture between these two procedures.

1. Thaw the fish completely if it has been frozen.

2. Using a small knife, make an incision on the belly side of the fish the full length of the body cavity. You can determine this easily by feel because it will be softer than the fleshy part. Reach inside, pull out all the body parts, including the gills, and discard them. Pay particular attention to the area around the gills, where some small pieces may tend to stick.

3. Carefully cut out the side fins, which are located just behind the gills. Leave the head, remaining fins, and tail intact.

4. Wash the fish carefully inside and out under cold running water. If any scales remain, remove them by scraping a knife in the direction opposite to which they lie.

5. If the fish is not to be used within 1 hour, place it in a bowl of water with plenty of ice, cover the bowl, and refrigerate it. Thawed fish should be used within 6 hours for the best flavor.

✳✳✳ ───────────────────────────

Hungry Shrimp
GOONG PAD NAM PRIG PAO

These shrimp are very popular in the United States. You might think that the Roasted Red Curry would overwhelm the delicate flavor of the shrimp, but it doesn't. Instead, it adds a rich accent to the subtle flavor of the shrimp. This recipe is quick and easy to prepare, and produces a moderate amount of sauce.

SERVES 4 OR 6

1 pound raw shrimp

3 tablespoons fish sauce
1½ tablespoons granulated sugar
½ cup water
¼ cup Roasted Red Curry (page 76)
1 tablespoon vegetable oil
1 teaspoon (2 cloves) finely chopped garlic

½ cup whole roasted unsalted peanuts
6 green onions, white parts only

Green lettuce
Coriander sprigs

1. Peel and devein the shrimp, leaving the tails intact. Set them aside.

2. Mix the fish sauce, sugar, water, and Roasted Red Curry in a small bowl, stirring until the sugar is dissolved completely. Set aside. Slice the green onion crosswise into pieces about ⅛ inch thick. Set aside.

3. Heat a wok, add the oil, and swirl it over the surface of the pan. Add the garlic and stir-fry until it is light golden. Add the shrimp and stir-fry over moderate heat until they turn pink, but do not overcook them. They will continue to cook as other ingredients are added.

4. Add the mixture from Step 2 and stir to mix it in well.

5. Add the peanuts and green onions and stir until they are hot. The onions should be crisp-tender and the peanuts should retain their texture.

6. Put a single layer of lettuce leaves in a serving bowl and pour the shrimp and sauce over them. Garnish with coriander sprigs and serve with rice.

✳✳✳ ─────────────────────────────

Crisp-Fried Fish with Hot Curry
PAD PED BLA TOD

This fish is spicier, richer, and hotter than the whole Deep-Fried Fish (page 216). In Thailand the fish is cooked until it is very crisp, almost like potato chips. In the United States it is usually not cooked that long, in deference to American tastes. Be sure to use a firm-fleshed fish, which will not fall apart during frying or folding into the sauce. If it does fall apart it will still taste good, but it won't be as attractive. The fish should be served as soon as it has been folded into the sauce because it will become soggy and uninteresting if allowed to stand.

SERVES 6 TO 8

2 pounds catfish, snapper, or other firm-fleshed fillets
Vegetable oil for deep-frying

½ cup vegetable oil
3 recipes Red Curry 2 (page 76)
2 tablespoons fish sauce
¼ cup granulated sugar

Coriander sprigs

1. Slice the fish into 1-inch squares and dry them with paper towels.

2. Pour about 1 inch oil in a wok or deep skillet and heat it to 375°. Deep-fry the fish, turning it frequently, until it is firm and crisp, about 3 minutes for red snapper or 5 minutes for catfish. (If you wish to prepare it in the traditional way, continue to fry the fish until it is crisp all the way through.) Set it aside on paper towels.

3. Heat a wok or large saucepan and add ½ cup oil. Add the Red Curry 2 and stir-fry over medium heat until the curry is fragrant and thick, about 5 or 10 minutes. The color will change to a dark red and the curry will develop a full aroma. Add the fish sauce and sugar and mix them in well. The curry should be thick but not pasty. If it is too thick, add water 1 tablespoon at a time until you have a smooth, thick sauce.

4. Add the fish and fold it in very gently, making sure that each piece is coated evenly. Avoid breaking the pieces of fish any more than you have to.

5. Remove the fish and sauce to a warm serving bowl and garnish with coriander leaves.

6. Serve immediately with rice. Do not try to keep it warm or the fish will get soggy.

✳✳✳ ─────────────────────────────────

Fish Cakes
TOD MAN

These fish cakes are probably unlike any you have had before; they are spicy, crisp, and chewy. The use of Kaffir lime leaves, fish sauce, green beans, and Red Curry 2 is an unlikely combination with ground fish, but it works beautifully. If available, Chinese long beans are traditional, but standard string beans work well. This recipe produces no sauce of its own, and we suggest you accompany the fish cakes with another dish that has a sauce so there will be something to flavor the ever-present rice. When you first cook them, the cakes will be puffy and light, but almost as soon as you remove them from the oil they will begin to collapse. Traditionally they are made with ground catfish, and the chewy, rubbery texture this produces is highly prized in Thailand. You may substitute any firm-fleshed fish.

MAKES 40 FISH CAKES

5 Kaffir lime leaves
¾ pound fresh green beans

1 pound ground fish
1 recipe Red Curry 2 (page 76)
1 egg
2 tablespoons fish sauce

Vegetable oil for deep-frying

Mint leaves
Coriander sprigs

Cucumber Sauce 2 (page 82)

1. Soak the Kaffir lime leaves in warm water for 15 minutes, and slice them crosswise into paper-thin strips. Slice the green beans crosswise into paper-thin slices.

2. Mix the ground fish, Red Curry 2, egg, fish sauce, and Kaffir lime leaves. Stir the mixture with a wooden spoon, or beat it on the lowest speed with an electric mixer, until the mixture thickens slightly, is mixed thoroughly, and will hold the shape of a patty easily, about 5 minutes. The stirring time will depend a great deal on the amount of water, if any, you used to grind with the Red Curry 2. The more water you added, the longer the stirring time is likely to be. Add the green beans and mix them in thoroughly. Shape the mixture into balls, using 1 to 1½ tablespoons mixture for each. Flatten the balls into patties less than ¼ inch thick. To keep the mixture from sticking to your hands, coat your hands lightly with oil or dip your hands in a bowl of water from time to time as you prepare the patties.

Ahead-of-time note: The mixture may be prepared up to 1 day in advance. Keep it covered in the refrigerator and bring it to room temperature before forming the patties.

3. Heat 2½ inches oil to 375° in a wok or deep skillet. Add the fish cakes one or two at a time, making sure not to crowd the pan. Deep-fry them until they are golden, about 3 minutes. Drain them on paper towels, place them on a serving platter, and garnish with mint and coriander leaves.

4. Serve hot or warm with Cucumber Sauce 2 and rice.

✳✳✳ ━━━━━━━━━━━━━━━━━━━━━━━━━━━━━━━

Ginger Steamed Fish
BLA NUANG

This dish gets its spicy, rich flavor almost entirely from the ginger root. It produces very little liquid sauce, but an ample amount of richly flavored solid "sauce," which is delicious with rice.

SERVES 4 TO 6

1 small whole fish (1–2 pounds), e.g., trout or small snapper

4 dried Oriental mushrooms
½ cup warm water

2 ounces (¼ cup sliced) ginger root
4 green onions, green and white parts
4 salted plums
2 ounces ground pork
2 tablespoons light soy sauce
3 tablespoons granulated sugar
¼ cup water

¼ teaspoon ground black pepper

1. If necessary, clean the fish following the instructions on page 218. Slit the skin diagonally in 3 or 4 places on both sides, cutting about halfway to the bone.

2. Soak the mushrooms in the warm water for 15 minutes, or until they are soft.

3. Peel the ginger root and slice it crosswise into pieces about ¹⁄₁₆ inch thick. Slice the green onions diagonally into pieces 1 inch long. Remove the seeds from the plums and chop the pulp finely. Remove the stems from the mushrooms and leave the mushrooms whole.

4. Mix all ingredients except the fish.

5. Place the fish on a decorative heat-resistant plate, cover with the mixture from Step 4, and steam for 20–25 minutes, until the fish is firm and opaque but not falling from the bones. Serve it on the plate on which it was steamed.

6. Serve with rice.

✳✳✳ ———————————————————————————

Spicy Steamed Fish
HOA MOAK BLA

This unusual dish is highly spiced and medium hot. It will probably make your guests wonder how you accomplished the effect, because the eggs add body to the very thin slices of fish. Surprisingly, they are recognizable as fish and aren't overwhelmed by the curry. Please use an attractive heat-resistant serving bowl to cook in because the fish looks best if served in the container in which it was cooked.

SERVES 6 TO 8

1 pound red snapper or other firm-fleshed fillets

2 eggs

1 recipe Red Curry 2 (page 76)
3 tablespoons fish sauce

¾ cup thick coconut milk

1 pound Napa cabbage
Boiling water

1 cup coriander sprigs

1. Wash and dry the fish. Lay each fillet on a cutting board and slice it crosswise at an angle into paper-thin slices. To do this, hold the knife so that it forms an angle of approximately 30 degrees with the cutting board. It is important to slice the fish very thinly. Place the slices in a large mixing bowl.

2. Separate the eggs and add the yolks to the bowl with the fish. Put the whites in a small saucepan and set them aside.

3. Stir the fish and yolks gently with a wooden spoon until the fish is coated uniformly and has absorbed most of the yolks, about 5 minutes. Add the Red Curry 2 and fish sauce and stir gently until the mixture is thick. Add ½ cup of the coconut milk, ¼ cup at a time, stirring constantly and gently to allow the fish to absorb the coconut milk. Continue to stir gently until the coconut milk disappears, about 5 minutes. Set aside.

4. Slice the cabbage crosswise into 2-inch-long pieces. Blanch it in boiling water until it is soft but not soggy, about 3 minutes. Drain in a colander and cool it under running water. Squeeze a handful at a time to remove as much of the liquid as you can without crushing the cabbage. It should be almost dry. Spread the cabbage evenly over the bottom of an 8 x 8 x 2-inch baking dish and set the dish aside.

5. Add the remaining ¼ cup coconut milk to the egg whites in the saucepan, and stir to mix thoroughly. Bring the mixture to a boil rapidly and remove it from the heat immediately.

6. Pour the fish mixture from Step 3 over the cabbage and spread it evenly. Pour the mixture from Step 5 over it. Sprinkle the coriander sprigs on top.

7. Place the baking dish in a steamer and steam for 15 to 20 minutes, until the fish is white, opaque, and firm.

8. Serve immediately, in the baking dish, with rice.

✳✳✳ ───────────────────────────────

Stir-Fried Mussels and Eggs
HOY MANG POO TOD

This dish is frequently sold by street vendors in Thailand, and is often considered a snack to eat on the way home from work, or after arriving home but before dinner is served. We think most FARANG ("foreigners") will find it a hearty meal in itself rather than a snack. If you prefer, you may buy "HOY TOD flour," which is a premixed combination of tapioca starch, rice flour, and salt. It's just as easy to make it yourself, however, and it is less expensive. If you use the premixed kind, you'll need 3 cups of it for this recipe.

SERVES 6 TO 8

2 cups tapioca starch
1 cup rice flour
½ teaspoon salt
2½ cups water
1 pound (after cleaning) mussels, clams, or oysters

1 bunch green onions, white and green parts

¾ cup vegetable oil (more if needed in Step 4)
2 tablespoons (1 ounce) finely chopped garlic
6 eggs

¼ cup white vinegar
¼ cup granulated sugar
¼ cup fish sauce

1½ pounds bean sprouts, plus more for side dishes

1 cup coriander sprigs

¼ teaspoon ground white pepper

Vinegar Sauce (page 83)

1. Mix the tapioca starch, rice flour, salt, and water to a smooth, thin batter. The batter will be only slightly thicker than whole milk. If you are using oysters, cut them crosswise into pieces about ¼ inch wide. Stir the seafood into the batter.

2. Slice the green onions diagonally into pieces about 1 inch long and set aside.

3. Heat a griddle or a 12-inch skillet (preferably cast iron) and add about 2 tablespoons of the oil. Add 1 teaspoon of the chopped garlic and stir-fry until light golden. Pour 1 cup of the batter into the skillet, tilting the pan so it spreads evenly. It will be very thin, about ¹⁄₁₆ to ⅛ inch thick, with pieces of seafood sticking up like little islands here and there. Break an egg onto the top of the batter and spread it around evenly, breaking the yolk as you spread it.

4. Cook the pancake over moderate heat until it is golden on the bottom, then turn it over and cook until it is golden on the other side. Total cooking time will be about 10 to 15 minutes. Do not try to rush the cooking time. It will probably break into several pieces when you turn it, and that's fine. Later you will be breaking it up into pieces anyway. Turn it once about every minute. If it begins to stick, add as much vegetable oil as is necessary to keep it from sticking. In Thailand, a great deal of oil is used in this dish. Remove it from the skillet and set aside. Repeat 5 more times with the remaining oil, garlic, batter, and eggs.

5. Break the pancakes into pieces 1 to 2 inches square.

6. Mix the vinegar, sugar, and fish sauce in a small bowl, stirring until the sugar is dissolved.

7. Heat a wok and add the pieces of pancake from Step 5 without adding oil. Add the bean sprouts and green onions and stir until they are crisp-tender, about 2 minutes. Add the liquid from Step 6 and stir it in thoroughly.

8. Remove contents to a serving bowl, garnish with the coriander sprigs and white pepper, and serve immediately with Vinegar Sauce, side dishes of additional bean sprouts, and rice.

❋❋❋ ━━━━━━━━━━━━━━━━━━━━━━━━━

Spicy Shrimp
PLA GOONG

As the name suggests, these shrimp are highly spiced and hot, but the mint tempers the "bite." The spiciness can be adjusted easily by reducing the amount of chilies, onions, or lemon grass to your own taste. We suggest you try the listed amount first, then adjust it if you need to. This recipe produces very little thin sauce. The shrimp are easily prepared in advance and work very well as a light summer meal.

1 pound raw shrimp

4 stalks lemon grass, bottom 6 inches only
2 green onions, white and green parts

2 tablespoons fish sauce
¼ cup lime juice
2 teaspoons ground roasted dried chilies (page 60)
¼ cup loosely packed mint leaves
Red lettuce leaves

1. Peel and devein the shrimp, leaving the tails intact. Grill them on a barbecue or under a broiler just until they turn pink. Place them in a mixing bowl.

2. Slice the lemon grass crosswise into paper-thin slices and place them in the bowl with the shrimp. Slice the green onions crosswise into pieces not more than ⅛ inch thick. Add them to the bowl.

3. Add the fish sauce, lime juice, ground chilies and mint leaves to the bowl and mix thoroughly. Line a serving bowl with lettuce and arrange the shrimp mixture on top.

4. Serve at room temperature with rice.

Ahead-of-time note: The ingredients may be prepared up to 6 hours ahead of time if the mint and liquid are not added and the mixture is not placed on the lettuce leaves.

• • •

Garlic Shrimp
GOONG GRATIEM

These shrimp are not hot and the shrimp flavor is clear and distinct. The recipe calls for a great deal of garlic and coriander root, but the flavors blend well and do not overpower the shrimp. There is relatively little sauce in this light, non-filling dish, so it could be served effectively with another that has more sauce. If it is served alone, use Lime Sauce for flavoring the rice.

The pink shrimp look particularly attractive when served on red lettuce leaves and, like other Thai garnishes, the leaves should be eaten. They provide a cool, crisp contrast to the soft, spicy shrimp.

SERVES 4 TO 6

1 pound raw medium shrimp

1 cup water
3½ tablespoons fish sauce
2 tablespoons granulated sugar

½ cup finely chopped coriander root
¼ cup (2 ounces) finely chopped garlic
1 tablespoon ground white pepper

¼ cup vegetable oil

Red lettuce leaves

Lime Sauce (page 84)

1. Peel and devein the shrimp, leaving the tails intact. Set aside.

2. Mix the water, fish sauce, and sugar in a small bowl, stirring until the sugar dissolves. Set aside.

3. Pound or grind the coriander root and garlic to a coarse paste in a mortar or blender. If you use a blender, it may be necessary to add the oil to aid in grinding.

4. Heat a wok, add the oil, and swirl it over the surface of the pan. (Do not add more oil if you used oil to grind the garlic and coriander root in Step 3.) Stir-fry the paste from Step 3 until it is light golden. Add the pepper and stir-fry for about 30 seconds. Add the shrimp and stir-fry until they are firm and pink, about 1½ minutes.

5. Add the mixture from Step 2 and stir and toss well with the shrimp over moderate heat.

6. Arrange a single layer of lettuce leaves in a serving bowl and spoon the shrimp over them.

7. Serve with Lime Sauce and rice.

Deep-Fried Fish with Pork and Ginger Topping
MOO PAD KING RAD BLA

The highly spiced topping in this dish gets its "bite" from ginger. When you read the recipe it may seem like an inordinately large amount of ginger, but it's necessary to produce the desired effect. The recipe produces a large amount of topping, which is delicious when eaten with rice. It does not produce much liquid sauce, but you may add a little more water than we recommend if you like.

SERVES 4 TO 6

2 ounces (about 16 pieces) cloud ears or Oriental dried mushrooms
1 cup warm water

2 green onions, white part only

2 tablespoons vegetable oil
1 teaspoon (2 cloves) finely chopped garlic
1½ cups (6 ounces) ginger, peeled and cut in julienne strips

¼ pound ground pork

2 tablespoons fish sauce
2 teaspoons granulated sugar
½ cup water
⅛ teaspoon ground white pepper

1 whole fish (1½ to 2 pounds), e.g., trout or small snapper
Vegetable oil for deep-frying

Coriander sprigs
Finely shredded carrot

1. Soak the ear clouds or mushrooms in the warm water for 20 minutes, until they are soft. Remove and discard the tough center stems. Slice the cloud ears or mushroms into thin strips and set aside. Slice the green onions diagonally into pieces about 1 inch long. Set aside.

2. Heat a wok, add the oil, and swirl it over the surface of the pan. Stir-fry the garlic until it is light golden. Add the ginger and stir-fry over moderate heat about 1 minute.

3. Add the ground pork and stir-fry until the pink color disappears completely.

4. Add the fish sauce, sugar, mushrooms or cloud ears, green onions, ½ cup water, and pepper. Stir until the ingredients are well mixed and hot, about 2 minutes. Set the mixture aside and keep it warm while you prepare the fish.

5. If necessary, clean the fish according to the instructions on page 218. Leave the head, tail, and fins intact. Make 2 or 3 diagonal slashes on each side of the fish, cutting about halfway to the bone.

Ahead-of-time note: The ingredients may be prepared to this point several hours in advance. Keep the fish and sauce refrigerated in separate containers. Heat the sauce to boiling before pouring it over the fried fish. It may be necessary to add more water if the solid ingredients have absorbed the water in which they were cooked.

6. Put 1½ inches oil in a wok and heat it to 375°. Dry the fish thoroughly and add it to the oil gently to avoid splattering. Fry until it is crisp and the flesh along the cuts is light golden, about 5 minutes. Turn it 3 or 4 times while frying. Remove the fish carefully and drain it on paper towels.

7. Transfer the fish to a warm serving platter and pour the topping over it. Garnish with the coriander sprigs and shredded carrot.

8. Serve immediately with rice.

●●● ━━━━━━━━━━━━━━━━━━━━━━━━━━━━━━━━━━━━

Deep-Fried Shrimp
GOONG TOD

These shrimp are mildly flavored, slightly sweet, and have a crisp crust, due in part to the use of red lime liquid. If red lime liquid is unavailable, you may omit it with good results. However, do make every effort to use coconut milk in the batter, because otherwise they would be too much like ordinary deep-fried shrimp. If fresh or frozen coconut milk is not available, use a good brand of canned.

SERVES 4 TO 6

1 pound raw medium shrimp
1 pound assorted vegetables (broccoli, green beans, eggplant, zucchini, etc.)

1 cup thick coconut milk
2 tablespoons red lime liquid (page 66)
1 tablespoon egg white (optional)
¼ teaspoon ground white pepper
¾ teaspoon salt
1 cup all-purpose flour

Vegetable oil for deep-frying

Garlic Sauce (page 84) or Plum Sauce (page 85)

1. Peel and devein the shrimp, leaving the tails intact. Butterfly each shrimp by holding it bottom side up and cutting through almost to the vein. Spread it flat to form a butterfly shape. Set the butterflied shrimp aside.

2. Remove and separate the broccoli florets; reserve the stems for another use. Remove the green cap from the eggplant, but do not peel it. Cut the eggplant lengthwise into slices about ¼ inch thick. Cut each of these pieces into strips about 1 inch wide and 2 inches long. Slice the green beans diagonally into pieces about 2 inches long and ¼ inch thick. Slice the zucchini diagonally into strips about ⅛ inch thick and 4 inches long. If you substitute other vegetables, slice them in similar patterns based on the shape of the vegetable and the time it takes to cook it. Firm vegetables should be sliced more thinly than soft ones.

3. Blend the coconut milk, red lime liquid, egg white, pepper, salt, and flour in a blender, food processor, or bowl using a wire whip to develop a smooth batter. Pour the batter into a bowl if you prepared it in a blender or food processor.

4. Pour 1½ inches oil in a wok and heat it to 375°. Dry the shrimp and vegetables thoroughly so the batter will adhere. Dip a few shrimp in the batter and deep-fry them until they are golden brown and crisp. Drain them on paper towels, set them aside, and keep them warm. Repeat with the remaining shrimp. Follow the same procedure for the vegetables. The firmer vegetables should be cooked first because they will hold their texture better while you are frying the others.

5. Serve immediately with Garlic Sauce or Plum Sauce. Do not try to keep this dish warm, because fried foods, particularly the vegetables, will become soggy, the soft vegetables being the fastest to deteriorate.

✳✳✳ ━━━━━━━━━━━━━━━━━━━━━━━━━━━━

Fish and Ginger
TOM SOM BLA

This dish receives its rich flavor from ginger and white pepper rather than from chilies. It produces ample sauce for flavoring rice, which should always be served with it. Traditionally, the bones are not removed from the fish before serving, but you may use fish fillets if you prefer.

SERVES 6 TO 8

1 3-pound whole fish, or fish fillets, e.g., catfish, snapper, or
    trout
3 cups water

2 green onions, white and green parts
2 ounces (¼ cup sliced) ginger root

2 ounces wet tamarind or ¼ cup tamarind concentrate
¾ cup water

½ cup (2 ounces) finely chopped yellow onion
2 tablespoons shrimp paste
½ teaspoon ground white pepper

3 tablespoons fish sauce
¼ cup granulated sugar

Coriander sprigs

1. Clean the fish if necessary (see page 218), and slice it crosswise into pieces 1 inch wide. (Traditionally, the fish is cooked with the bones in.) If you are using fish fillets, they should be sliced the same way. Place the fish and the water in a large saucepan.

2. Slice the green onions diagonally into 1-inch pieces. Peel the ginger and slice it into thin julienne strips. Set these ingredients aside.

3. (Omit this step if you are using tamarind concentrate.) Soak the tamarind in ¾ cup warm water about 15 minutes, until it is soft. Press the pulp through a sieve, being sure to scrape and save all pulp that adheres to the outside of the sieve. Discard the residue in the sieve.

4. Pound or grind the yellow onion, shrimp paste, and pepper to a smooth paste in a mortar or blender. If you use a blender, add just enough water to aid in grinding. Add the paste to the fish in the saucepan. Simmer the mixture until the fish is firm and opaque, but do not overcook it or it will fall apart.

5. Add the green onion, ginger, tamarind solution, fish sauce, and sugar. (If you used tamarind concentrate, add an additional ½ cup water.) Bring the mixture to a boil, then remove it from the heat immediately.

6. Place the fish and sauce in a warm serving bowl and garnish with coriander sprigs. Serve with rice.

• • •

Hot-and-Sour Mussels
DOM YOM HOY MANG POO

These mussels are hot and spicy, with a touch of lime to help blend the flavors. The recipe produces a large amount of thin sauce, which is more like a broth than a sauce and is excellent for flavoring rice. In addition to being tasty, this dish is very attractive, because the dark shells of the mussels contrast beautifully with the beige broth and green coriander leaves. It is one of our favorites, and we suggest it may be one of yours too. Clams may be substituted.

SERVES 4 TO 6

2 tablespoons finely chopped yellow onion
1½ teaspoons shrimp paste
½ teaspoon ground black pepper

2 Serrano chilies
½ cup coriander sprigs

1 quart water
1½ pounds fresh mussels in their shells
¼ cup fish sauce

3 tablespoons lime juice

1. Pound or grind the onion, shrimp paste, and pepper to a smooth paste in a mortar or blender. If you use a blender, add just enough water to aid in grinding.

2. Remove the stems, but not the seeds, from the chilies, and mash the chilies with the side of a cleaver or wide-bladed knife until they split open. Set aside. Chop the coriander sprigs coarsely and set aside.

3. Pour the water into a medium-size pot and add the paste from Step 1. Bring it to a boil rapidly. Add the mussels and bring the liquid back to a slow boil over moderate heat. Cover the pot and boil gently about 3 minutes, until the mussels open their shells. Do not overcook them, or the mussels will become tough. Add the fish sauce and chilies and remove the mixture from the heat.

4. Add the lime juice and coriander sprigs and stir to mix them in completely. Transfer the preparation to a large warm serving bowl.

5. Serve with rice.

Fish Balls
LOOK CHIN BLA

Fish balls can be used in soups, cooked with curries, or barbecued or deep-fried for use as a separate dish. If served as a separate dish, they should be accompanied by Lime Sauce or one of the Cucumber Sauces. Ground fish often can be purchased in Thai or Oriental markets in 1-pound containers, and is found in the seafood or frozen food section. You could also prepare your own by grinding mild, lean fillets such as sole, perch, bass, scrod or snapper in a food processor or putting them through the fine blade of a meat grinder. Shrimp balls (LOOK CHIN GOONG) are made in exactly the same way with shrimp meat. For shrimp balls, you should have 1 pound of raw shrimp, not counting the weight of the shells.

MAKES 1 POUND (ABOUT 30 BALLS)

1 tablespoon (½ ounce) finely chopped garlic

1 pound ground fish or shrimp
¼ teaspoon ground white pepper
2½ tablespoons fish sauce

2 quarts water

1. Pound the garlic to a coarse paste in a mortar, or mash it with a fork. In either case, a few grains of salt will be helpful.

2. Place all the ingredients except the water in a food processor and process them until they form a fine puree.

3. Bring the water to a slow boil in a large pot. Form balls of the puree, using about 1 tablespoon mixture for each. Wet your hands periodically to keep the mixture from sticking to them, and form the balls so there are no pockets of trapped air.

4. Drop the balls into the water and cook until they rise to the surface, usually less than 1 minute. Remove them from the water with a strainer and drain on a wire rack.

5. Use the balls immediately, store them in a covered container in the refrigerator for 1 day, or freeze them in a tightly closed container for later use.

14
Variety Meats

IN THAILAND, just about every part of an animal except the hair is used for food in one form or another, and virtually nothing is wasted. The cuts of meat used in the recipes in this chapter are often ignored in the United States, but are used frequently in many other countries. It is a shame to ignore them, because they are delicious when properly prepared and provide inexpensive and nutritious meals. We hope you will try some of the more familiar ones and venture out from there to try some of the more exotic preparations.

✳✳✳

Stir-Fried Chicken Giblets
KRUANG NAI PAD KING

This is a rich, spicy dish which will add a commonly available meat to your meals. The combination of ginger and chilies is spicy and hot and you may wish to reduce the number of chilies, but please do not omit the ginger, because it blends beautifully with the natural flavor of the meat and is the heart of the preparation. It is very important not to overcook the meat,

because it will become tough, dry, and uninteresting. If you prefer, use only gizzards or livers or hearts, or any combination.

SERVES 4 TO 6

2 ounces (¼ cup sliced) ginger root
1 medium (¼ pound) sweet green (bell) pepper
¼ pound (1 cup finely sliced) yellow onion
3 green onions
2 Serrano chilies

½ cup water
1½ tablespoons fish sauce
2 tablespoons oyster sauce
2 tablespoons granulated sugar

1 pound chicken giblets

3 tablespoons vegetable oil
1 teaspoon (2 cloves) finely chopped garlic

¼ teaspoon ground white pepper

Red lettuce leaves

1. Peel the ginger root and slice it crosswise into pieces
not more than ⅛ inch thick. Remove the stem and seeds from the
bell pepper and cut the pepper into 1-inch squares. Peel the yellow
onion and slice it into 1-inch squares. Set these ingredients aside
in a bowl. Slice the green onions diagonally into pieces about 1
inch long and set them aside in a separate bowl. Remove the
stems, but not the seeds, from the chilies and slice the chilies
lengthwise into long, thin strips.

2. Put the water, fish sauce, oyster sauce, and sugar in a
small bowl and stir until the sugar is dissolved. Set aside.

3. If you are using gizzards, remove the tough white part
and discard it. Slice each giblet horizontally part of the way
through, and spread each into a butterfly shape so they will be
thin enough to cook quickly before they get tough. If some of the
pieces are already thin, do not butterfly them.

4. Heat a wok, add the oil, and swirl it over the surface of
the pan. Add the garlic and stir-fry until it is light golden. Add

the giblets and chilies and stir-fry over moderate heat until the red color of the giblets is almost gone, about 2 minutes. Do not overcook them or they will become tough. They do not need to be completely done because they will continue to cook in subsequent steps and are tenderer if they are a little pink in the center after the cooking is completed.

5. Add the ginger, bell pepper, and yellow onion. Stir-fry until the vegetables are just crisp-tender.

6. Add the mixture from Step 2 and stir about 1 minute. The sauce will not be thick.

7. Line a serving bowl with lettuce leaves and pour the giblets and sauce over them. Sprinkle with ground pepper and serve with rice.

✳✳✳ ━━━━━━━━━━━━━━━━━━━━━━━━━━━━━

Spicy Pigs Feet
KA MOO PALO

SERVES 4 TO 6

1 pound pigs feet

1 tablespoon finely chopped coriander root
1 tablespoon (½ ounce) finely chopped garlic

¼ cup + 1 tablespoon fish sauce
¼ cup granulated sugar
2 teaspoons black soy sauce
3 cups water
½ teaspoon five-spice powder
⅛ teaspoon ground black pepper

2 tablespoons oil

Assorted Pickled Vegetables (page 137)
Lime Sauce (page 84)

1. Place the pigs feet over and near very hot coals in the barbecue, or not more than 1 inch from a hot broiler. Char the skin quickly without cooking the meat. This must be done very quickly to prevent the meat from cooking. Another effective way to do this is to use a propane blowtorch. With a sharp knife, scrape away all the black, charred part of the skin.

2. Pound or grind the coriander root and garlic to a coarse paste in a mortar or blender. If you use a blender, add the oil to aid in grinding.

3. Mix the fish sauce, sugar, soy sauce, water, five-spice powder, and pepper in a bowl, stirring until the sugar is dissolved. Set aside.

4. Heat a wok, add the oil, and swirl it over the surface of the pan. (If you have ground the garlic and coriander root in the oil, do not add more here.) Stir-fry the paste from Step 2 until it is light golden.

5. Dry the pigs feet thoroughly with a paper towel and add them to the wok. Stir-fry until a light golden crust is formed. Add the liquid from Step 3 and stir to mix well.

6. Cover the wok and bring the mixture to a boil. Reduce the heat and simmer for 1 hour, or until the meat is very tender and separates from the bones. Remove the bones or leave them in according to your preference. Traditionally, they are not removed.

Ahead-of-time note: This dish may be prepared up to 2 days ahead of time and stored, covered, in the refrigerator. Reheat it just before serving.

7. Serve hot with pickled vegetables, Lime Sauce, and rice.

✳✳✳ ─────────────────────────────

Spicy Chinese Sausage
GOON CHEUNG YAM

This easy-to-prepare dish combines hot, sweet, sour, spicy, and salty flavors. The hot, spicy effect is moderated by crisp, cool cucumbers. The proportions are flexible and can be modified to meet your own taste and the ingredients you have available. Spicy sausage is another of Kamolmal's father's favorite dishes. Whether he is preparing it to eat himself or for others, he takes the same special care in selecting the sausage and preparing the ingredients.

SERVES 4 TO 6

1 pound Chinese sausage

½ pound cucumber
2 ounces (½ cup sliced) yellow onion
2 green onions, white and green parts
3 Serrano chilies

2 tablespoons fish sauce
¼ cup white vinegar
1 teaspoon black soy sauce
¼ cup granulated sugar

½ cup coriander sprigs

1. Fry the sausage in a dry skillet or broil or barbecue it until done, about 5 minutes. Allow it to cool to room temperature and cut it diagonally into strips about ⅛ inch thick and 3 inches long. Place the strips in a mixing bowl.

2. Peel the cucumber and cut it diagonally into slices about ⅛ inch thick. Peel the yellow onion and cut it vertically into very thin slices. Slice the green onions diagonally into pieces about ½ inch long. Remove the stems, but not the seeds, from the chilies and slice the chilies crosswise into paper-thin slices. Put all of these ingredients in the bowl with the meat.

Ahead-of-time note: The ingredients can be prepared to this point several hours in advance. Add the liquids and the sugar just before serving.

3. Add the fish sauce, vinegar, soy sauce, and sugar and mix thoroughly until the sugar has dissolved completely. Garnish the top with coriander sprigs.

4. Serve at room temperature with rice.

Stir-Fried Beef Heart and Bok Choy
PAD HUAJAI NUE GOB PAK

If you have never had beef heart you may be surprised at the delicious flavor and interesting texture of this dish. Unless you tell your guests what it is, they may not be able to guess. From the cook's point of view, it is easy to prepare and cooks quickly. The heart and accompanying sauce can be completed from start to finish in less time than it takes to cook rice. There is very little sauce, so it is a good idea to serve the heart with one or more other dishes of your choice that have a substantial amount of sauce. If you have not tried "innards" before, this is a good recipe to begin with. If you have, and like them, you will find this one a delight. In most markets you will find that the heart has already been sliced and cleaned for you. If not, slice the heart lengthwise into flat pieces about ¼ to ½ inch thick and rinse them thoroughly before beginning with Step 1.

SERVES 4 TO 6

½ pound beef heart
2 large stalks bok choy

2 tablespoons vegetable oil
1½ teaspoons (3 cloves) finely chopped garlic

2 tablespoons fish sauce

Green lettuce leaves
¼ teaspoon ground black pepper

Lime Sauce (page 84) or Vinegar Sauce (page 83)

1. Trim the fat and outer covering from the heart if that hasn't already been done by your butcher. Slice the heart cross-wise into strips not more than ⅛ inch thick and 1 to 2 inches long. Set aside. Slice the bok choy diagonally into pieces about 1 inch long and ¼ inch thick. Set aside.

2. Heat a wok, add the oil, and swirl it over the surface of the pan. Add the garlic and stir-fry until it is light golden. Add the beef heart strips and stir-fry until the red color disappears. Do not overcook or they will get tough.

3. Add the bok choy and fish sauce. Stir over moderate heat until the bok choy is crisp-tender. If the mixture becomes dry before the bok choy is done, add 1 or 2 tablespoons water.

4. Arrange a single layer of lettuce leaves in a serving bowl. Pour the cooked mixture over the lettuce leaves and sprinkle with ground pepper.

5. Serve with Lime Sauce or Vinegar Sauce and rice.

✳✳✳ ─────────────────────────────

Spicy Assorted Meats
TOM KREUNG NAI

We include this recipe for those who truly love special dishes and aren't afraid to try the unusual. We have listed four different cuts of meat, but you may use any combination of two or more according to availability and your own preference. The selection we have made offers contrasting textures ranging from the chewy tripe and intestines to the soft liver. If you like innards, the flavor and texture of this preparation are hard to beat.

SERVES 8 TO 10

1 pound each beef heart, tripe, liver, and small intestines

2 quarts water
2 stalks of lemon grass, bottom 6 inches only
2 tablespoons kah *pieces*
10 Kaffir lime leaves

¼ cup fish sauce

4 Serrano chilies
½ cup white vinegar
½ pound bean sprouts
1 cup coarsely chopped coriander sprigs

1. Clean the outside of the intestines by rubbing them thoroughly with salt or alum. Turn them inside out and clean the now-exterior surface with salt or alum. (Chopsticks are very useful for turning them inside out.) Rinse them thoroughly and place them in a large pot. Add the water, lemon grass, *kah,* and Kaffir lime leaves. Bring the mixture to a boil rapidly, reduce the heat, and boil slowly for 15 minutes.

2. Add the heart, liver, and tripe. Boil slowly for 45 minutes.

3. Remove the meats from the liquid and slice them into 1-inch long or square pieces, depending on the original shape. Put the meat pieces back in the pot and boil gently, covered, for 1 more hour, or until the meats are tender. Add hot water periodically to keep the level at the point it was when you started. A total of 4 or 5 cups may be needed over the entire cooking time. Remove the mixture from the heat and add the fish sauce.

4. Pound the chilies in a mortar until they are soft. Then chop them finely and mix with the vinegar. Set aside in a small serving bowl. Divide the bean sprouts evenly in 6 soup bowls. Ladle the hot stew over them, and garnish with coriander sprigs.

5. Serve with the chili-vinegar mixture and rice.

Stir-Fried Pork Belly
PAD MOO SAM CHON

Granted, the name of this dish doesn't sound too appealing unless, perhaps, you grew up on a farm and learned long ago not to judge the flavor of food by its name. If we had labeled it Stir-Fried Fresh Bacon it might have sounded better. However, even though the cut of meat is basically the same as that from which bacon is made, it is most likely to be known as pork belly in your butcher shop or market. Traditionally, pork stomachs were used in this dish. We have substituted pork belly because it is more widely available and, equally important, more appealing to a wider number of people. This preparation is chewy, rich in flavor, and only mildly hot. Please don't be afraid of it. The pork can be cooked well in advance and requires no attention other than to be sure the water does not boil away. The broth in which the pork is cooked can be used instead of water in other pork dishes.

SERVES 4 TO 6

1 pound fresh pork belly

4 ounces (1 cup sliced) yellow onion
3 green onions, white and green parts

2 tablespoons fish sauce
1 teaspoon granulated sugar
1 cup water

2 tablespoons vegetable oil
2 teaspoons (4 cloves) finely chopped garlic
¼ teaspoon ground black pepper

Vinegar Sauce (page 83) or Lime Sauce (page 84)

1. Simmer the pork belly, covered, about 2 hours in enough water to cover it. (If the pork belly is already sliced when you buy it, reduce the cooking time to 1 hour.) Remove it from the water, let it cool to room temperature, then slice it into strips about 2 to 3 inches long and not more than ⅛ inch thick. Set aside.

2. Peel the yellow onion, slice it vertically into thin strips, and set aside. Slice the green onions diagonally into pieces about 1 inch long and set them aside in a separate bowl.

3. Mix the fish sauce, sugar, and water in a bowl, stirring until the sugar is dissolved. Set aside.

4. Dry the pork strips with paper towels. Heat a wok, add the oil, and swirl it over the surface of the pan. Stir-fry the garlic until it is light golden. Add the meat and stir-fry until the strips are heated through, but not crisp. Even if you have dried the meat well, it will pop and spatter, so be careful as you fry it. Add the yellow onions and stir-fry until the strips are translucent. Add the pepper and mix it in well.

5. Add the mixture from Step 3 to the wok and stir it with the other ingredients while it comes to a boil over moderate heat. Add the green onions and stir briefly until they are crisp-tender.

6. Serve with Vinegar Sauce or Lime Sauce and rice.

Grilled Beef Liver

YAM TOB NUE

This liver could be called "liver and onions," but oh what a difference from what we usually think of by that name! This one is strong with the flavor of raw onion. If you do not like that flavor you may break with tradition and stir-fry the onions briefly. The two types of onion add bite, and the fish sauce, lime juice, and water serve to blend the flavors. The toasted rice adds texture. The liver absolutely must not be overcooked and dry or the effect will be lost. This dish is quick, easy, and inexpensive. It can be prepared well in advance except for the final mixing, and it works very well as a summer patio preparation.

SERVES 6 TO 8

1 pound beef liver
1½ cups water

2 ounces (½ cup sliced) red onion
4 green onions, white and green parts
¼ cup fish sauce
¼ cup lime juice
3 stalks lemon grass, bottom 6 inches only
¼ cup mint leaves
½ cup ground toasted rice (page 66)
1 teaspoon ground roasted chilies (page 60)

Green lettuce leaves

Assorted raw vegetables (green beans, zucchini,
    tomatoes, broccoli, etc.)

1. Grill the liver over charcoal, broil it, or cook it in a wok without oil until it is done on the outside but pink and moist on the inside. Do not overcook it or it will become dry, hard, and flavorless. The cooking time will depend on the thickness of the slices.

2. Slice the liver crosswise into strips not more than ⅛ inch thick. Return the liver to the wok, turn the heat to high, add the water, and bring it to a boil rapidly. Stir thoroughly until the mixture barely begins to thicken, then remove the wok from the heat. The liver strips will lose the pink color on their surface, but still be pink and moist inside. Place the meat and liquid in a mixing bowl and prepare the other ingredients while the liver cools to room temperature.

3. Peel the red onion, remove the root portion, and slice the onion vertically into paper-thin pieces. Slice the green onion crosswise into pieces about ⅛ inch thick.

Ahead-of-time note: All the ingredients may be prepared in advance to this point. Mix them just before serving.

4. When the liver and the liquid are at room temperature, add all remaining ingredients except the lettuce and raw vegetables.

5. Line a serving bowl with a single layer of lettuce leaves and pour the liver and sauce over them.

6. Serve at room temperature with assorted raw vegetables and rice.

15
Eggs

EGG DISHES ARE very much appreciated in Thailand and are used as main dishes at any meal. When Kamolmal first arrived in the United States she was amazed at the low cost of eggs and she promply set about cooking one egg dish after another for family and friends. When she and her husband Choompol opened their first restaurant they had several egg dishes on the menu and were surprised to learn that Americans rarely order egg dishes for dinner and only occasionally for lunch. The recipes in this chapter describe a few of the many ways in which eggs are prepared in Thailand. When you read the recipes you may be surprised at the unusual methods used. Fried Eggs with Tamarind Sauce is one such recipe, where the eggs are first hard-cooked, then deep-fried, and finally sliced and covered with sauce. Try it—it is delicious, and it could serve as an inexpensive and easy main course, one that can be prepared well in advance.

Stir-Fried Cucumbers and Eggs
PAD TANG QUA

This unlikely combination of ingredients produces a mild, tasty dish. We think you will be surprised at how good it is. The cucumbers may exude a great deal of liquid if you do not have an intense heat source. If they do, it serves as a good sauce for rice.

SERVES 4 TO 6

1½ pounds cucumber
½ pound boneless pork chops or pork loin or
boned chicken breasts

¼ cup vegetable oil
2 cloves (1 teaspoon) finely chopped garlic

3 tablespoons fish sauce
2 eggs

1. Peel the cucumbers, slice them diagonally into pieces ⅛ inch thick, and set them aside. Slice the pork or chicken across the grain into strips ⅛ inch thick and 1 to 2 inches long. Set aside.

2. Heat a wok, add the oil, and swirl it over the surface of the pan. Stir-fry the garlic until it is light golden. Add the pork or chicken strips and stir-fry until the pink color disappears.

3. Add the fish sauce and cucumber and mix them in well. Add the eggs, breaking the yolks, and stir until they are set.

4. Serve with rice.

Steamed Eggs
KAI TOON

These eggs require an unusually large amount of liquid for their preparation, and a large amount of liquid remains in them after cooking. The first time you prepare the mixture you may think that it can't possibly work or that you or we have made a mistake in the ingredients. It does, and we haven't. When the eggs are served, the liquid will ooze out of them and may be used to flavor rice. The eggs will puff slightly but not as much as a soufflé. The texture can be described best as being somewhere between a custard and a soufflé, and the flavor is subtle. In Thailand, this dish is often served to young children or to the elderly, particularly those who have no teeth. It certainly need not be reserved for those alone, since it is a very tasty dish.

SERVES 4 TO 6

2 tablespoons vegetable oil
1 tablespoon finely chopped garlic

1 green onion, white and green parts
¼ cup coriander sprigs

3 eggs
2 cups water or chicken stock
1 tablespoon fish sauce
½ teaspoon lime juice

Lime Sauce (page 84)

1. Heat a wok, add the oil, and swirl it over the surface of the pan. Stir-fry the garlic until it is light golden.

2. Slice the green onion crosswise into paper-thin pieces. Chop the coriander sprigs coarsely.

3. Combine all the ingredients except the Lime Sauce and beat them thoroughly with a fork.

4. Pour the mixture into a small, attractive heatproof serving bowl, soufflé mold, or Charlotte mold and place it in a steamer. Steam the mixture for 15 minutes. Be sure the water in the steamer does not boil away during the steaming. Check the eggs for doneness. They should be set throughout, have a texture somewhere between a custard and a soufflé, and be moist but not runny in the middle. A final test is to make a small hole in the center. The liquid that fills it should be clear. If not, continue to steam the eggs until it is.

5. Serve the eggs in the container in which they were cooked. Accompany with Lime Sauce and rice.

Variation: One-quarter cup of uncooked finely chopped meat of your choice may be added with the other ingredients.

• • •

Fried Eggs with Tamarind Sauce
KAI LOOK KUEE

These eggs are also known as "Son-in-Law Eggs." It is an unusual way to turn ordinary hard-cooked eggs into a treat, and illustrates the cleverness with which Thai people approach cooking. The combination of ingredients produces a tart–sweet sauce that is a perfect accompaniment to the bland hard-cooked eggs. The eggs will form a thick, chewy skin that is slightly crisp and crunchy. The dish can be prepared up to the last stage well in advance.

SERVES 4 TO 6

8 eggs

3 ounces wet tamarind or ¼ cup + 2 tablespoons tamarind concentrate
¾ cup water

½ cup granulated sugar
2 tablespoons fish sauce
¾ cup water

½ medium yellow onion
¼ cup vegetable oil
¼ cup (2 ounces) finely chopped garlic

Vegetable oil for deep-frying

½ cup coriander sprigs

1. Hard-cook the eggs in simmering water and peel them when they are cool enough to handle.

2. (Omit this step if you are using tamarind concentrate.) Soak the tamarind in ¾ cup warm water for 15 minutes, or until it is soft. Put it through a sieve, pressing out all the liquid you can and scraping all the pulp from the outside of the sieve. Discard the residue in the sieve.

3. Combine the tamarind solution or concentrate, sugar, fish sauce, and ¾ cup water. Bring the mixture to a slow boil and cook until it is thick, about 10 minutes. Set aside and keep it warm.

Ahead-of-time note: The eggs and sauce may be prepared to this point several days in advance. Store the eggs in the refrigerator in a closed container with enough water to cover them. Store the sauce in the refrigerator in a separate closed container. Bring the eggs to room temperature or place them in warm water for 5 minutes before proceeding with the recipe. Heat the sauce to boiling before pouring it over the eggs.

4. Peel the onion, remove the root portion, and slice the onion vertically into thin pieces. Heat a wok, add the oil, and swirl it over the wok surface. Stir-fry the garlic until it is light golden, remove it from the oil, and set aside. Stir-fry the onions in the same oil until golden brown and barely crisp. As the onions begin to brown, watch them carefully to make sure they don't burn. Remove from the oil and set aside.

5. Heat 1 inch oil to 350° in a wok. Dry the eggs with paper towels and fry them until they are golden brown all over, about 5 minutes. They will develop blisters as they brown, and a thick skin will form. Remove the eggs from the oil, drain them on paper towels, and slice them in half lengthwise.

6. Place the eggs on a serving platter and pour the sauce from Step 3 over them. Cover the top of the sauce with the fried onions and garlic and garnish with coriander leaves.

7. Serve with rice.

Variation: Well-done fried or poached eggs may be substituted. For added texture with poached eggs, dry them thoroughly and place them about 1 inch from the heat in a preheated broiler. Broil until they develop crisp edges.

Egg Crepes
KAI SOD SAI

As the name suggests, these crepes are made entirely of egg. They are cooked essentially the same way one would any other kind of crepe and they are easy to prepare. It is helpful to have a small wok made especially for cooking egg crepes, but they may be cooked in a regular wok or in a skillet with sloping sides. The advantage of the small wok is that it is much easier to handle than a standard-size wok, and the crepes are easier to fill and remove from it. Standard crepe pans are too small to allow the egg to be spread to the necessary thinness.

SERVES 8

2 large yellow onions
1 large tomato
½ cup coriander sprigs

3 tablespoons vegetable oil
1 teaspoon (2 cloves) finely chopped garlic
1 pound ground pork, chicken, shrimp, or beef
¼ cup plus 1 tablespoon fish sauce
¼ cup + 2 tablespoons granulated sugar
¼ cup + 1 tablespoon white vinegar

⅛ teaspoon ground white pepper

Vegetable oil for frying the crepes
8 extra-large or jumbo eggs

Coriander sprigs for garnish

1. Peel the onions, remove the root portion, and slice the onions vertically into ⅛ inch slices. Remove the stem portion and slice the tomato vertically into ⅛-inch slices; set aside with the onions. Chop the ½ cup coriander sprigs coarsely and set aside.

2. Heat a wok, add the oil, and swirl it over the surface of the pan. Add the garlic and stir-fry until it is light golden. Add the ground meat and stir-fry until the pink color disappears. Add the sliced onions and tomato, fish sauce, sugar, and vinegar. Bring the mixture to a boil and stir until it is dry. Add the ½ cup coriander sprigs and stir them in well.

3. Remove the mixture from the heat and let it cool to room temperature. Add the pepper and mix it in thoroughly. Separate the mixture into 8 equal portions.

Ahead-of-time note: The filling may be prepared up to 1 day in advance and stored, covered, in the refrigerator. Bring it to room temperature before proceeding with the recipe.

4. Coat a small wok very lightly with oil and heat it over moderate heat. Break one egg into a small bowl and beat it lightly until the yolk and white are well mixed but not frothy.

5. Grasp the wok handle with one hand and, using the other hand, pour the egg into the wok all at once. (Be careful here—the wok will be very hot and if it has metal handles they will be hot too, so pot holders should be used.) Lift the wok immediately and swirl the egg around on the surface until it coats the wok as thinly as possible. Keep the wok over heat during this procedure so that the surface of the pan remains hot.

6. When the egg is set and barely dry on the top, place one portion of the filling in the center of the crepe. Lift the edges of the crepe and fold them over the filling, forming a rectangular packet. Press the top of the packet firmly with a spatula.

7. Pour about 2 teaspoons oil around the edge of the crepe and cook until the crepe is golden. Turn it over and brown the other side.

8. Remove any excess oil from the wok with a paper towel and repeat the process with the remaining eggs. Place the crepes on a serving platter and keep them warm or let them cool to room temperature.

9. Garnish with coriander sprigs and serve warm or at room temperature.

Hard-Cooked Eggs with Brown Sauce
KAI PALO

This recipe sounds too simple to provide the tasty result it produces. The rich, flavorful sauce contrasts well with the bland eggs and penetrates the whites to add color. The sauce is relatively thin, but may be made thicker by reducing the amount of water according to your taste. Allow 2 eggs per person, more if it is the only dish to be served.

SERVES 4

8 eggs

2 tablespoons (1 ounce) finely chopped garlic
¼ cup finely chopped coriander root

¼ cup vegetable oil

2 tablespoons fish sauce
2 teaspoons black soy sauce
2 tablespoons light soy sauce
2 tablespoons palm sugar
1 teaspoon five-spice powder
¼ teaspoon ground black pepper

2 cups water

½ cup coriander leaves

1. Hard-cook the eggs in simmering water. When they are cool enough to handle, peel them and set aside.

2. Pound or grind the garlic and coriander root to a smooth paste in a mortar or blender. If you use a blender, add the oil to aid in grinding.

3. Heat a wok and add the oil. (If you used the oil to grind the coriander root and garlic, do not add more here.) Stir-fry the paste from Step 2 until it is light golden. Add the fish sauce, both types of soy sauce, palm sugar, five-spice powder, and black pepper. Stir to mix them well.

4. Add the peeled eggs to the sauce and turn them gently so they're covered all the way around with sauce. Add the water and stir gently to combine the ingredients thoroughly.

5. Simmer the mixture for 20 minutes.

Ahead-of-time note: The ingredients may be prepared and combined to this point up to 3 days in advance. Cover the mixture and refrigerate it. Reheat the eggs and sauce completely before serving.

6. Remove the eggs and sauce to a serving bowl and garnish with coriander leaves. Serve with rice.

••••————————————————————————

Sweet-and-Sour Crepes
KAI NAM DANG

These richly flavored crepes provide a meal in themselves, needing little accompaniment other than rice. There is a large amount of tasty sauce. If possible, use a small wok for preparing the crepes. These crepes are one of the favorite dishes in Kamolmal's parents' restaurant in Bangkok, and her father is very skilled in their preparation. This recipe is based on the procedures he uses.

SERVES 4

2 tablespoons finely chopped coriander root
1 tablespoon (½ ounce) finely chopped garlic
½ pound ground pork, chicken, or shrimp
¼ teaspoon ground white pepper
2 teaspoons fish sauce
½ cup shredded carrot
½ cup shredded Napa cabbage
½ cup thinly sliced celery

¼ cup oil (more if needed in Step 2)

4 extra large or jumbo eggs

3 cups Sweet-and-Sour Topping (page 86)

¼ teaspoon ground white pepper
½ cup coriander sprigs

1. Pound the coriander root and garlic to a smooth paste in a mortar. Combine this paste with the ground meat, pepper, fish sauce, and vegetables. Divide the mixture into 4 portions of equal size. Form each portion into a patty about 5 inches long, 2 inches wide, and ¼ inch thick.

2. Heat a wok, add the oil, and swirl it over the surface of the pan. Fry one of the patties over moderate heat until it is golden brown on both sides and the meat is done. Remove it from the wok and keep it warm. Repeat with the other patties, adding more oil if necessary.

3. Beat 1 egg lightly until it is well mixed but not frothy. Coat a small wok lightly with oil and heat it over high heat. Pour the egg into the wok and move the wok around, over moderate heat, until the egg forms a thin skin. Cook briefly until the egg is set but not completely dry.

4. Place a meat patty in the center of the crepe. Fold one side of the crepe over the meat, then fold the opposite side of the crepe over that. Leave the ends unfolded. Remove the crepe from the wok and keep it warm. Repeat with the other eggs and the remaining patties.

5. Place the crepes seam side down on a warm platter and cover them with Sweet-and-Sour Topping. Sprinkle with additional ground pepper to taste and garnish with coriander sprigs. Serve with rice.

16
Tofu

TOFU HAS BECOME more widely available in the United States in recent years due, at least in part, to the increasing emphasis on a good diet and health foods. It is a versatile, high-protein, low-fat, low-calorie food that has been eaten in Asia for centuries. We provide a small sample of the many ways tofu is prepared in Thailand, and hope that these dishes inspire you to develop additional preparations of your own and to explore the world of tofu cooking through books devoted exclusively to it.

✳✳✳

Stir-Fried Tofu and Bean Sprouts
PAD TOHOO GOB TUA NGOG

Very often tofu dishes are criticized for being too bland. In the true Thai manner, this one is richly flavored. It is quick and easy to prepare and the soft tofu contrasts beautifully with the crunchy bean sprouts. When served with rice it provides a complete meal.

1 pound firm fresh tofu

3 Serrano chilies
4 green onions, white and green parts

¼ cup oyster sauce
2 tablespoons fish sauce
1 cup water

3 tablespoons vegetable oil
1 tablespoon sesame oil
2 teaspoons (4 cloves) finely chopped garlic

1 cup (3 ounces) bean sprouts

⅛ teaspoon ground white pepper

Lime Sauce (page 84)

1. Put the tofu on a pad made from 4 paper towels and cover it with a pad of 4 more paper towels. Put a plate on top of that, and a 2-pound weight, e.g., a can of tomatoes, on top of the plate. Let the tofu stand for 30 minutes so the excess water is pressed out. Cut the tofu into ½-inch cubes and set aside in a bowl.

2. Remove the stems, but not the seeds, from the chilies and slice the chilies lengthwise into thin strips. Add them to the tofu. Slice the green onions diagonally into pieces about 1 inch long and ¼ inch thick. Set aside.

3. Mix the oyster sauce, fish sauce, and water. Set aside.

4. Heat a wok, add both kinds of oil, and swirl them over the surface of the pan. Stir-fry the garlic until it is light golden. Add the tofu, chilies, and bean sprouts. Stir-fry over moderate heat until the bean sprouts are crisp-tender, about 2 minutes. Add the liquid from Step 3 and the green onions. Stir over high heat until all the ingredients are heated through and the mixture is boiling.

5. Put the mixture in a serving bowl and sprinkle with pepper.

6. Serve immediately or keep it warm while you prepare other dishes. Serve with Lime Sauce and rice.

✳✳✳ ━━━━━━━━━━━━━━━━━━━━━━━━━━━

Spicy Tofu
LAB TOHOO

This dish is highly spiced, but if you prefer a milder version it is easy to reduce the amount of chilies or red onion or both. In any case, the mint adds a pleasant, cooling contrast to the ground chilies. Fresh vegetables are essential to provide a crisp texture and moderate the spiciness.

SERVES 2 TO 4

½ pound firm fresh tofu

1 ounce (¼ cup sliced) red onion
1 green onion, green and white parts
¼ cup mint leaves
2 pounds raw assorted vegetables (cabbage, green beans, zucchini, broccoli, etc.)

2 tablespoons fish sauce
2 tablespoons lime juice
½ teaspoon ground toasted rice (page 66)
1 tablespoon ground roasted chilies (page 60)

Green lettuce leaves

1. Cut the tofu into ¼-inch cubes. Set them aside on paper towels to drain for 15 minutes or more.

2. Peel the red onion and slice it vertically into paper-thin slices. Slice the green onion diagonally into pieces about ⅛ inch thick. Set both types of onion and the mint leaves aside. Cut the vegetables into serving-size pieces and set them aside.

3. Heat a wok and add the tofu without oil. Stir-fry until the tofu is heated through, but not crisp. Put it in a mixing bowl.

4. Add all the remaining ingredients except the lettuce and assorted vegetables. Mix thoroughly. Line a serving bowl with a single layer of lettuce leaves and pour the mixture on top of them.

5. Serve at room temperature with rice and assorted raw vegetables.

Deep-Fried Tofu

TOHOO TOD

This is a simple, tasty, and nutritious dish that is especially good for a quick lunch, late-night snack, or an appetizer or cocktail food. The tofu will puff slightly and the outside will be crisp and brown, while the inside will remain white and soft. These contrasting textures add an interesting touch to the tofu, which is bland and uninteresting raw.

SERVES 4 TO 6

2 pounds firm fresh tofu

Vegetable oil for deep-frying

Tofu Sauce (page 89)

1. Put the tofu on a pad made from 4 paper towels and cover it with a pad of 4 more paper towels. Put a plate on top of that, and a 2-pound weight, e.g., a can of tomatoes, on top of the plate. Let it stand for 30 minutes to press out the excess water.

2. Slice each cake of tofu vertically across the center. Slice each of these horizontally in half to form a total of 4 pieces from each cake. If you prefer tofu that is crisper, slice it more thinly.

3. Heat 1 inch oil to 375° in a wok. Dry each piece of tofu with a paper towel and deep-fry it until golden and crisp on the surface. This will take several minutes, but do not overcook them or they will become dry, hard, and uninteresting. The inside should be soft, spongy, and white or light tan. Be careful when turning the tofu so that it does not break apart.

4. Serve immediately with Tofu Sauce for dipping.

Spicy Tofu and Bean Threads
DOM YOM TOHOO

How can tofu taste so good? This dish is quick and easy to prepare, is full of flavor, and produces much thin sauce for flavoring rice. If you prepare the liquid in advance you may wish to add additional green onions when reheating it, to have the crisp texture. Do not pour the liquid over the bean threads until serving time.

SERVES 4 TO 6

4 green onions
½ pound firm fresh tofu
1 quart water
¼ cup + 1 tablespoon fish sauce

1 ounce bean threads

3 tablespoons granulated sugar
¼ cup lime juice
½ teaspoon ground roasted chilies (page 60)

1 teaspoon crisp-fried garlic and its oil (page 65)
1 tablespoon ground roasted unsalted peanuts (page 66)
½ cup coriander sprigs

Vinegar Sauce (page 83)
Ground roasted chilies (page 60)

1. Slice the green onions diagonally into pieces about ⅛ inch thick and 1 inch long. Cut the tofu into ¼-inch cubes. Bring the water to a boil in a large saucepan and add the tofu, green onions, and fish sauce. Let the liquid return to a rapid boil over moderate heat, then remove saucepan from the heat.

2. Soak the bean threads in room-temperature water about 15 minutes. They will become pliable and transparent. The best way to describe the texture is "al dente." Set them aside in a colander to drain.

3. Add the sugar, lime juice, and ground roasted chilies to the tofu mixture from Step 1.

4. Put the drained bean threads in a serving bowl and pour the cooked mixture over them. Sprinkle the top with crisp-fried garlic and its oil, ground roasted peanuts, and coriander sprigs.

5. Serve with Vinegar Sauce, additional ground roasted chilies, and rice.

Variation: Add 1 tablespoon Roasted Red Curry (page 76) or more to taste.

17
Vegetables

IN THAILAND, vegetables are frequently eaten raw. Unlike some other Asian countries, the Thai people grow their vegetables in "clean" soil. They play an important role in the Thai diet, and add interesting textures and flavors as well as important sources of nutrition. Thai vegetable dishes often contain meat, but not enough to warrant classifying them as meat dishes. The first part of this chapter contains recipes without meat and the second part has recipes that contain some meat. Whenever possible, fresh vegetables should be used. In Thailand, vegetables are picked from the home garden or purchased daily to insure freshness. In the United States that may not be possible in some parts of the country at certain times of the year and it may be necessary to substitute frozen products. Bean sprouts, a popular vegetable in Thailand, are available to anyone at any time of year because they can be grown in your own kitchen and need neither soil nor sunlight to sprout. We provide instructions for growing your own on page 59.

Stir-Fried Eggplant
PAD MA KUA YAOW

This recipe uses either American or Japanese eggplant; the dish has a slightly sweet flavor with a hint of garlic. It is probably unlike any eggplant dish you may have had before, and if you already like eggplant, chances are good that you'll love this. If you don't already like eggplant, we hope you change your mind about that vegetable, which is one of our favorites. Some of the eggplant will disintegrate and form a thick sauce in combination with the liquids. Some will retain its shape and be soft, creamy, and brown.

SERVES 4 TO 6

1½ pounds eggplant

½ cup water
1 tablespoon granulated sugar
2 tablespoons oyster sauce or 2 teaspoons fermented soybeans
2 tablespoons fish sauce

½ cup vegetable oil
1 tablespoon (½ ounce) finely chopped garlic

1. Remove the green cap from the eggplant, but do not peel it. Cut the eggplant into ½-inch cubes. If you use American eggplant some of the pieces will not have skin attached. If you use Japanese eggplant each piece will have some skin attached. If the eggplant is not young and fresh, sprinkle it lightly with salt, let it stand in a colander for 15 minutes to exude liquid, then rinse it thoroughly and pat the pieces dry with a paper towel.

2. If you are using fermented soybeans, rinse them well and remove any small stones you may find. Mash the beans to a smooth paste in a mortar or with a fork. Mix the water, sugar, oyster sauce or fermented beans, and fish sauce in a small bowl. Stir until the sugar is dissolved, then set the liquid aside.

3. Heat a wok, add the oil, and swirl it over the surface of the pan. Stir-fry the garlic until it is light golden. Add the eggplant, reduce the heat to moderate, and stir-fry until the cubes have absorbed the oil. Continue to stir-fry over moderate heat until the oil reappears on the surface of the eggplant. You may be tempted to add more oil, but don't—the final product would be much too oily. This will take about 3 to 5 minutes. Be sure to stir frequently so the eggplant doesn't stick to the pan or burn.

4. When the oil reappears on the surface of the eggplant, reduce the heat to simmer and cook, stirring frequently, until the eggplant is done, about 7 minutes more. The eggplant may brown a little. If it does, so much the better. If it doesn't, that's all right.

5. Increase the heat to high, add the liquid from Step 2, and stir until most of the liquid has been absorbed by the eggplant.

6. Serve immediately or keep it warm while you prepare other dishes. Serve with rice.

• • •

Stir-Fried Bean Sprouts and Chives
PAD TUA NGOG

In Thailand, bean sprouts are a popular vegetable and this recipe clearly indicates why. It is crisp and lightly spiced with sesame oil and chives. Be sure to use the full amount of chives, because the bean sprouts are bland and need a great deal of seasoning. This crisp preparation is particularly good as a contrast to soft, bland foods such as steamed eggs. Bean sprouts are often considered additives to other dishes, but this preparation demonstrates that they can serve as the focal point. The green part of green onions may be substituted if chives are not available, but the flavor will be stronger.

SERVES 6 TO 8

1 pound (6 cups) bean sprouts

2 tablespoons vegetable oil
2 tablespoons sesame oil
1 teaspoon (2 cloves) finely chopped garlic

½ cup coarsely chopped chives
1 tablespoon fish sauce
2 tablespoons oyster sauce

⅛ teaspoon ground white pepper

Lime Sauce (page 84)

1. Soak the bean sprouts in a bowl of cold water for 15 minutes. Drain them thoroughly in a colander just before beginning Step 2.

2. Heat a wok, add both types of oil, and swirl it over the surface of the pan. Add the garlic and stir-fry until it is light golden. Sesame oil scorches easily, so keep the heat at a moderate level.

3. Add the bean sprouts, chives, fish sauce, and oyster sauce. Stir about 2 minutes, until the bean sprouts are crisp-tender and the ingredients are mixed thoroughly.

4. Remove the mixture to a serving platter and sprinkle it with ground pepper.

5. Serve immediately with Lime Sauce and rice. Do not try to keep this dish warm, because the bean sprouts will get soggy.

Variation: Remove the stems, but not the seeds, from 2 Serrano chilies and slice the chilies lengthwise into thin strips. Add them in Step 3.

••• ━━━━━━━━━━━━━━━━━━━━━━━━━━━━━━━━━━━

Stir-Fried Banana Squash
PAD FUKTONG

This recipe produces a slightly sweet, golden-yellow dish that looks a little like sautéed carrots with small flecks of brown on the surface. The main recipe produces a dish with a small amount of sauce. The variation produces a relatively dry dish, although you could add a little more water according to your own taste. Pumpkin may be substituted.

SERVES 4 TO 6

1 pound banana squash or pumpkin
4 cups boiling water

1 tablespoon vegetable oil
½ teaspoon (1 clove) finely chopped garlic
1½ tablespoons fish sauce
2¼ teaspoons granulated sugar
⅛ teaspoon ground white pepper
½ cup water

Lime Sauce (page 84) or Spicy Fish Sauce (page 83)

1. Remove the tough rind from the banana squash or pumpkin and cut the flesh into 1-inch squares. Parboil it in the boiling water for 2 minutes, then drain thoroughly in a colander.

2. Heat a wok, add the oil, and swirl it over the surface of the pan. Add the garlic and stir-fry until it is light golden. Add the squash and stir-fry over moderate heat until the cubes are fork-tender, about 3 minutes. Add the fish sauce, sugar, pepper, and water, stirring until the sugar has dissolved completely.

3. Pour the squash and sauce into a warm serving bowl and serve it immediately or keep it warm while you prepare other dishes.

4. Serve with Lime Sauce or Spicy Fish Sauce and rice.

Variation: Break 1 egg into a small mixing bowl and beat it lightly with a fork until well blended. Add it to the squash in Step 2 after the squash is cooked and before adding the other ingredients. Stir-fry quickly to distribute the egg and squash evenly, and proceed with Step 3.

•••

Stir-Fried Broccoli
PAD BROCCOLI

In Thailand, Chinese broccoli is used rather than the type of broccoli sold in most U.S. markets. We have used American broccoli in this recipe because it is much more widely available, because many Thai people in this country prefer it, because it is less likely to be bitter than the Chinese variety, and because it provides a crisper texture. You may, of course, substitute Chinese broccoli if it's available and if you prefer it. Whichever type you use, be sure to use the leaves as well as the stems and florets. Unfortunately, many Americans discard the leaves, which are flavorful and nutritious.

SERVES 4 TO 6

1 pound broccoli
4 cups boiling water

2 tablespoons vegetable oil
1 tablespoon (½ ounce) finely chopped garlic
1 cup water
2 tablespoons brown bean paste

⅛ teaspoon ground black pepper

Vinegar Sauce (page 83), Lime Sauce (page 894), or Spicy Fish Sauce (page 83)

1. Remove the leaves and florets from the broccoli and set them aside. Peel the stems and slice them diagonally into pieces about ¼ inch thick. Parboil the broccoli until it turns bright green, about 1 minute.

2. Heat a wok, add the oil, and swirl it over the surface of the pan. Add the garlic and stir-fry until it is light golden. Add the broccoli and stir-fry until it is well coated with oil and has turned deep green, about 1 minute. Reduce the heat to moderate. Add the water and bean paste and stir until the broccoli is crisp-tender.

3. Put the broccoli on a warm serving platter and sprinkle with the ground pepper. Serve it immediately or keep it warm while preparing other dishes.

4. Serve with Vinegar Sauce, Lime Sauce, or Spicy Fish Sauce and rice.

Hot-and-Spicy Mushrooms
YAM HED

The smoothness of the mushrooms in this dish contrast well with the spiciness of the ground chilies, and the mint adds a refreshing coolness. The mushrooms should be well cooked but still firm. Canned mushrooms may be substituted, with some loss in texture, but they should be cooked only long enough to warm them thoroughly.

SERVES 4 TO 6

3 pieces kah
¼ cup uncooked rice

2 pounds fresh mushrooms
Water or chicken broth

1 green onion, white and green parts

2 tablespoons fish sauce
¼ cup lime juice
1 teaspoon ground roasted chilies (page 60)

¼ cup mint leaves

1. Toast the *kah* and rice in a dry wok or skillet until they are dark golden. When they begin to change color, watch them closely, because they can burn easily from that point on. Grind them together to a fine powder in a mortar, blender, or electric coffee or spice grinder.

2. Cut the mushrooms into quarters unless they are very large, in which case cut them into sixths or eighths. Put them in a saucepan and add enough water or chicken broth to cover them by about ½ inch. Cover the pan, bring the liquid to a slow boil, and cook the mushrooms until they are tender but still firm, about 2 to 3 minutes.

3. Slice the green onion diagonally into pieces ⅛ inch thick and set aside.

4. Drain the mushrooms and discard the cooking liquid or save it to use as a broth in other dishes. Add the fish sauce, lime juice, ground *kah* and rice, ground chilies, green onion, and mint leaves. Stir the mixture well and let it stand about 15 minutes to allow the flavors to develop and penetrate the mushrooms.

5. Serve warm with rice.

✳✳✳ ─────────────────────────────────

Spicy Green Beans
PAD PED TOU KAG

These beans are rich, flavorful, and crisp. They go particularly well with milder meat dishes, such as Thai Dried Beef. They are best when made with young beans; frozen or canned beans should never be substituted.

SERVES 4 TO 6

1 pound green beans

½ cup vegetable oil
1 recipe Red Curry 2 (page 76)
2 tablespoons fish sauce
2 tablespoons granulated sugar
½ cup water

1. Slice the green beans diagonally into pieces ⅛ inch thick and about 2 inches long. Blanch them in boiling water for 30 seconds, drain, and set aside.

2. Heat a wok, add the oil, and swirl it over the surface of the pan. Add the Red Curry 2 and stir-fry it over moderate heat until it is dark-colored and fragrant. Add the green beans and stir-fry until they are crisp-tender. Add the fish sauce, sugar, and water and bring the mixture to a boil rapidly.

3. Put the cooked beans and sauce in a warm serving bowl and serve immediately or keep them warm while you prepare other dishes. Serve with rice.

Deep-Fried Vegetables
PAK TOD RUAM MIT

These vegetables are similar to fried vegetables found in other cuisines, e.g., Japanese tempura, but they are prepared with a uniquely Thai batter that adds the subtle, sweet flavor of coconut.

SERVES 8 TO 10

2 pounds assorted vegetables (broccoli, eggplant,
*   zucchini, sweet potato, cauliflower, etc.)*

1 cup thick coconut milk
2 tablespoons red lime liquid (page 66)
1 tablespoon egg white (optional)
¼ teaspoon ground white pepper
¾ teaspoon salt
1 cup all-purpose flour

Vegetable oil for deep-frying

1. Remove and separate the broccoli florets. Cut the broccoli stems lengthwise into long strips about ⅛ inch thick. Slice the eggplant lengthwise into pieces about ⅛ inch thick. Cut each of these into pieces about 1 inch wide and 2 inches long. Slice the zucchini diagonally into slices about ⅛ inch thick and 4 inches long. Cut the other vegetables into pieces of similar sizes.

2. Blend the coconut milk, red lime liquid, egg white (if used), pepper, salt, and flour in a blender, food processor, or bowl using a wire whip to develop a smooth batter. Pour the batter into a bowl if you prepared it in a blender or food processor.

3. Pour about 1 inch oil in a wok and heat it to 375°. Dry the vegetables so the batter will stick to them, then dip them in the batter and deep-fry them until they are crisp and golden brown. The firmer vegetables should be cooked first because they will hold their texture better while you are frying the others.

4. Serve immediately.

Stir-Fried Bamboo Shoots with Chilies

PAD PRIG NOMAI

This is a very popular dish in Thailand. Garlic, onion, and chilies add a rich flavor to the bland bamboo shoots to produce a very tasty dish. Traditionally, this dish is very hot and spicy, but you may modify the amount of flavorings to suit your own taste.

SERVES 6 TO 8

½ pound boneless pork chops or pork loin
16-ounce can bamboo shoots

6 Serrano chilies
½ cup (2 ounces) finely chopped yellow onion
¼ cup (2 ounces) finely chopped garlic

¼ cup vegetable oil

¼ cup mint leaves
¼ cup fish sauce
½ cup water

Mint leaves

1. Slice the pork across the grain into slices not more than ⅛ inch thick and 1 to 2 inches long. Set aside. Rinse the bamboo shoots thoroughly under running hot water to remove the "tinny" taste. Drain them thoroughly and slice into thin julienne strips if they are not already in strips. Set them aside in a separate bowl.

2. Remove the stems, but not the seeds, from the chilies and chop the chilies finely. Pound or grind the onion, garlic, and chilies to a coarse paste in a mortar or blender. If you use a blender, add the oil to aid in grinding.

3. Heat a wok, add the oil, and swirl it over the surface of the pan. (If you used the oil in grinding, do not add more.) Stir-fry the paste from Step 2 until it is light golden. Add the pork and stir-fry until the pink color disappears completely.

4. Add the bamboo shoots, mint, fish sauce, and water.

Bring the mixture to a boil rapidly, then remove it from the heat immediately. Place it in a serving bowl and garnish with mint leaves. Serve with rice.

Stir-Fried Cabbage with Shrimp
PAD KALAMPLEE GOB GOONG

This easily prepared dish is deceptive in appearance. It looks like a big bowl of dull, semisoft cabbage with a shrimp poking out here and there. Nevertheless, it has a lovely, subtle flavor. There is relatively little sauce, but what there is flavors the accompanying rice well, and the lime sauce adds a tart-hot accent.

SERVES 6 TO 8

1½ pounds Napa cabbage
½ pound raw shrimp

¼ cup + 2 tablespoons vegetable oil
1 tablespoon (½ ounce) finely chopped garlic

3 tablespoons fish sauce

Lime Sauce (page 84)

Fresh red chilies

1. Chop the cabbage coarsely or slice it into 1-inch lengths and set aside. Shell and devein the shrimp, leaving the tails intact. Set aside.

2. Heat a wok, add the oil, and swirl it over the surface of the pan. Add the garlic and stir-fry until it is light golden.

3. Add the shrimp and stir-fry until they are pink. Do not overcook them.

4. Add the cabbage and fish sauce. Stir and toss about 5 minutes to mix them well, but not long enough for the cabbage to lose all its crispiness.

5. Scoop out the contents to a large serving bowl and garnish with chilies that have been cut into decorative shapes.

6. Serve with Lime Sauce and rice.

Stir-Fried Baby Corn and Shrimp

PAD GOONG GOB KAOW POAD OAN

SERVES 6 TO 8

¼ ounce dried Oriental mushrooms
½ cup warm water
4-ounce can bamboo shoots

½ pound raw shrimp

¼ pound sweet green (bell) pepper
4 green onions, white and green parts
½ pound canned baby corn

1 tablespoon tapioca starch
2 tablespoons water

1 tablespoon vegetable oil
1 teaspoon (2 cloves) finely chopped garlic

2 tablespoons sesame oil

3 tablespoons fish sauce
1 tablespoon granulated sugar
¼ cup water if needed in Step 7

⅛ teaspoon ground white pepper

1. Soak the mushrooms in the warm water for 15 minutes. Remove the stems and slice the caps into thin strips. Set them aside. Slice the bamboo shoots into thin julienne strips if they aren't already; then rinse them under running water and set aside in a colander to drain.

2. Peel and devein the shrimp, leaving the tails intact. Set them aside.

3. Remove the stems and seeds from the bell peppers and slice the peppers into 1-inch squares. Slice the green onions diagonally into pieces 1½ inches long. Slice the baby corn diagonally into pieces about ⅛ inch thick. Set these ingredients aside in a bowl.

4. Mix the tapioca starch and water. Set aside.

5. Heat a wok, add the vegetable oil, and swirl it over the surface of the pan. Stir-fry the garlic until it is light golden. Add the shrimp and stir-fry until they turn pink.

6. Add the vegetables from Steps 1 and 3 and the sesame oil. Stir-fry until the ingredients are heated through, about 3 minutes. Sesame oil scorches easily, so keep the heat at a moderate level.

7. Add the fish sauce, sugar, and if needed, ¼ cup water. There should be enough liquid at this point to make about ½ cup sauce. Stir the tapioca starch mixture, add it to the wok, and stir until the mixture thickens. Put in a serving bowl and sprinkle with ground pepper.

8. Serve with rice.

●●●───────────────────────────────

Cabbage Stuffed with Chicken and Shrimp
KA LAM MOEN

This dish really can serve as a main dish. It is rich and smooth with an earthy flavor. It is essential to serve it with Lime Sauce to accent the flavors of the cabbage and meat. When steaming it, it is best to place the cabbage rolls on a heatproof plate, rather than directly on a steaming rack, to preserve the juices which will be produced. If you are using a bamboo steamer that is essential. You will need two heads of cabbage because you will use only the larger outer leaves; the smaller inner leaves can be saved for another purpose.

SERVES 6

2 heads Napa or green cabbage

1 ounce dried Oriental mushrooms
1 medium carrot
1 stalk celery
4-ounce can bamboo shoots
2 tablespoons (1 ounce) finely chopped garlic
¼ cup finely chopped coriander root

½ pound raw shrimp
½ pound boned chicken breasts

2 green onions, white and green parts

2 egg yolks
2 tablespoons fish sauce

Lime Sauce (page 84)

1. Separate the leaves from the cabbage and blanch them about 2 minutes in boiling water. You will need about 12 large, outer leaves from regular cabbage or about 24 large outer leaves from Napa cabbage. Squeeze the water from them carefully, or drain them thoroughly in a colander, and set them aside. The leaves of Napa cabbage come apart easily, but green cabbage leaves are more difficult to separate. With regular cabbage, place the head in boiling water, remove a few leaves, and continue to repeat the process until you have 12 large leaves. Save the unused cabbage for another purpose.

2. Soak the mushrooms in hot water for 15 minutes, or until they are soft. Remove the stems. Chop the mushrooms, carrot, celery, and bamboo shoots finely and place them in a mixing bowl. Pound the garlic and coriander root to a coarse paste in a mortar.

3. Peel, devein, and remove the tails from the shrimp. Grind the shrimp and chicken together in a food processor or meat grinder. Place the mixture in the bowl with the vegetables.

4. Slice the green onions diagonally into pieces about ¼ inch thick and add to the mixing bowl.

5. Add the egg yolks, fish sauce, and ground paste from Step 2, and mix thoroughly.

6. Spread a cabbage leaf flat on a working surface and place 2 tablespoons mixture about 1½ inches from the bottom end. Fold the bottom end of the leaf over the mixture, then fold the sides toward the center. Roll the leaf up moderately tightly, and allow for slight expansion of the filling during cooking. Repeat with the other leaves.

7. Steam the stuffed leaves for 15 minutes, or until the filling is completely cooked.

8. Serve with Lime Sauce and rice.

18
Beverages

• • •

Thai Iced Tea
CHA YEN

Thai iced tea is a very sweet, milky drink to which some people are absolutely addicted. It is one of those foods that you either like a great deal or don't care for at all. Please use only Thai tea, because it blends with the two types of milk much better than any other kind. Standard tea will, to put it simply, create a disaster. The tea may seem too strong when you first brew it, but remember that a lot of milk will be added.

½ cup Thai tea
3 cups water

14-ounce can sweetened condensed milk

1½ cups evaporated milk or half-and-half

1. Place the tea in a bag made of muslin or other fine cloth. (See the description of the Thai tea strainer on page 14.) Bring the water to a rapid boil, pour it over the tea, and let it steep for 3 minutes. Pour the liquid back through the tea 5 or 6 times until it is a deep orange color and is flavored strongly.

2. Strain the tea well, pressing out all the liquid that you can. Add the sweetened condensed milk to the warm liquid and mix it well. Allow the mixture to cool to room temperature.

3. Just before serving, fill each glass with cracked ice and fill it half to three quarters full of tea. Add evaporated milk or half-and-half to fill the glass, and stir well.

Variation: If you prefer a darker colored and stronger flavored tea, substitute ¾ cup granulated sugar for the sweetened condensed milk.

●●● ━━━━━━━━━━━━━━━━━━━━━━━━━━━━━━━━━━

Thai Coffee
GAFA YEN

Like Thai tea, Thai coffee is very sweet and milky. It is prepared in the same way and can be used interchangeably with tea. Only Thai coffee should be used in brewing. It may seem too strong when first brewed, but remember that a lot of milk will be added.

⅓ cup Thai coffee
3 cups water

14-ounce can sweetened condensed milk

1½ cups evaporated milk or half-and-half

1. Place the coffee in a bag made of muslin or other fine cloth. (See the description of a Thai tea strainer on page 14.) Bring the water to a rapid boil, pour it over the coffee, and let it steep for 3 minutes. Pour the liquid back through the grounds 4 or 5 times until it is a dark brown color.

2. Strain the coffee well, pressing all liquid out of the grounds. Add the sweetened condensed milk to the warm liquid and mix it well.

3. Just before serving, fill each glass with cracked ice and fill it half to three quarters full of coffee. Add evaporated milk or half-and-half to fill the glass, and stir well.

Variation: If you prefer a darker colored coffee, substitute ¾ cup granulated sugar for the sweetened condensed milk.

Strong Coffee or Tea

Follow the instructions in the variations above for making tea or coffee, but omit all the milk products. The color will be very dark and the flavor very strong. Serve hot or cold.

Mild Tea

Mild tea is very pale in color and has a subtle flavor. It is often served at home or in restaurants instead of water, and some people in restaurants have been known to send their "water" back because it looked dirty. If that happens to you, please check first to make sure that you have not been served the traditional pale tea. We do not provide specific instructions or quantities because standard tea-making principles apply. We suggest using Jasmine tea and brewing it very, very weakly, and according to taste. Serve hot or cold.

Beer

Thai beer is available in Thai markets, and your local liquor store can probably get it on special order. As far as we know, the most widely available brand in America goes by the name SINGHA although another brand called AMARIT is available in some locales. Either is very good. Because of the alcohol content it must, by law, be labeled "ale" in the United States. Beer or ale is very good with hot and spicy dishes and complements their flavors. Any good beer or ale can be used.

19
Sweets

SWEETS ARE frequently eaten as snacks throughout
the day in Thailand, rather than being served after meals as desserts. The most likely dessert to be served after a home meal
would be fresh fruit, although prepared sweets might be served
for a special occasion or holiday. Jellied sweets are made with
agar, which sets at higher temperatures than the gelatin we are
accustomed to and therefore is very useful for serving on hot days
because it will not melt easily. Thai sweets take some getting
accustomed to and frequently are not popular outside of Thailand
because of their unusual ingredients, flavors, and textures. We
have included them here to illustrate the kinds of sweets available
in Thailand and to give you the opportunity to try them to see if
you like them.

Baked Mung Bean Custard
KANOM MOGANG

Yes, this sweet dish really is topped with fried onions! To
the Thai that doesn't seem unusual, but the Western custom of

preparing sweets with cinnamon does. It's a great example of acquired tastes and customs. Some of the people who tried the recipes in this book during its development liked this sweet a great deal, and others couldn't bear the thought of the ingredients.

MAKES 16 PIECES

¾ cup yellow mung beans
4 cups water

1¼ cups palm sugar

1½ cups egg white (about 12 large eggs)
1 cup thick coconut milk

¼ pound (1 cup sliced) yellow onion
½ cup oil

1. Soak the mung beans in 2 cups water until they have doubled in size, at least 2 hours and preferably overnight.

2. Discard the soaking water and boil the beans in 2 cups fresh water until they are soft, about 15 minutes. Drain and puree the cooked beans in a food processor until they are a smooth paste.

3. Preheat the oven to 350°.

4. Stir the egg white and sugar until they are well mixed, but do not beat them or make them frothy. Add the coconut milk and pureed beans to the mixture.

5. Pour the mixture into a saucepan and cook over low heat, stirring constantly, until the mixture begins to thicken. Pour the mixture into an 8 x 8 x 2-inch baking pan and put it in the oven on the middle rack. Bake about one-half hour, or until a toothpick inserted into the center comes out clean.

6. Peel the onion, remove the root section, and slice the onion vertically into very thin slices. Heat a wok and add the oil. Stir-fry the onion until it is dark golden. When the onion begins to change color it will burn very easily, so be careful. Set it aside in the oil in which it was fried.

7. When the custard is done, remove it from the oven and spread the fried onions and oil over it. Allow it to come to room temperature before serving, and slice it into 16 pieces.

Deep-Fried Bananas
KLUAYKAG TOD

These bananas are quick and easy to prepare, and will get rave reviews from your guests. This recipe is a favorite of Kamolmal's mother, who taught her how to cook it as a child. The outside is crisp with a hint of coconut flavor, and the inside is naturally sweet and creamy. The bananas should be completely ripe, but not overripe and soft. If you use packaged coconut, try to get the unsweetened kind. If only the sweetened variety is available, reduce the amount of sugar in the recipe by 1 tablespoon. If you are grating your own fresh coconut it isn't necessary to remove the brown skin, but you may if you wish. The bananas should be served immediately so that the crust doesn't get soggy. They may be sprinkled with powdered sugar if you like.

SERVES 8 TO 10

1½ cups all-purpose flour
1½ cups unsweetened shredded coconut
1¾ teaspoons salt
2½ tablespoons granulated sugar
2 tablespoons red lime liquid (page 66)
1¾ cups water
¼ cup sesame seeds

4 pounds bananas

Vegetable oil for deep-frying

1. Thoroughly mix all the ingredients except the bananas and oil.

2. Heat 1½ inches oil to 375° in a wok. While the oil is heating, slice 2 or 3 bananas in half lengthwise and then cut each piece in half crosswise. Each slice should be between ¼ inch and ½ inch thick. If the bananas are exceptionally thick, you may need to slice them lengthwise into three slices.

3. Put the pieces of banana in the batter and stir gently to coat them well. Put a few pieces of banana at a time in the hot oil and fry until they are golden brown and crisp. Drain them on paper towels and keep them warm while the remaining pieces are fried. Repeat with the remaining bananas, doing 2 or 3 at a time.

4. Serve immediately.

...———————————————————————————

Coconut Ice Cream
IDEM GATI

This dessert is technically not "ice cream" because it contains no dairy products, much less cream. But, traditionally, it is called ice cream and is rich and delicious no matter what the name. In Thailand it is made with kernels of cooked fresh corn and young coconut, which can be found in the frozen food section of Thai and Oriental markets. If you find that too unusual, use only shredded young coconut, or omit the corn and the coconut.

SERVES 8 TO 10

2 ears corn (optional)
6 cups thick coconut milk
1 pound package shredded young coconut (optional)

Unsalted roasted peanuts

1. If you are using corn, boil the ears until they are firm and done, about 5 minutes. Remove the kernels from the ears.

2. Mix the coconut milk, corn, shredded coconut, and sugar, stirring until the sugar has dissolved. Put the mixture in an ice cream freezer and follow the manufacturer's instructions for freezing.

or

Place the mixture in a pan in your freezer and freeze until it is icy and almost set. Scrape it into a mixing bowl and beat it thoroughly with a wooden spoon, or on low speed with an electric mixer. Return it to the freezer and freeze until it is set.

3. Before serving, remove the ice cream from the freezer and let it get soft. Traditionally, it is served very soft, almost in the liquid state.

4. When you serve the ice cream, sprinkle the top with whole, unsalted, roasted peanuts.

Coconut Rice Pudding
TACO SAKU

<small>MAKES 16 PIECES</small>

½ cup long-grain rice
2 cups water

1½ cups water
½ cup small tapioca pearls
¼ cup + 1 tablespoon granulated sugar

1¼ teaspoons salt
2½ tablespoons granulated sugar
2 cups thick coconut milk (more if needed)

1. Soak the rice in the water overnight.

2. Bring 1½ cups water to a boil. Put the tapioca pearls in a sieve and rinse them very quickly under running water. Add them to the boiling water and stir until they become translucent. Add the sugar to the tapioca and water and stir until the sugar dissolves.

3. Remove the mixture from the heat and pour it into small custard cups or an 8 x 8 x 2-inch baking pan. Traditionally, the custard is poured into banana leaves that have been formed into the shape of a cup.

4. Wash the soaked rice in 2 or 3 changes of water until the water runs clear, and drain it well. Grind the uncooked rice with the salt, sugar, and 1 cup of the coconut milk until it is pureed.

5. Put the ground rice mixture into a pan with the remaining coconut milk. Cook over medium heat until it thickens slightly. Reduce the heat to low and cook for 10 to 15 minutes more, until it is very thick but still pourable. If the mixture begins to dry out or gets too thick to pour, add more coconut milk as needed.

6. Remove the pan from the heat and pour the mixture evenly over the layer of tapioca pudding.

7. Serve at room temperature.

Sweet Egg Threads

FOY TONG

This is a very good sweet that requires few ingredients, but it does require some skill and practice in preparation. The first time you do it you may feel like the sorcerer's apprentice, because you will be watching the egg thread, holding the Foy Tong maker, keeping a finger over the holes in the maker, and removing the cooked egg threads, all at one time. It does take some practice to produce the little golden balls of sweet goodness, but it is worth it. Some people think the optional flavoring has a medicinal odor and taste, so omit it if you don't like it or if it is not readily available.

SERVES 6 TO 8

2 cups granulated sugar
2 cups water
1 teaspoon nam nommao *(optional flavoring)*

15 egg yolks *(save the whites to make coconut custard)*

1. Combine the sugar and water and bring to a boil over medium heat. Boil it gently for 15 minutes or until it thickens slightly and forms a thin syrup. Reduce the heat to simmer, and simmer the liquid throughout the preparation of the Sweet Egg Threads.

2. While the syrup is boiling, separate the egg whites from the yolks, strain the yolks through a fine sieve, and add the optional *nam nommao* to them. (Cover and refrigerate the egg whites for use within 24 hours, or freeze them for later use. A convenient way to freeze them is in plastic ice cube trays. When they are frozen, remove them to a plastic container for storage in the freezer.)

3. Pour the egg yolk into a Foy Tong maker, a paper cone of the type we describe following this recipe, or a pastry tube fitted with a very small tip. Whatever you use, the opening(s) should be about 1/16 inch in diameter. Hold your finger over the opening(s) until the Foy Tong maker is over the syrup. Release enough of the egg yolk to form a single layer of fine threads that cover the surface of the syrup. Put your finger back over the opening to stop the flow of egg. The egg threads will become firm upon touching the hot syrup. As soon as they are completely set and firm, remove them from the syrup with a strainer or slotted spoon and form them into loose balls. Set them aside while cooking the remainder of the egg yolk.

Ahead-of-time note: The balls may be prepared up to 1 week in advance and stored, tightly covered, in the refrigerator.

4. Serve the balls cold or at room temperature. Chilling firms them up a little and makes them slightly crisp.

Preparing Your Own Foy Tong Maker

Take an 8½ x 11-inch sheet of waxed paper and roll it into a cone so that the bottom is completely closed. Fasten the seam with tape. Cut off enough of the tip to form a hole about 1/16 inch in diameter. *Or:* Fold up about 1 inch of the bottom of the cone and fasten it securely with tape. Cut 2 holes about 1/16 inch in diameter in the flat surface you have created by folding.

● ● ●

Steamed Sweet Rice
KAO NIEW MA MUANG

This sweet is a little less sugary than many of the other preparations in this chapter, and resembles rice pudding. This is another recipe Kamolmal learned from her mother, who makes it less sweet than is usually found in Thailand. In Thailand, very sweet, soft mangoes are used. Most mangoes in the United States are firmer and less sweet, but they can be used with equal success.

SERVES 8

4 cups glutinous rice

½ cup yellow mung beans

1 cup thick coconut milk
2 cups thin coconut milk
4 teaspoons salt
½ cup sugar

Mangoes

1. Cook the glutinous rice according to the instructions on page 96.

2. Toast the mung beans in a dry wok or skillet over high heat until they are brown and crisp. If mung beans are not available, you may substitute toasted cooked rice. To prepare that, take leftover cooked rice and let it get dry and hard. Then toast it in a dry wok the same way you would toast uncooked rice.

3. Combine 1 cup thick coconut milk and ½ teaspoon of the salt in a saucepan. Bring to a boil and remove from the heat immediately. Stir until the salt is dissolved, pour the liquid into a serving pitcher, and set aside.

4. Combine the 2 cups thin coconut milk, 3½ teaspoons salt, and the ½ cup sugar. Mix until the salt and sugar are dissolved completely.

5. Put the rice in a mixing bowl large enough to allow for stirring in the ingredients from step 4. Add the coconut milk mixture from Step 4, mix well, and cover the bowl. Let the mixture stand for 5 minutes or until the rice has absorbed the liquid.

6. Stir the mixture thoroughly but gently and put it on a serving platter. Peel the mangoes, slice them lengthwise along the seeds, then crosswise into pieces about ½ inch thick. Turn the mango and repeat on each side until all the flesh is separated from the seeds. Lay them decoratively beside the steamed rice. Sprinkle the toasted mung beans over the steamed rice and mangoes.

7. Serve the steamed rice with the remaining coconut milk, which each diner may pour over it according to taste.

● ● ● ────────────────────────────

Agar with Syrup
WUN NAM CHUAM

This dessert is crisp and cooling on a hot summer day. It is sweet, but not filling, and is easy to prepare. It is made frequently in Thailand, but is rarely available in Thai restaurants in the United States.

SERVES 8 TO 12

1 tablespoon agar powder
3 cups water

½ cup granulated sugar
½ cup water

Crushed ice

1. Combine the agar powder with 3 cups water in a saucepan and stir until the powder has dissolved. Bring the mixture to a boil, remove it from the heat immediately, and pour it into an 8 x 8 x 2-inch baking dish. Place it in the refrigerator for 1 hour or more, until it is completely set.

2. Dissolve the sugar in ½ cup water in a saucepan. Bring to a boil and cook until it gets slightly thick, about 10 minutes.

3. Slice the jelly into thin julienne strips and place it on a bed of crushed ice on individual plates. Pour the sugar syrup over the jelly. Serve immediately.

Ahead-of-time note: The agar and syrup may be prepared up to a day in advance and stored separately in the refrigerator. Store the agar in enough cold water to cover it, and store the syrup in a closed container. Drain the agar completely and slice it before putting it on the ice. Reheat the syrup, adding a little water if necessary to bring it back to the consistency it had before being refrigerated.

● ● ● ━━━━━━━━━━━━━━━━━━━━━━━━━━━━━

Deep-Fried Sweet Potatoes
MAN RANG NOK

This dessert is very sweet and rich. The preparation is unusual because the sugar syrup is poured directly into hot oil after the potatoes are fried. It really does work, and if the syrup is thick it will not cause the oil to spatter as you might think it would. After the potatoes sit at room temperature for about 30 minutes the patties will become slightly crisp and chewy. Yams may be substituted for sweet potatoes.

MAKES 30 TO 35 PATTIES

2 pounds sweet potatoes

½ cup water
½ cup palm sugar

Vegetable oil for deep-frying

1. Peel the sweet potatoes and shred them lengthwise into very thin julienne strips about 3 inches long. This can be done with a knife or cleaver, but it is tedious and time-consuming. The most efficient way is to use a 2 × 2 mm. julienne blade of the food processor. If you use a food processor, put the potato pieces in the feed tube horizontally so that the potatoes are sliced lengthwise. Set them aside.

2. Dissolve the sugar in the water over medium heat, and stir it over the heat until it forms a thick syrup that is barely pourable.

3. Pour about 2 inches oil in a wok and heat it to 375°. Put about one fourth of the potato strips into the hot oil and fry them until they are golden brown, about the color of French-fried potatoes. Pour one fourth of the sugar syrup onto the potatoes while they are still in the oil, and stir to mix the potatoes and syrup completely.

4. Remove the potatoes from the oil and place them on a large platter or ungreased cookie sheet. Using two forks, form the potatoes into slightly mounded rounds about the size of silver dollars or a little larger. The potatoes will be very hot, so do not try to use your fingers, and work quickly to complete the work before the potatoes become firm. When the patties are formed, place them on a double layer of paper towels to drain.

5. Repeat Steps 3 and 4 for the remaining potatoes and syrup. Discard the oil or save it for preparing this dish again, but do not use it for other purposes because it will retain the flavor of the sugar syrup.

6. Serve within 3 to 4 hours of preparation for the best texture and flavor.

Coconut Balls
MA PROAW GAW

Makes 25 to 30 balls

2 cups granulated sugar
1 cup water

4 cups (½ pound) unsweetened shredded coconut

1 teaspoon nam nommao *(optional flavoring)*

1. Use a wok or large skillet for this recipe, a pot that will hold all the ingredients comfortably and that allows for easy stirring. Put the sugar and water in the wok or skillet and bring it to a medium boil slowly. Stir frequently until the sugar has dissolved.

2. Add the coconut and stir constantly until almost all the liquid is absorbed and the mixture is barely moist. Add the optional flavoring if desired and stir to mix it in thoroughly. Remove the container from the heat.

3. Using two soup spoons, form the coconut into balls of about 1½ to 2 tablespoons mixture each. The mixture will be very hot, so do not try to form the balls with your fingers! It will be necessary to work quickly to get the balls formed before the mixture begins to dry out and set. As they are formed, place the balls on a sheet of aluminum foil or an ungreased cookie sheet.

4. Allow the balls to dry thoroughly, about 4 hours, at room temperature. If they are not to be served on the day of preparation, store them at room temperature in an airtight container for up to 2 weeks.

• • •

Thai Tea Cakes
KANOM KROK

This recipe was given to Kamolmal by her grandmother, who really enjoyed preparing it, especially for the children of the family. These light, slightly sweet cakes are eaten in Thailand in much the same way that donuts are eaten in the United States, usually in the morning with coffee or tea. They have a rich coconut flavor, with only a hint of onion flavor and are a popular item prepared by street vendors. They are always eaten hot. To prepare them, you must use a pan that has small cup-like depressions to hold the batter. In Thailand there is a special clay cooking vessel used only for making these cakes. They are generally not available in the United States, and are very fragile. An excellent substitute is a cast-iron Danish Ebelskiver pan. Another good substitute is a cast-iron cornstick pan, which will produce long narrow cakes rather than the traditional round ones. Lacking either of these, you may use a muffin tin whose cups hold no more than 2 tablespoons batter.

MAKES 35 TO 40 CAKES

2 cups raw long-grain rice
3 cups water
2 cups finely chopped fresh coconut
1 quart water
½ cup cooked long-grain rice
2 teaspoons salt

3 green onions, green part only (optional)
1½ cups thick coconut milk
¾ cup granulated sugar
1 teaspoon salt

1. Soak the raw rice overnight in 3 cups water, then drain it and discard the soaking water. Blend the first five ingredients to a smooth puree in a blender. Because of the quantity, you will need to do this in two or more batches; the actual number of batches will depend on the capacity and power of your blender. Thorough blending will take 2 or 3 minutes on high speed ("liquify"). It's a good idea to let your blender cool a little between batches to keep it from overheating and to avoid possible damage.

2. Chop the green onions coarsely and combine them with the thick coconut milk, sugar, and salt. Stir until the sugar and salt have dissolved. Set the mixture aside.

3. Heat the cooking tin over moderate heat until a drop of water skitters around on the surface and evaporates quickly. Fill each depression in the pan about three quarters full of the mixture from Step 1. Immediately put enough of the mixture from Step 2 on top to fill the depression. Cover the pan immediately. If you do not have a cover that fits, use aluminum foil. Cook over moderate heat until the edges of the cakes turn brown. The tops will be light colored and moist, and the bottom surfaces will be crisp and light brown. If the center does not set completely and collapses a little after you remove it from the pan, don't be concerned. That's one of the ways they can be cooked. If you prefer a firmer cake, cook until the center is set completely, but make sure not to burn the bottom.

4. Remove the cakes from the pan and keep them warm while you cook the remainder. Serve hot, with coffee or tea.

• • •————————————————————————

Sweet Rice Tarts
KANOM TOUPAB

MAKES 30 TO 35 TARTS

3 cups uncooked glutinous rice
1½ cups yellow mung beans
Water

½ teaspoon salt
2 cups shredded fresh or unsweetened packaged coconut

2 tablespoons sesame seeds
½ cup granulated sugar

1. Soak the rice overnight in water to cover. In a separate container, soak the mung beans overnight in water to cover. After soaking, grind the rice and water to a fine puree in a blender. Drain the mung beans and set them aside. Drain the water from the rice puree, using a fine cloth bag such as a Thai tea strainer. Press most of the water out by massaging the bag, but leave the rice moist enough to hold together. Knead the rice puree until it is smooth, about 5 minutes.

2. Cook the mung beans about 15 minutes in just enough boiling water to cover them. Drain the mung beans and mix them with the salt and ½ cup of the shredded coconut.

3. Pour about 2 quarts water in a large saucepan and bring it to a medium boil. Form the kneaded rice puree into small balls about 3 inches in diameter. Flatten each ball into a thin circle about ⅛ inch thick. Put them into the boiling water a few at a time, and cook until they float to the surface. Put them into room temperature water immediately.

4. Form each rice patty into a small cup shape, and put 2 tablespoons of the mixture from Step 2 in the center of the cup. Fold the edges over to form a half-circle. Put the remaining 1½ cups shredded coconut in a bowl and gently toss the tarts in it to coat them lightly.

5. Put the sesame seeds in a dry wok or skillet and roast them over moderate heat until they are light golden and fragrant. Crush them in a mortar, or grind them in a blender, to form a medium fine powder. Mix them with the sugar.

6. Serve the tarts with the mixture from Step 5, for each diner to add as desired.

Mail Order Sources

THE FOLLOWING sources were filling mail orders at the time of preparation of this book. Each of them provides a slightly different service and line of products, and we hope this list will be useful in your search for good ingredients and equipment.

Ann's Dutch Import Co.
4357 Tujunga Ave.
North Hollywood, CA 91604
Wide variety of Indonesian and Dutch products, including such things as Sambal Oeleck, various soy sauces, prepared saté sauces, lemon grass, etc.

Cardullo's Gourmet Shop
6 Brattle St.
Cambridge, MA 02138
Does not have a catalogue, but will quote prices on specific items on request.

Kam Man Food Products, Inc.
200 Canal St.
New York, NY 10013
Does not have a catalogue, but will respond to inquiries and give prices for specific products.

Logee's Greenhouses
55 North St.
Danielson, CT 06239
Sells lemon grass plants and other herbs and spices for growing at home.

Park Seeds
254 Cokesbury Road
Greenwood, SC 29647
This is the only mail-order source we have located that sells seeds for the tiny, fiery hot Thai chilies. Has a wide selection of other chili seeds as well as some unusual vegetables.

Mrs. DeWildt
R.D. #3
Bangor, PA 18013
Price list includes principally Indonesian ingredients, some of which are common to Thai cooking, such as lime leaves, mung beans, *kah* (listed as *galangal*), dried lemon grass, dried shrimp, etc.

Suggested Additional Reading

Haydock, Y., & Haydock, B. *Japanese Garnishes*. New York: Holt, Rinehart, and Winston, 1980.

A well-illustrated guide to preparing garnishes from carved vegetables and fruits. The garnishes they describe are similar enough to Thai garnishes to be of great value. Diagrams and instructions are straightforward and easy to follow.

Haydock, Y., & Haydock, B. *More Japanese Garnishes*. New York: Holt, Rinehart, and Winston, 1983.

A sequel to the 1980 book listed above.

Hom, K., & Steiman, H. *Chinese Technique*. New York: Simon and Schuster, 1981.

This book takes you step-by-step through the basics of preparing ingredients for cooking, stir-frying, steaming, and deep-frying. Each step is shown in detail with well-done black and white photographs.

Shurtleff, W., & Aoyagi, A. *The Book of Tofu*. Brookline, Mass: Autumn Press, 1975.

An incredibly detailed and complete work on the history, preparation, and uses of tofu and related soy products. In addition to many recipes and procedures it even tells you how to prepare tofu in your own home.

Sittitrai, P. *The Art of Vegetable and Fruit Carving*. Bangkok: Institute of Technology and Vocational Education.

This small book has color photographs of some of the spectacular ways in which food is carved in Thailand. Unfortunately, the English instructions are not always clear, but by referring to the color illustrations and the detailed line drawings, and using a little patience, it is possible to create the carvings shown.

Su-Huei, H. *Chinese Appetizers and Garnishes*. Taipei: Sun-Chuan Publishing, Ltd., 1982.

This is a beautiful book complete with detailed color photographs showing the various steps in carving vegetables and fruits into surprising shapes. What it lacks in written clarity is more than made up for with the color photographs.

Tropp, B. *The Modern Art of Chinese Cooking*. New York: Morrow, 1982.

This book could easily be viewed as the *sine qua non* in the field of Chinese cuisine. The discussions of equipment, procedures, and ingredients (some of which are used in Thai cooking) are complete, clear, and based on the author's thorough understanding of Chinese philosophy and culture. Her wit and wisdom make for entertaining reading even when you're not cooking.

Von Welanetz, D., & Von Welanetz, P. *The Von Welanetz Guide to Ethnic Ingredients*. Los Angeles: J. P. Tarcher, Inc., 1983.

An incredibly complete guide to specialty ingredients for cuisines from around the world, classified into geographical regions.

Warren, W., Black, S., & Rangsit, M. R. P. *Thailand*. Singapore: Apa Productions (HK) Ltd., 1983.

An excellent guidebook to Thailand which discusses the history, geography, and customs of the Thai people. Unfortunately, it deals little with food.

Index

Hot or spicy dishes (*cont.*)
    Stir-Fried Beef with Mint, 171
    Stir-Fried Chicken Giblets, 237
    Stir-Fried Mussels and Eggs, 225
    Stir-Fried Pork, 190
    Stir-Fried Tofu and Bean Sprouts, 258
    Stuffed Yellow Chilies, 168

I
Ice Cream, Coconut, 285
Innards in Thai cuisine, 2, 237
Intestines, in Spicy Assorted Meats, 243

K
Knives, 11

L
Lard, 51
Lemon grass, 47, 65
Lettuce, 31, 48
Lime(s)
    about, 48
    pickled
        about, 48
        in chicken soup, 125
    Red, *see* Red lime
    Salad Dressing, 90
    Sauce, 84
Liver, beef
    grilled, 246
    in Spicy Assorted Meats, 243

M
Mangoes, in Steamed Sweet Rice, 288
Maw, *see* Fish maw
Measuring, 67–71
Mee Krob, *see* Noodles, Sweet Thai
Melon, winter *see* Winter melon
Menus
    appetizers and snacks in, 24
    buffet, 26
    guidelines, 23–28

    hot and spicy, 25
    light meal, 25
    mild and hot, 25
    mild, 25
    planning, 3–4, 23
Microwave oven, 12
Mild dishes
    Barbecued Beef with Peanut Curry, 153
    Barbecued Chicken 1, 205
    Barbecued Chicken 2, 206
    Beef Musman, 178
    Beef Noodle Soup, 120
    Beef Tendon Soup, 130
    Beef with Broccoli, 177
    Cabbage Stuffed with Chicken and Shrimp, 276
    Chicken and Cashews, 203
    Chicken Balls, 210
    Chicken Fried Rice, 99
    Chicken Soup with Pickled Limes, 125
    Chicken with Richly Flavored Rice, 207
    Chive Dumplings, 156
    Coconut Chicken Soup, 119
    Crisp Rice, 97
    Deep-Fried Bread and Pork, 162
    Deep-Fried Shrimp, 231
    Deep-Fried Tofu, 261
    Deep-Fried Vegetables, 272
    Egg Crepes, 253
    Fish Balls, 236
    Fish Maw Soup, 122
    Fried Chicken Curry Won Tons, 159
    Fried Eggs with Tamarind Sauce, 251
    Fried Spring Rolls, 160
    Galloping Horses, 145
    Garlic Shrimp, 228
    Garlic-Pepper Pork, 189
    Glutinous (Sweet) Rice, 96
    Green Salad, 136
    Grilled Beef Liver, 246
    Ground Pork and Shrimp, 191

Winter melon (*cont.*)
  in Chicken Soup with Pickled
    Limes, 125
Wok(s)
  cleaning, 16–17
  covers, 18
  scoops, 18
  seasoning, 17
  selecting, 15

Won Ton(s)
  Fried Chicken Curry Won Ton,
    159
  Sauce, 87
  Steamed Won Tons, 154
  Won Ton Soup, 131

Z
Zucchini garnish, 29